In the Alley of the Friend

Middle East Literature in Translation
Michael Beard and Adnan Haydar, *Series Editors*

Select titles in Middle East Literature in Translation

Abundance from the Desert: Classical Arabic Poetry
Raymond Farrin

Arabs and the Art of Storytelling: A Strange Familiarity
Abdelfattah Kilito; Mbarek Sryfi and Eric Sellin, trans.

A Child from the Village
Sayyid Qutb; John Calvert and William Shepard, eds. and trans.

Contemporary Iraqi Fiction: An Anthology
Shakir Mustafa, ed. and trans.

Gilgamesh's Snake and Other Poems, Bilingual Edition
Ghareeb Iskander; John Glenday and Ghareeb Iskander, trans.

Jerusalem Stands Alone
Mahmoud Shukair; Nicole Fares, trans.

Moroccan Folktales
Jilali El Koudia; Jilali El Koudia and Roger Allen, trans.

Thou Shalt Not Speak My Language
Abdelfattah Kilito; Waïl S. Hassan, trans.

In the Alley of the Friend

On the Poetry of Hafez

Shahrokh Meskoob

Translated from the Persian by
M. R. Ghanoonparvar

Syracuse University Press

Syracuse University Press wishes to acknowledge and thank the board of directors of the Mehr Foundation for its generous support of this project.

Syracuse University Press
Syracuse, New York 13244-5290

First Edition 2018

18 19 20 21 22 23 6 5 4 3 2 1

Originally published in Persian as *Dar Kuy-e Dust* (Tehran: Kharazmi Publishers, 1978).

∞ The paper used in this publication meets the minimum requirements of the American National Standard for Information Sciences—Permanence of Paper for Printed Library Materials, ANSI Z39.48-1992.

For a listing of books published and distributed by Syracuse University Press, visit www.SyracuseUniversityPress.syr.edu.

ISBN: 978-0-8156-3617-5 (paperback) 978-0-8156-5460-5 (e-book)

Library of Congress Cataloging-in-Publication Data

Names: Miskūb, Shāhrukh, author. | Ghanoonparvar, M. R. (Mohammad R.), translator.
Title: In the alley of the friend : on the poetry of Hafez / Shahrokh Meskoob; translated from the Persian by M. R. Ghanoonparvar.
Other titles: Dar kuy-e dust. English
Description: First edition. | Syracuse, New York : Syracuse University Press, 2018. | Series: Middle East literature in translation | Includes bibliographical references.
Identifiers: LCCN 2018044866 (print) | LCCN 2018044882 (ebook) | ISBN 9780815654605 (E-book) | ISBN 9780815636175 (pbk.)
Subjects: LCSH: òHåafiòz, active 14th century—Criticism and interpretation.
Classification: LCC PK6465 (ebook) | LCC PK6465 .Z894813 2018 (print) | DDC 891/.5511—dc23
LC record available at https://lccn.loc.gov/2018044866

Manufactured in the United States of America

Contents

Translator's Introduction

In the Alley of the Friend is the translation of an original book in Persian, *Dar Kuy-e Dust*, by one of the most original Persian men of letters in the twentieth century about the poetry of perhaps the most original Persian poet of all time, Hafez, who is often referred to as *Lesan ol-Gheyb* or the "Tongue of the Invisible." Like the majority of Persian speakers around the world, especially in Iran, literate and illiterate alike, I grew up with the poetry of Hafez, but I claim no expertise in Hafez studies. With this excuse and also since this book is about Hafez, I will refrain from expressing any thoughts about that great poet, leave that task to the author, and instead say a few words about Shahrokh Meskoob.

Shahrokh Meskoob (1924–2005) was an artistic intellectual and an intellectual artist, a learned philosopher and historian, a talented translator, an astute scholar and social and literary critic, and a poet and writer of immense talent, whose remarkable style of writing and use of poetic language is inspirational for Persian speakers. Even more inspirational is his innovative approach to writing about major classics of Persian poetry, such as Ferdowsi's *Book of Kings* and Hafez's *Divan*. As Hafez is perhaps the most cited and memorized Persian poet, and due to the wealth of lore about his life and poetry, a great deal has been written over the centuries, and especially in the past one hundred years, about the *Divan*. Meskoob's approach, however, is highly innovative and different from all previous scholarship. Although thoroughly informed by the necessary historical and cultural background and equipped with pertinent philosophical, mystical, and literary knowledge, Meskoob follows a path distinct from conventional scholarship in Hafez studies.[1] The author tells us in his foreword that *In the Alley of the Friend* is an attempt to find his way into the garden of the *Divan*, an excursion in that garden, and a description of what he observes. His is not, however, an excursion to observe the exterior of the garden, the mere exploration of what he calls the linguistic and rhetorical "magic" of the poet, but an exploration of the interior, of the inner workings and thinking of the mind that produced these ghazals, these love songs. To do so, rather than speaking about Hafez, Meskoob seems to summon the spirit of the poet through his poems, to act as a medium or a channel, as it were, and to allow Hafez to speak through him. Meskoob's first-person narrative often appears to become Hafez's, and his *I* and the *I* of the ghazals are fused and become one and the same.[2] This fusion and at times unexpected shift in the points of view in the narrative can initially be confusing to the reader, as they might appear to add to the seemingly insurmountable ambiguity that characterizes Hafez's poetry. But if we trust Meskoob, and as Geoffrey Squires says in the following observation about Hafez and Meskoob, "we let ourselves go with him, follow him," he opens new vistas in our reading and understanding of Hafez and functions as the tongue of the Tongue of the Invisible.

> Hafez is "difficult" if we try to arrive at a single, definitive meaning or interpretation of his poems. This is our normal impulse or procedure with poetry. We feel if we work hard enough we will eventually get it, pin it down. But Hafez resists this. His work is essentially, systemically, open. There is no limit to the sense of his images. More than that, I think that for Meskoob and indeed Hafez this is how the world is, not convergent but divergent, bottomless, endless. The world allows closure in certain limited, defined respects, but essentially it is open, infinite, *iihaam*, polyvalent. And that is the normal situation, not the exception. Usually we think of ambiguity as a kind of failure, an inability to define things properly, but I think Meskoob's exploration of Hafez's imagery goes in the other direction. Definition is the exception not the rule. We have to learn to live with this fundamental openness, which we cannot and never will be able to close. Some people would label this a mystery, but it is not in the usual sense of *mystical*. It all depends how we approach Hafez. If we try to corral him, delimit him, then of course he is astoundingly difficult, but if we let ourselves go with him, follow him, then he is oddly easy.[3]

"Hafez studies," Meskoob tells us, is a slippery slope, an observation that has proven to be true in regard to translating the poetry of Hafez as well.[4] And I have learned through my experience of translating *In the Alley of the Friend* that translating Meskoob is also a slippery slope for the translator. His highly precise use of the Persian lexicon—employing terms that are accurate but uncommon—and in the case of the present book, his use of the often ambiguous words and phrases from the poetry of Hafez have frequently paused and postponed the process of translating this text.

Meskoob likens the ghazals to small flowerbeds, among other things, beside which he stops in his excursion to pick a flower or two. In other words, much of Meskoob's text consists of words, phrases, and paraphrases he borrows from various ghazals or other poems with which he builds the narrative of his reading of Hafez. With the exception of a few footnotes in the chapters of his book where he makes reference to specific poems, the author takes for granted that his readers can identify the borrowed segments from the ghazals he uses in his narrative, which at times appear within quotation marks but often do not. Given this habit, we can safely assume that Meskoob's intended audience consists of the Persian literati who are thoroughly familiar with, and even know by heart, the ghazals of Hafez. For the average reader of this translation, on the other hand, who most likely does not know Persian and has no access to all the poems alluded to in this book, I have identified and cited the couplets that contain the majority of the aforementioned hemistiches and phrases from the ghazals in endnotes and bracketed segments of the author's footnotes. In addition, when a phrase, a line, or a couplet is alluded to or cited within quotation marks several times in the text, I have repeated the couplets that contain them in the relevant endnotes.

It is the consensus among English-speaking scholars of Persian poetry that the best translations of Hafez are the most recent renditions by the British poet Dick Davis and the Irish poet Geoffrey Squires. In his *Faces of Love: Hafez and the Poets of Shiraz*,[5] Davis provides us with the translations of seventy-nine ghazals in full, and in his *Hafez: Translations and Interpretations of the Ghazals*,[6] Squires has rendered in part or fully 248 of the 486 ghazals. I have made extensive use of Squires's translations, and to a lesser extent, those of Davis, especially when they lend themselves to Meskoob's narrative.[7] In other instances, I have provided fairly literal, though hopefully coherent, translations to avoid deviating from Meskoob's text. In addition, on occasions, I have either used or cited a few other translations of particular ghazals, including those in Robert Bly and Leonard Lewisohn's *The Angels Knocking at the Door: Thirty Poems of Hafez.*[8]

In quoting the ghazals and other poems by Hafez, Meskoob uses the edition of the *Divan* that was edited by Mohammad Qazvini and Qasem Ghani and first published in 1941.[9] The ghazal numbers in the brackets of the footnotes and in the endnotes refer to this edition. Davis, Squires, and Bly and Lewisohn use the *Divan* edited by Parviz Natel-Khanlari first published in 1980.[10] The ghazal numbers in the Khanlari edition are different from those numbered by Qazvini and Ghani. After locating every ghazal that was translated from the Khanlari edition, I have used the corresponding Qazvini and Ghani ghazal numbers in the endnotes.

In the rendition of any text from one language and culture to another, particularly between two languages such as Persian and English that seem not only linguistically but also culturally alien to one another, each translator faces dilemmas at every step of the way, and although he or she usually negotiates a path through most of them, there often remain certain culture-specific concepts that appear to defy translation. In the rendition of this text, the translator is faced not only with the challenge posed by Meskoob's distinctive language style and usage, but also the difficulties in rendering a number of concepts from the *Divan* that have been regarded by many translators as untranslatable, particularly because of their specific usage or usages in Hafez's poetry. While some translators have tried to find, often inadequate, equivalents for these concepts, others have merely transliterated the Persian terms and provided explanations for them. For instance, the two terms *kuy* (alley) and *dust* (friend), which Meskoob has chosen for the title of his book and which are taken from Hafez's poems, may not fully encompass in English all the meanings the original terms convey to Persian readers, since for example, both terms connote much closer intimacy than do their English renditions. In addition, since the title of Meskoob's book for many, if not most, Persian readers indicates that his book is about the *Divan*, I have added a subtitle to the original.

In the ghazals and also in Meskoob's narrative, the word *friend* sometimes may refer to God, sometimes to a beloved, sometimes to an actual friend, and often, ambiguously to all three. It becomes even more ambiguous given that the third-person pronoun in Persian is gender free. Moreover, the Persian alphabet does not have uppercase and lowercase letters. Hence, I have refrained from using the uppercase letters *F* in *friend* and *H*, as in *he* or *his*, presumably referring to God, to retain the ambiguity that characterizes both the ghazals and Meskoob's narrative.

An important word in the poetry of Hafez is *rend*, an anti–religious establishment persona with whom Hafez identifies, which some translators render as "libertine" in English. Depending on the context and usage by Meskoob, I have used the terms "libertine" or "free-spirited libertine" in this translation. Hafez also identifies with *sahebdelan*, which I have rendered as "people of the heart" or "the kindred spirits who follow their own hearts."[11]

In his poetry, Hafez often refers to his "Magian elder." Likewise, at times Meskoob refers to Hafez as "my elder" or "my rose-colored elder," and on occasions as "Khajeh" or "Khajeh-ye Shiraz." The word *khajeh* in Persian is an archaic honorific used for a person of some social standing and affluence. In the case of Hafez, based on his available biographical information, this honorific was most likely used because of his widespread reputation during his own lifetime as a poet. For this reason, I have opted to translate the term as the "bard" or the "Bard of Shiraz," accordingly.

In a few instances, Meskoob places words and phrases in quotation marks for emphasis, and they are not actual quotes from the ghazals. The author's footnotes are marked in the text with symbols, and my endnotes with Arabic numerals.

As I have stated earlier, I have tried to avoid undermining Meskoob's unique and highly individual and insightful exploration of Hafez's poetry by adding any biographical information about Hafez or including the opinions and interpretations of generations of scholars about his poetry. Instead, I direct interested nonspecialist readers to the relatively brief but extremely helpful introductions and explanations of such astute and erudite Hafez scholars and translators as Dick Davis, Geoffrey Squires, and Leonard Lewisohn, whose works I have used in my translation as well as the endnotes. Davis's introduction and explanatory notes to his *Faces of Love: Hafez and the Poets of Shiraz* offer an insightful background to Hafez and his poetry in the context of the historical, political, cultural, and literary milieu of Hafez's time in fourteenth-century Shiraz. In his extensive annotations to his *Hafez: Translations and Interpretations of the Ghazals*, as a poet and translator, Squires walks us through not only his personal experience with Hafez's poetry but also various aspects of Persian prosody. Squires's bibliography provides a list of other translations of Hafez's work as well as secondary sources for further reading. Leonard Lewisohn's brief essay in *The Angels Knocking at the Door: Thirty Poems of Hafez* presents biographical as well as literary background to Hafez and his ghazals.

In rendering the Persian names and terms in the English alphabet, I have used more of a simplified transcription rather than a transliteration method, although in many instances they are the same. Hence, no diacritical marks are used to distinguish between consonants that are pronounced alike in Persian and represented by different letters. Also, I have used no diacritical marks to distinguish between the pronunciation of the letter *a* as in *tall* and the short *a* as in *hat*. The apostrophe (') is used to represent the letter *eyn* and the sign *hamzeh* but is omitted in the initial position. The spelling of Meskoob's name does not follow the aforementioned transcription system, but rather his own preference.

This translation is based on the first printing of *Dar Kuy-e Dust*, published in Tehran by Kharazmi Publishers in 1978. Readers interested in the original poems cited by Meskoob can easily find them online. To find ghazal 39, for instance, simply search "Ganjoor Hafez ghazal 39."[12] In the appendix, I have also provided the original Persian of the set-off couplets in this translation, identified and alphabetized by the first line of the English translation of the couplet. Bracketed numbers in the appendix refer to ghazal numbers.

Finally, in this project, I am indebted to many individuals. First, to Shahrokh Meskoob, whose friendship was a source of inspiration for me, especially when I translated and wrote about his *Goftogu dar Bagh*[13] (*Dialogue in the Garden*) in my book, *Translating the Garden*, in 2001.[14] Over many years of teaching Persian literature, I always evaded questions I was asked about Hafez by students and friends alike, since I was uncertain about my understanding of the ghazals. The translating and close reading of *In the Alley of the Friend* has in a way reinforced my previous hesitation; but it has also equipped me with a fresh outlook and, as Meskoob calls it, a new window, through which I can share not only Meskoob's reading of Hafez, but perhaps my own, with others.

My debt to Dick Davis and Geoffrey Squires is immense. Over many years, whether from our too few conversations or from reading his many pieces of writing about Persian literature, Dick Davis has taught me a great deal. And Geoffrey Squires was actually my first truly inspiring teacher of English literature over fifty years ago in Iran. Squires, who was kind enough to read and comment on an earlier draft of this translation, has been most generous with his time and so very gracious when pointing out my often incomprehensible renditions and lexical and grammatical transgressions. Once again, I thank him, and I treasure our newfound friendship after having lost track of each other for so many years. I also thank him for his generous permission to quote many couplets from his translations in this work. I am most grateful for all I have learned from both of them.

My dear friend Ali Banuazizi encouraged me to translate this book. I thank him for his encouragement, his confidence in me, and his indispensable published interview with Meskoob, which provided additional insight regarding our departed friend.[15] On the murky path of this project, M. Mehdi Khorrami has always been there to shine a ray of light to help me see more clearly. I am grateful for all his help and for volunteering to read this translation and point out some of my errors. Likewise, I would like to express my gratitude to my friend of many decades, Michael Beard, for his enthusiastic support of this project and for his suggestion to add the original Persian verses in the appendix.

Despite all the difficulties that I have encountered in this project, translating *In the Alley of the Friend* has been not only an expression of gratitude to Meskoob for personal reasons, and more importantly for his valuable contributions to Persian culture, but also a labor of love. My wife, Diane, and I have spent many hours together ruminating, mulling over, arguing about, and enjoying not only Meskoob's writing but also, through him, Hafez's ghazals. I am most indebted to her and her meticulously critical mind and editorial skills for any degree of possible success in the rendition of Meskoob's observations during his excursion in the garden of Hafez's *Divan*.

Finally, I would like to express my gratitude to the editors, artists, and staff of Syracuse University Press, including Suzanne Guiod, Kelly Balenske, Fred Wellner, and Brendan Missett, for their assistance and their highly professional work.

Foreword

A few years ago I wanted to write a treatise about the trilateral relationship of man, the world, and God: If the idea of God exists, what is the nature and characteristic of man's connection to himself and to the world? And what if the idea does not exist? And today, how does the presence or absence of this idea build and advance our relationship with the world? What meaning does it give to our life? I did not intend to investigate religion or any other idea or concept; however, I had gone to the sources to cleanse and refresh my spirit. Nevertheless, I wanted to base my work only on the Gathas. In other words, I wanted to organize my thoughts according to the structure, the connections, and the continuity of the worldview of these hymns and *shape* my own thinking within this warp and weft in order for the idea to be born and become universal.

Once I began writing, however, my path was blocked. Subconsciously, Zoroaster's hymns reminded me of the ghazals[1] of Hafez. In both, the same presence at the dawn of creation and at the end of time, the same eagerness to see the friend, the same self-reflection and seeing him with the heart's eye, and choosing to reside in the house of light and song, or the alley of the friend, effervesce like water from a spring or light from dawn. And it is as if light is the *face* of existence.

In any case, each time, a ghazal greeted a stanza of a hymn and took over my mind, leaving no room for anything else. Early on, I thought it was a coincidence and paid no attention to it. But because this occurred repeatedly, I became hesitant. Eventually, after an entire month during which I made no progress, I closed the notebook, and, freeing my mind of other preoccupations, I went on a pilgrimage to the poet who had summoned me. Several months passed and I was bewildered. It was as though

I had never read Hafez, or perhaps I had never been in the right mood for such a happy experience. And now, this book is the souvenir of that journey and that bewilderment.

Thus it was that involuntarily I stumbled upon a path that I did not choose. I did not want it, since I knew that speaking about Hafez was a daunting task. He is closer to us than any other poet, and at the same time, he is more remote than any other poet. We have all had some dealings with him in one way or another. Some of us have become familiar with him, and some have expressed devotion to him. He has been within us and has lived inside us as long as we have let him be as he is; but as soon as we have tried to delve into him through "scholarship," logical analysis, and so on, he has slipped out of our grasp and disappeared before our myopic eyes. It is as though he is a living body, and as soon as we open it up to learn the secret of his life, we take his life. "Hafez studies" is a slippery slope. This writer has merely taken an excursion for a while in the garden of Hafez's *Divan* and said a few words about what he has seen. This excursion and observation, however, has been undertaken with some preparation and on a particular path, not an accidental wandering.

In our history, the teaching of sciences has always been by degrees. Religious jurisprudence, medicine, mathematics, theology, philosophy, poetic techniques, and so on were external matters that had their own particular logic and function. The seeker of knowledge had to travel, step by step, to further and loftier stages. But since the truth was not divisible by degrees, the wayfarer would be provided with it in its entirety from the beginning. The child would begin with the Koran. The Koran was the divine word, and as a result, the eternal truth. And the truth was an internal matter, which the travelers on the path would enjoy every step of the way, to the extent that their fortune and efforts would allow; and mystical knowledge would open up to them like a flower, or dawn, layer by layer. Truth was there, just like God and the sun, and the wayfarer needed to wipe clean the dust or stains from his mirror to see its manifestation as clearly as he could. The stages and levels of discovering mystical knowledge would blossom internally in the wayfarer.

As he reaches new stages, and new levels of mystical knowledge dawn in him, with the passage of time, our Hafez completes the degrees of "knowledge of the word and wisdom"[2] and acquires the magic of the word. The essence of the word, however, "is no more than one point"[3] that the poet has reiterated in every language; but what he says is not a repetition of what has been repeated, since every time it is in a different arena and at a different level, and every time he has found and then uncovered that singular truth in a different context. Hence, in this study, the *Divan* of Hafez has been viewed as a singular and complete whole, like an intrinsically organized garden and an inherently stable firmament, not as an anthology of miscellaneous poetic ideas that are arranged side by side in the form of scattered ghazals.

Looking at the *Divan* of Hafez in this way, the ghazals can be considered small flowerbeds, heavenly bodies, or limbs and organs of a living body, each of which is in its proper place, like "lines, moles, eyes, and eyebrows."[4]

A garden and firmament can be seen from within, not from without. Hence, with this perception, the *Divan* does not constitute an "object" in front of us. One must find a way into it. One can make an excursion into the garden, and one can travel—like light—in the firmament. In order to understand and perceive the garden and the firmament, however, one cannot open them up and examine each piece separately, because then there would remain neither a garden nor a firmament. All that would remain is a heap of fragments.

If we consider the ghazals to be the limbs and organs of a living body, these small flowerbeds and "forms" are no longer useless and distinct, like the beads from a broken string. They are linked to one another, and hence, they have meaning in and of themselves. Searching for these links would perhaps provide us with a path to the intellectual structure of the *Divan*, the map of the "garden" and design of the "firmament," and contemplating the warp and weft that form the basic foundation of the ghazals might perhaps provide us with a clue to the workings of the imagination of the poet. After all, the foundation of every ghazal is built on the basis of a design, and every form on the basis of an image.

If we view the entire *Divan* as a living phenomenon, we must then search for the ways to observe and become familiar with it within the "phenomenon" itself; we must assess it from within and become familiar with its mechanisms and how its components function within each other in order for our internal excursion to be more illuminating and insightful than an observation from outside. For instance, if we are able to fall like a drop into the veins of this body, we might be able to move through it with the blood in circulation and the movement of its systems.

Of course, here and there and when relevant, this "phenomenon" has been placed in the context of history, society, and the world in comparison to other things, such that we can occasionally take an external look at its body and its surroundings and see its "meaning" in relationship to other "phenomena." Nevertheless, following that perception, the method of observation is fundamentally phenomenological.

Blessed by the presence of Hafez, the garden or the firmament is within our field of vision. If we want, however, to find our way toward the design of a thought process through the "small flowerbeds" or "images," or if we want to formulate a mindset through the *Divan* and make it "formable" so that it can be perceived, inevitably, the excursion and observation itself must have a system and a plan; otherwise, the observer will be lost in his distraught wandering and futile action.

The poet has provided us with the signs and trails—ghazals—for our excursion in this garden or traveling in this firmament; but we ourselves must find the sightseeing paths. From one flowerbed to another and from one image to another, each one of us finds his own path, and anyone who comes across the *Divan* of Hafez has his own relationship and experience with it.

The path of this treatise is a journey and a quest from darkness to light and back to darkness, from incomplete to complete to incomplete, and from man to God to man: from friend to friend! At the beginning, we will talk about the creation of light and the enlightened of the world, about the cup, wine, the tavern, and the Magian elder. Then there is a chapter about the gravitation of the mystic follower toward the mystic leader, about our gravitation toward Hafez and Hafez's toward the Magian elder, about the wish to flee and to stay within oneself. Then comes love, which is the impetus for being and the substance of existence and nonexistence. Being in the abode of nature and experiencing it fervently and also finding a way to the "hereafter" is the topic of another chapter. Then there is a contemplation of human ethics that bestows light upon the world and a contemplation of social man, who despite attachment to living with others does not become helpless in the trap of social events and flies beyond them. The conclusion is on poetic creation, an internal quest that uncovers its existence in poetry and becomes external. Here the conversation has to do with going beyond the self to reach the essence of the self, for the self to blossom and arrive at the friend, to depart from the self and fly to the alley of the friend!

Hence, this treatise is a journey from divine creation to poetic creation. In the first creation, the poet is "present," and in the other, God is "present." Two friends witness the conception of existence, the evolving and being of each other.

But because the friend of our Hafez, both within man and also outside him, is of two different worlds, the person who seeks to benefit from the poet to reach the alley of his own friend must bring to his imagination an ideal of absolute perfection. We are not talking about believing in a God who is standing there watching you. But if a person is unable to contemplate God in his own imagination, even if he takes many sips of the pure wine of the poems, he will not gain access to the entirety of the garden of Hafez and will not share his secret. In contrast, for those who consider the poet to be a "liberated" mystic or a superficially faithful believer and who then turn his poetry into a lifeless corpse, the Hafez of such readers does not reach beyond the level of a rend, a free-spirited libertine, who is the enemy of falsity and injustice. He would be perceived as an ethical social man, and many of his other dimensions would remain hidden.

This book is the travel diary of a traveler to the alley of the friend. On this journey, the couplets and ghazals have served as guiding stars, and the traveler has followed one and then another to complete his path. Even though the stars come from the friend, since I have chosen the path myself and whenever I have wished, I have paused by a shrub or a flower and rested alongside a meadow, and sometimes instinctively traveled and revisited the paths taken all over again. Since I have ridden on the wings of my own imagination, the value of this book is no more than that of a travel diary of a traveler. In other words, this is only one of the windows through which one can view the "garden" of Hafez. No doubt, one can shed other lights on this "firmament" and undertake other journeys of exploration.

In the Alley of the Friend

From This Hidden Fire . . .

Everyone has a star that is born with him and leaves this world with him. The star of fortune of the poet is the sun that existed at the beginning of time, and will remain forever. It has me in itself, and because of it, I am present at the beginning and at the end, since my star is my place of birth and my resting place. The bird sleeps on the mountain, the fish in the sea, and the poet in light, having bright dreams. He sets his imagination in flight, into the sky like a star in daylight and in the darkness of the night. Because the unruly steed of his imagination, his white colorful steed with sprawling mane and noble face, gallops with long, strong legs in waking and in sleep, it does not sleep and does not stop. And once he releases his star into the sky, in its light, he sees all that is worth seeing, since he now possesses a clear vision and embodies universal insight. How magnificent is the sun and what a friendly light is in my bosom, more brilliant and more clear-sighted than the eye of the sun!

> The flaming torch of the sun
> that rises in the eastern sky
> is lit from the hidden fire inside my breast*

The fire in my breast is restless, in drunkenness and in sobriety and in being and not being. How could my sun rest? When the silence of the

* Hafez's poems using the same spelling (with a few exceptions) are quoted from Qazvini and Ghani, eds. *Divan-e Hafez* (Tehran: Amir Kabir Publishers, 1969). [From ghazal 87; the translation of this couplet is from Geoffrey Squires, trans. *Hafez: Translations and Interpretations of the Ghazals* (Miami: Miami University Press, 2014), 419.]

nocturnal place of sleep comes softly and stealthily to conceal my light, my runaway sun is at work on the other side of night, to rise again and return. My night is not mere darkness, it is illumined darkness.

If a ray of light does not shine from my breast, my night and day and my moon and sun are the darkness of the night of the winter solstice; with blind eyes, I am present in nonexistence and in my prison, I observe the invisible. When can I find a place to escape from "the house of nature,"[1] this "shackled frame of the body,"[2] and open my eyes to reality, to the truth?

My midnight sun is the midday sun. I sleep in light, and in sleep I see clearly, because the source of the river of the sun is in the nocturnal darkness in which Adam's clay is molded in the measuring cup that reveals the entire universe and in which the water of life finds its way, like light.*

God molded Adam's body with clay and formed him into the shape he had envisioned. It was lifeless, lying on the ground, and did not have the ability to exist. Then God breathed into his mouth. The breath of God became the soul of man, and his body came to life. When God measured and molded the clay of man, man's form and figure capable of thinking came forth. But this form is no other than that which God nurtures and had in his mind. Hence, God created the form of his idea and gave form to his idea. Thus, man is a form of God's idea, or his formable idea.

In this manner, God's idea came to be, since everything can be perceived once its form can be imagined. Neither can absolute shapelessness be seen nor can it be perceived intuitively and inherently. Hence, in creating Adam, God became perceptible, and thus he created himself. In the words of the poet, he removed the veil from the face of thought, and man

* Last night I saw the angels
    tapping at the wine-shop's door,
And kneading Adam's dust
    and molded it as cups of wine.

[From ghazal 184; the translation of this couplet is from Dick Davis, trans. *Faces of Love: Hafez and the Poets of Shiraz* (New York: Penguin, 2013), 40. See also Squires, *Hafez*, 356, and Robert Bly and Leonard Lewisohn, trans. *The Angels Knocking at the Door: Thirty Poems of Hafez* (New York: HarperCollins Publishers, 2008), 39–40. For "the cup that reveals the entire universe," see endnote 16, and for "water of life," see endnote 11.]

perceived God, and then he could drink from the same cup from which the celestial denizens—those concealed, remote, and inaccessible ones—drank, and he accepted the covenant with God.[3]

In the rapture of this timeless and eternal unity, the powerless hands of the cruel and foolish—or according to the poet, "mad"—man accepted the friend's burden of trust.[4] He was cruel and foolish in agreeing to such a covenant. Had he known what he was doing, he would have split open like a mountain from fright; but because he did not know, he was cruel to himself. Like a flash of light in time, leaving before arriving, having the desire for eternity in his heart, and from the abyss of Satan grabbing for the zenith of God at every moment! "What is in the mind of this droplet that dreams the impossible," that he imagines he is the regent of God on earth?[5]

This is the fire that was cast on Adam's being one day, and when it was manifested to Moses on Mount Sinai and he asked, "Am I not your Lord?" he said, "You are." And when he accepted the covenant, his soul burned with the desire to see, but he was unable to see. A fire in the rays of which an insignificant candle laughs is but a plaything. The fire was that which was in the soul of Moses and made him a wanderer of deserts, throwing caution to the wind, on endless paths to see the friend and to spread the message, that which God wanted in the world.

Everyone, based on his own imagining, reveals a way for man to complete this mission and bring the burden of trust to some destination, and everyone who is on some path is at war with another who is not his traveling companion. The war of the seventy-two factions![6] In the dust of this struggle, truth remains obscured, and everyone is content with some fantasy and argues his case.

Nonetheless, let us leave behind the self-righteous fabricators of fanciful stories. The poet leaves behind these blind alleys and arguments and returns to the friend, and he sings in harmony and shares his heart with him. Now, in gratitude for this reconciliation, humans, spirits, stars, and spheres are all intoxicated dancers.

The poet does not contemplate creation; rather, in his own mind—which is of the same make and essence as the conceivable and evolving mind of God—he observes its happening. He has the gift of seeing the notion that says that since the time they began adorning the face of speech, "No one has drawn aside the veil / of Thought as Hafez has."[7]

In the darkness of yesternight, the poet saw that timeless time before creation, when not only was man being created, but also God was becoming God. In the nocturnal visit of this man who says, "we wanted him and he was filled with desire"[8] for us, the dawn of man and God is a single thing. In this unity, two friends become contemporaries, and man, as well, like God, is present at the time when there was no time and at the time when there will be no time. Man is from before the beginning and eternal, because he is with God, because God desires him, and God's desire is absolute, such that it cannot be quantified, a rapturous inevitable love that envelopes all of existence! Such a lover inevitably needs a beloved. The existence of the beloved in a love that cannot be nonexistent—and exists because it does—is a necessity beyond all free will. Our need for him, however, is also a need outside our own free will. Because we do not exist without his existence, we need him to exist, and since we seek him in ourselves and outside ourselves, in being and in death, our need is an eager quest for love.

Two beings filled with longing, two singular lovers, this is both a pleasant and a painful existence that the poet contemplates, and because of which he is alive. Even though we would not exist and could not be without him, without us, he would be a formless notion; and because he created us in the form of his idea, he emerged from his formless, boundless, and chaotic void and was able to see himself. He placed a mirror before himself.

But where and who is outside of him? The entire world is the mirror of his face. Man is in the world, and he looks into this mirror to once again find and recognize himself through it and repeat the statement of the "master of eternal beginning":[9] Man is the reflection of the face of God's idea, and when he looks at his idea, he returns to himself. The thought he manifests, however, is not merely of man but of the entire world. Hence, as man attains his self, he gains access to the entire world, and the all-encompassing eyes of his thought can see every boundless shore.

The poet is a man of clear vision, and clear vision occurs in light. The poet's seeing, however, is not merely with physical eyes that can only view external things outside the being of the seer. He sees the interior of things and the relationship that connects them and gives them life and soul. These cannot be perceived with the external eye. He views existence from the other side of light and darkness that can be seen, like the nocturnally vigilant god, the angel of good tidings,[10] who brings the message of divine blessing. Like Khezr,[11] who drinks the water in the heart of the dark region of hidden eternal light, the poet too is a "recluse." He is clear-sighted in seclusion and darkness; he sees by the internal light and inner eye; he has an alert heart. As for we who are the prisoners of our few senses and cannot go beyond the seeing and hearing of the body, our lamp is extinguished in the storm of darkness, and our ears cannot hear in the tumult of eating and sleeping. But he has chosen to live in the seclusion of darkness, on the other side of our vision that appears to be dark. He is present at a time and place in which we are absent: in the invisible world. And the invisible world is far away; it is strange and mysterious.

That is where he gains access to the water of life, opens his eyes to see the friend, and is released from sorrow, the sorrow of being a captive within the constricting walls of the body and remaining blind at the bottom of the bottomless pit.

> it has grown dark within
> perhaps from the hidden world
> someone will come and light a lamp[12]

My inner self as well is the realm of the invisible that keeps me invisible to myself. Inner blindness has kept me so removed from my origin and my truth that I do not know myself and my world, as though I am not within myself and another is within me. Something else made of anger and greed, of the burning temptation to dominate others and nature, is in command of me. Egotism has so filled me and so inflamed me, as though I am everyone and the entire world, and nothing and no one else exists but me. In this case, everything and everyone lose their attributes, because they can be seen only from my perspective. As a result, they are separated from their own nature, appear other than they are, and lose their "freedom." Hence, I take away the truth of things, leaving them hollow and empty.

But since it is impossible for one individual to dominate everyone and possess all that can be possessed, it is I who have lost my freedom; I have become a "thing," such that "any lingering attachments"[13] enslave me and keep me away from my truth, my reality, to the point that I become empty and "invisible" to my own self, and my self becomes my invisible realm that I no longer see.[14] The liberated poet resides in the secluded place of this invisible realm that is free of the tumult of my pseudolife: in this alley of the friend, which is his "Sinai desert."[15] And he is the light in that invisible remote place. Blessed by his light, darkness is destroyed, and if an eye is eager to see, it becomes enlightened by the vision of the invisible realm. Up to now, things were only seen in terms of their benefit or loss for me; but now, with the lamp which that recluse has lit, further beyond, I see people and things in the world that—in a different way and with a different meaning outside limited me, in relationships devoid of my egotism and intent—can also exist in harmony and friendship. The poet removes the mask from the unseen face of existence, leading me into its mysterious inner recesses, and in doing so, removes the veil of imagination from before my eyes and opens my eyes. He is a link that connects me to all that is other than myself. It is through his light that I see. He is the midnight sun and the cup that reveals the entire universe.[16]

And this nocturnal darkness, in which the poet resides and in the seclusion of which he dreams of creation, is a pregnant night that gives birth at dawn. Who else is the offspring of dawn but sunlight? Such a night is the source of light, and night like a mother nurtures her bright child within her veins. It is a night of good tidings in the bosom of which one is awake waiting for dawn to rise in the sky with its golden chariot and luminous horses. A darkness, a Khezr, and a cup of water.[17]

But the demonic darkness of Ahriman is different. No spot of light shines in it such that one could gaze at it with the eyes of the heart. It is a pervasive darkness the end of which you will never reach, no matter how far you go, and you will see nothing, no matter how long you look. "Companionship with oppressors is like sinking into the darkness of the night of the winter solstice,"[18] as though it is not followed by a dawn, as though it will never end; no matter how long you sit and wait, you will spend your life in darkness, unless you sever your covetousness for companionship and friendship with them and abandon them. "The ill-tempered ascetic"[19] also belongs to the same group of "upstarts" and "the arrogant," and with every morning that dawns, he descends like black night with the religious rulings he has in his hand and a scroll of what is permitted or prohibited, a morals police chief who "became a high priest and forgot his own debauchery."[20]

They are darkness, and they are imprisoned in the "darkness of bewilderment."[21] They are not even Alexander, who in search of the water of life[22] wandered in the region of darkness, because they search for nothing but themselves. Hence, they are darkness itself, and bewildered, they will remain in their own dark soul and heart.

The nocturnal darkness of Hafez, despite the terrifying waves and whirlpools,[23] is not of this sort. He is a Joseph lost in the well for whom the moon and the sun are searching, and once he comes out of his own inner recesses, he bestows light on the thirsty land of Egypt and the country of the eager eyes of lovers—the eyes of Zoleykha, Potiphar's wife, and the eyes of the soul of Jacob. In his boundless mind, the moon and the sun are awake.

> Last night in my sleep I dreamed that a moon had risen
> the brightness of whose face
> put an end to the darkness of separation[24]

Happy is "the auspicious night" that is followed by such a "blissful dawn,"[25] and the poet, longing for such a dawn, keeps vigil and is anxious at night. He is moving in a desert of massive darkness, like a ray of light in the warp and weft of the night, and because of wakefulness, he does not allow the silence and stagnation of the darkness of the world to sleep in his concealed hands. A moonlit stream softly moves toward the dawn in this long dream. At dawn, the "mysterious messenger of the tavern" places in his hand the cup of the sun that can reveal the universe, and reveals to him the secret of both worlds.[26]

Seeing clearly is awareness, seeing clearly with the eye of the heart and revelation that lights the spirit like a lamp; and the light of the lamp shines on all that exists. The world and I both, like a singular body, like the body of the sun, light up; we are both the eye and the vision, and as we see, so we are seen. We are hidden manifestations who are manifest in our concealment and, with the exception of ourselves, we who are an unrevealed secret, we face no secret. Then even after death, I boast of seeing in nonexistence. Is it not true that I know the secret of both worlds?

And it is at dawn that the tavern elder places the cup that reveals the universe in my hands, and when I look into the mirror, I see your beauty, and my heart becomes aware. Happy is the awareness of the poet who awakens at dawn longing for the "face of the sun," and the sun bestows upon his spirit the light of its face.[27] When the aspirations of a poet of this kind mingle with the breath of those who rise at dawn, the poet is freed "from the shackles of life's sorrows": "Last night, at dawn, in my distress, salvation was given to me."[28]

The messenger angel of God is the messenger and the revealer of the secrets of the invisible realm, and God himself is the guardian of night, who in the mysterious darkness of the night safeguards the world against harm from demons, to entrust it to the caravan of light. The rooster is the good harbinger of dawn and belongs to it. Our "Tongue of the Invisible"[29] is the "monarch of the kingdom of dawn"[30] who hears the "good tidings" of the invisible voice of dawn with the ears of his spirit.

At dawn, my good fortune came to my bedside
And told me, arise, the beloved king has come.[31]

But this dawn is not before the sun appears, when darkness has lost its hue and has removed its veil from the body of nature; rather, it is a dawn in nocturnal darkness, in the heart and depth of night, and at precisely the time when the end of night arrives, later and farther away than at any other time. When the darkness of the world has surrounded the poet and imprisoned him, the light of dawn shines on his spirit, and the sorrow that had been lodged in him becomes insignificant and is destroyed. The one "who has chosen seclusion and rises at dawn"[32] lights up in ultimate darkness, like the North Star that has a bright heart on dark nights and, if a patch of cloud does not block our view, shows the pilgrims the way to the realm of light. Similar to the light of the water of life, which is in a dark cave, the dawn of the poet is an internal light in external darkness. Otherwise, the poet would not say, "at dawn, in that darkness of night."[33] After all, dawn is not morning. Hafez's dawn is not always at the end of night; it is often in the heart of it. A night that has such a dawn is the "night of revelation," with the brightest sun and greatest manifestation of sight. The poet resides in the east of this manifestation, precisely where light emerges. When he is distanced from there, he is alienated from being a poet, and he is no longer the cup that reveals the universe; he is the dust of the road. "I am the visionary cup that reveals the world / and the dust of the true path."[34]

Now I return and say that the sun's cup that reveals the universe is the poet's star of good fortune, and blessed by its light in this nocturnal darkness that engulfs him, he loses himself and becomes intoxicated by the manifestation of the beauty of the face of the friend.

"With the reflection of your face in the mirror of the cup" of my heart, now a ray of your essence and manifestation of your beautiful face is in me.[35] Blessed by your magnanimous light, my beautiful spirit is bright, and I see myself in you. But if I did not have a ray of you, I would be dark and unable to see. Hence, it is your favor that gives sight to my eyes, and now that I can see, I recognize myself again. From now on, I will look into the mirror: "from now on, my face and beauty's mirror."[36] But since you blew into me a manifestation of your beauty, I am also your mirror:

in the beauty of your face   admire God's handiwork
in the mirror of my heart   behold the divine.[37]

Look at the friend to see yourself, and look at yourself to see the friend. Two mirrors that reflect each other: light in light.

The brightness of the friend's face shone in the cup of your heart and made of it a cup that reveals the universe. Jamshid is the discoverer of wine, the possessor of the sun, and the king of light.[38] Old age and death do not exist in his realm, and everyone enjoys eternal spring and youth. And because the source of light is in his paradise, the denizens of his paradise do not know the meaning of darkness. The cup of Jamshid, which is the goblet of the sun and the gem of light, not only bestows light on everything and makes the gift of seeing possible, but is itself the seer of all things; and for anyone who has it, all veils are removed from before his eyes, and he will learn all the secrets of the world. Nothing remains concealed from his path-finding eyes. He holds a cup in his hand, or his hands are a cup with which and in which he sees the entire world: a full-length mirror that reflects everything. When the sun rises, in its light the earth and the sky become illuminated; but the cup of Jamshid is the imagining of that sun that not only brightens the secret heart of the earth and the sky, but contains the image of all the high and low secrets.

> Veils are removed from the earth and the heavens
> For anyone who serves the cup that reveals the universe.[39]

This is the organ of sight that, as it sees, can be seen itself. It sees the world, and the world can be seen in it. Hence, if it looks at itself, it sees everything. And when it sees everything, it sees its own truth. It is an image of an internal sight in which the outside and inside are one.

Keykhosrow,[40] who was the king of the Persians, possessed just such a cup that revealed the universe; and Hafez, who is the poet of lovers, has such a cup in his heart, which is the secret place of God's treasures. His heart, which is in search of the cup of Jamshid, searches in vain for it here and there, and pleads with strangers.[41] Man's heart is the full-length mirror and the cup that reveals the entire universe. But was this ray of the beauty of the friend manifested only in the heart of man? He is the creator of the entire universe. Hence, his manifestation can occur at any time and in any place, in everything and in the midst of all things, and more than anything else, in the cup of inebriating wine.

For a person like me, who every day passes through the corridors of making a living and retires, settling behind a desk, spending my life at a job that is futile and weary, and struggling in the entangling snares of daily routines, living means chewing up and spitting out my life. Guided by the expediency that arranges my relationships with others and provides me with my daily bread, I walk with the feet of a minor intellect that crawls like a worm, hoards like an ant, and rips asunder like a wild boar. Every day, the same smiles, the same repeated lies, and the same injustices boil up from the ground and pour down from the sky. What dark and lasting weariness! It is as though my life were passing through an underground tunnel.

Inebriation from wine is the antidote that frees me for a few moments from the twists and turns of entanglement in expediency. "Oh wine, may my whole life and body be sacrificed for you."[42] Even if not much else is to be said about wine, at least for a moment, it "makes one unaware of the temptations of reason."[43] How long in the greater or lesser scheme of things should one writhe around himself like a snake and with wounded hands and feet blindly grope in the dark and not get anywhere? He could see that the human spirit suffers injustice and his life is fraught with pain, that divine justice is in the hands of the powerful and the "upstarts," and that the angel is the captive of the demon. The vultures devour the carcasses of the fallen, and the hyenas fight over their corpses. The hypocrites are rewarded, and the truthful are punished. Without a sip of wine to erase the memory of sorrow from the poet's heart, the dread of events uproots his foundation.[44] He desires a potent wine that can bring down a champion, so that "for a while I may forget / the iniquity of these times."[45]

But all this aside, the wine that can free us for a moment is indicative of another wine that affects the "essence of the soul" and takes us somewhere beyond this chaos that has no purpose.[46] In the same way that inebriation means separation and freedom from reason, this mystical inebriation is rapture and respite from the tangible needs and freedom from the confines of human fate. The "wine" of this inebriation is a ray of light from him, and the brightness and beauty of seeing the friend is manifested in the cup of wine that is the source of this inebriation. Wherever the brightness of his beauty shines, that place, like the human heart, becomes a mirror "reflecting God."[47] The brightness of his face is everywhere; and wherever it is, there is the human heart, just as the human heart is everywhere. For our Hafez, the cup, the mirror, and the heart are three synonymous concepts born at the same time.

The radiance of his face was reflected in the mirror, and the brightness of the face of the cupbearer, in the cup; and the heart "grasped at her tresses." Love arrived! "The beauty of your face reflected in the mirror" and certain illusory thoughts appeared in my "mirror of illusions," with vain hopes that I imagined to be true, and I was deceived by my own imagination. From the brightness of the face of the friend, many strange images and colorful forms appeared in the mirror of imagination, and creation was born.[48] The world is the mirror and the cup of wine, and the heart is the cup that reveals the universe and the cup of Jamshid. "The heart that reveals the unseen and holds the cup of Jamshid" is the universe.[49] And the wine in this cup is the brightness of the face of the friend, like the sun that in the cup of the sky is the brightness of the face of the universe.

> If you must have sunlight at midnight, cast off the veil
> From the rosy face of the daughter of the vine.[50]

Neither does this "midnight sun" have any ray of his face, nor is it an allusion to somewhere or something else. It is none other than that which they take from the vine, place in the wine cellar, and, once it is clarified, even drink its dregs.

There is a revolving firmament that, with its stars of fortune, with night and day and seasons and the moon and the sun, and with its images and sleight of hand, creates time in its revolution, and because we have fallen into the rotation of days, inevitably, we are moving along with it; and in the same way that it brought us at one time, it will take us away at another time. Its work is a meaningless game, one without purpose, and if it does have a purpose, the knower of the world does not know it. In any case, since our lives pass in time, our suffering comes along with the passing of days and bears us away, as though if this passing were not constant, the time for my suffering would not arrive. Hence, there is a simultaneity between the days that come from the revolving firmament and my misfortune. The firmament is blind and absentminded and can neither see nor feel my pain. My soul is steeped in sorrow, and my spirit is silent. A hand is smothering my heart in darkness. Where is a meteor to split the heart of this darkness? Wine in a vat that will erase the darkness of suffering and return the brightness to my heart.

> If your heart is about to burst
> From the injustice of the firmaments, Hafez,
> Throw a meteor at the demon of sorrow.[51]

When I had reached the point of being at the end of my rope because of the injustice of the world, I opened the door of the dark wine cellar, removed the veil from the purple face of the sun that was hidden in it, and drank the sun; and with its rays my heart brightened and became free.

I have been struck by an arrow of the firmament
Give me wine so that inebriated
I can knot the cord of Gemini's quiver
Then splash a sip from the cup on this palanquin
And hurl the hubbub of the harp into the azure sky.[52]

On the night when the demon raids, wine is the midnight sun that frees me from the injustice of the world and the fear of nonexistence that is with me in life and in death.[53] Fear of the silent desert of sleepers in which every traveler disappears embitters my life; it slips like a dream into my wakefulness and does not allow me to be free. From early dawn, the night is the fellow traveler of the sun that brings it down from the middle of the sky and stabs it in the back with the dagger of sunset; but the sun—which runs like the wind through the fertile field of night—sees the morning. The cup of the poet's heart on that journey, at which all roads end, is overflowing with "midnight sun," and even without the hope of a morning, it gains victory over the fear of dark loneliness,* because with the help of the mirror that he has, "he boasts of sight in nonexistence."[54]

O tie a cup to my shroud
so that on the day of resurrection
with wine I may dispel the fear of judgment[55]

The wine that paves the path of life and eases death for me is not merely a sign of and an allusion to "the brightness of the face of the cupbearer in

* "Bring the ship of wine, so that we may ride happily / Away from this sea whose shores are invisible." [From ghazal 428; Squires translates this couplet as follows: "bring me a vessel of wine / so that I may cross the sea / to that undiscovered shore." Squires, *Hafez*, 102.]

the cup";[56] rather, it is wine itself, because it drives the demon from my heart, and "when the demon departs, the angel arrives."[57] The good news of "the messenger angel of the invisible realm"[58] replaces "the demon of suffering."[59] Two wines, each from a different world, blend; the essences of the heavens and the earth become united and one in the mind of our Hafez. In this condition, "the lamp of the cup," as wide as the sky, and the purple color of the wine achieve the brightness of the candle of the sun.[60] "The sun of wine from the east of the cup" rises, and in its light, "from the garden of the face of the cupbearer, a thousand tulips" bloom.[61] The dallying of the darkness of sorrow withers in the cup of the heart, and the garden of sight blossoms. Moonlight loses color in the rays of the cup, and the sun lights up the morning harvest with the light of the lamp of wine.[62] Wine is as bright as the insightful heart of the poet.

The poet seeks the sun of truth, the essence of the cup that reveals the universe, or the cup of Jamshid, so that from the brightness of the wine that it contains, like Jamshid and Keykhosrow, he can behold existence and nonexistence. But since this wine was given to him before the dawn of creation, before any Jamshid or Keykhosrow, they are the ones who have drunk Hafez's wine and found a way into the heart of creation.

like Jamshid drink from that visionary cup
whose rays disclose the secrets of heaven and earth[63]

In truth, who is this man? How can a person who lived such a short and difficult life during the darkest period of history within the confines of the four walls of a city boast of knowing the secrets and being the king of two worlds?* How can a person whose pillow is merely a clay brick hope

* See the following ghazal [488]:

Dawn   in the tavern   and the mysterious voice
that acts as my guide   said

come back again   you that for so long
have frequented this place.
[Squires, *Hafez*, 325]

to step on the peak of the Seven Planets? The difference between the lowly life and the soaring desire of this mendicant is the difference between earth and heaven. But the poet traverses that distance accompanied by Khezr and does not seek the water of life without his guidance, because he knows that it passes through the realm of darkness. "Fear the danger of going astray!"[64]

Khezr is the guiding angel, the divine face of the soul, a reflection of his face in the mirror of the heart, or the other self of the poet, who rises in the "darkness" of dawn from the pinnacle of the soul; he is his Magian elder. During the period of restrictions and prohibitions when the poet lived and when wine, like freedom, was forbidden on religious grounds, some kindred spirits would surreptitiously make wine; but selling wine was the work of a few non-Muslim Zoroastrians who were not worried about their reputations and being disgraced. Taverns were located in remote areas and isolated neighborhoods in order not to offend the public morality of the faithful. Only the infamous haunters of a pothouse and carefree, wise kindred spirits knew the secret path to it. The old magi would secretly make wine in a back room or a cellar. The cellar where the vats were kept was the dark house; the daughter of the vine was veiled, and the water of life was in darkness. My body is the veil of the spring of the heart and the cellar of vats, the veil of the sparkle of wine. Light is at the heart of darkness.

Khezr shows the way to the water of life, and the old Magi, to the essence of a ruby that "holds no engraved image other than truthfulness."[65] The tavern is the place of the truthful, and the breath of the truthful is the morning and light of the world: "Strive to be truthful and the sun will be born from your breath."[66] What Solomon could have such breath of Christ?[67] The beggars at the door of the tavern are the owners of this "kingdom of poverty," and the smallest part of this kingdom stretches from "the moon to the fish."[68] Simorgh,[69] this legendary bird of truth, spreads its wings over the entire world, and its eyes, like the spear of the sun, penetrate all that exists. Hafez the mendicant, who shares the cup of wine with the celestial denizens, boasts of this indigent Christlike kingdom.

Is there any transient albeit aware mortal who would boast of such hopeful dreams and not suddenly return to his own insignificance, and not remember that he is like a candle in the wind? That is why after that high flight of aspiration, he suddenly falls to the ground of his human and beloved limitations and says: You do not understand, and you cannot boast of poverty. What are you doing, and how do you want to bring the high heavens under your feet? Descend from the zenith of the heavens; do not abandon the gathering of Turan Shah, who is an insignificant minister with a bit of wealth; and do not abandon this comfort with the hope of reaching lofty heights.[70]

Placing one's head at the threshold of a tavern, the walls of which, despite being low, reach up to the heavens, is like being in paradise. Such a wine worshipper with his short arms grabs the sanctuary of the heavens from his earthly abode, as though such a tavern, with its crumbling walls and roof but with the essence of the sun in its cellar of vats, is the workshop of creation, just as the ruin that is the human body, despite old age and decrepitude, is the secret place of the heart and the house of the artistry of God. The tavern and the body both have two secret treasures, each a light in their prison that longs for manifestation and freedom.

Adam's clay was kneaded in the tavern, and it was formed into the shape that God held in his imagination. In "the tavern of love, they leaven human nature,"[71] this bewildered nature that remains in the grand talisman of the body, this flying bird that has fallen into the cage of the body and whose heart flies toward the friend! The tavern of Hafez is an ocean at the bottom of which is the sole pearl of love, and the diving poet plunges in search of a gem in the waves and storm, and this "sea whose shores are invisible"[72] is a ruin that contains the light of the friend, which is the house of light. The person who wipes his eyes with the dust of the tavern nurtures his eyes with light and is able to look into the cup that reveals the universe, which is the mirror of secrets. The Sufis and dervishes wait in vain to see the beloved friend in the monastery in order to tread the path of love. The secret of the monastery is revealed through the "blessing of the cup."[73] One must find a way to the "threshold of the tavern."[74] And the one who finds the secret of the two worlds reads it in the line of the cup; and he who also finds his way from the image in the dust to the wondrous secrets of the heart's cup that reveals the universe "turns dust into gold with a glance,"[75] and because of the attributes of gold, the quality of things changes. Not that the worthless mudbrick and dust would acquire the glimmering of gold; rather, the cloak of darkness falls off the human frame, and man's "illuminated persona" emerges. Such a spectator, with the elixir of gold that he has in the eye of his heart when he looks at the world, from the brightness of the light, the body of existence, sees beautiful colorful images.

> at every moment the image of your face
> blocks the road of my imaginings
> to whom shall I tell the things
> I see in this shadow play[76]

Neither the body nor the tavern remain within their strict boundaries, neither the body within its frame nor the tavern within nature. The body shows the way to the friend through the path of the heart, and the tavern through wine. Two windows of light, one in the dark house of the body and the other in the monastery of the Magi,[77] show man the way to the spring of the sun. The seeker of the spring, however, must undoubtedly go beyond "the house of nature."[78]

The nature of the world and of man is not some carrion that has been created without reason, futile and in vain, deserving detestation. The body is neither corruption nor darkness, and the asceticism of the Manichean monks is not pleasing to our poet. He is enamored with gazing at the garden of the world, and he considers every moment of it a rare opportunity for enjoyment. To be "beside a spring, by a stream,"[79] with a book, a cup, and a companion, is a joy that he would not exchange for this or the next world. Because of some unexplained coincidence, being able to live for a few days and walk on earth is a rare opportunity that you pilfer from the claws of miserly time. Beneath the ground is the house of failed dreams; but to become enamored of nature and to remain helpless watching these enchanting images and not see anything beyond is to fall into the trap of appearances. Nature is a manifestation of truth, but it is not the complete truth. When you gaze at the growth of plants, the flight of birds, the loneliness of stars, and the weeping of the rain with the heart's eye; when you hear the sounds of the day and the silence of the mountain with the ear of your intellect; and when you wash your wandering soul in the running water, you join the sea along with the stream and overflow with the memory of the friend.

This same world, with its pains and regrets, that abandons its offspring on earth and like a very patient vulture awaits their death and decay, is the workshop of God's creation: like the human body, like Hafez's tavern! The world is not merely these ruins in which humans in the name of reason run about like madmen. This workshop, with the light that it contains, takes you outside its four walls. God's workshop of creation is a house in which, if you are able to see, the house of God is discernable. The tavern is an image of an exalted creation, because a nature that extends beyond "the house of nature" and beyond itself finds its way to the alley of truth.

Somewhere far away, water bubbles forth and saturates the parched body of the earth. A stream is a sign of the existence of the spring and its flowing in a narrow channel. This narrow stream is connected to that bubbling spring in the same way that the low roof of the tavern is connected to the seventh heaven! And the poverty of those who frequent this tavern is the wealth of both worlds.

In this house of ruins, a messenger brings the good tidings of paradise. The tavern of the poet is not the raw substance of silent nature. In the realm of imagination, it may be another form of this house with two doors, the world as a caravanserai: the Magi's tavern and the light of God, darkness and a window to liberation! And the poet himself is astounded by "what light he sees, and from where."[80]

The path of the journey of the haunters of the tavern traverses darkness, and the danger of going the wrong way looms like an ambush by bandits. One should not thus embark without the guidance of Khezr. A traveler without a guide who has knowledge of the secrets will remain helpless on the path and will not reach the desired destination. The unknown route of this journey is not the sort of knowledge that can be found in a book. There may be knowledgeable people who have learned a great deal about the movement of the stars, the how and why of things, and the ways and the protocols of affairs, but they are confused and take the wrong path in the world. They are like a blind man with a torch and a cane; they search the bowels of nature and destroy it; and they imagine the means of making a living, the manipulation of politics, and sleight of hand in order to eat and sleep to be truth. Imagine having a lamp in hand but with eyes that are blind in the house of the heart.

Such knowledge ruins my world and destroys my soul. Even if the knowledge of ascetics, religious jurists, theologians, and Koranic interpreters could not ruin the world of that memorizer of the Koran,[81] it would at least make the life of kindred spirits like him bitter. Philosophers, alchemists, astrologers, and soothsayers did not provide answers to the poet's unanswerable questions, and the pretentious physicians did not remedy his pain. Among the mystics and Sufis, he was not fond of any of the elders. His recollection of them brought a sneer, and their names would be uttered by him with the sarcasm that hypocrites deserve. After all, even though they too repudiated the learned, with their various theories about the stages of the spiritual journey and its rules, the rites and ceremonies of wearing the habit, and the protocols of being an elder leader and a novice follower, as well as other complicated proceedings, they had turned the love for the friend into a secret science. In contrast to a few reclusive kindred spirits, many were those who wore the Sufi habit and their leaders, who especially in those days were the confidants of bloodthirsty rulers. The Sufi elder was a drinking companion of the religious inquisitor and an associate and intimate friend of the prominent figures of the government and the political elite of the country. The faith of the Sufis was the wealth of the elder, the sect, and the hierarchy of the organization of the government; and the followers were his subjects. He was the commander of all the followers and an ally of other rulers. Before God's people, he would pretend to prostrate himself on his prayer rug and would not rest in his beneficence; but in private, he acted "in a wholly different way,"[82] and in every instance, hypocritically.

The poet, that clever, free-spirited libertine, could see that neither the knowledge of the former group nor the piety of the latter would accomplish anything. But he also knew that whoever embarks on a quest for the water of life without the help of Khezr would in the end return like Alexander, empty-handed.

God created man and the world with intermediaries: through the Essences,[83] the Holy Spirit, the First Intellect,[84] and so on. In every religion and creed, reuniting with him involves learning from the prophets, saints, and guides, or going through various stages and following the path of physical and spiritual experiences. In Iranian mysticism, the idealized elder and leader who is the manifestation of either the Holy Spirit, Gabriel, or Khezr is the knot that ties the human hand to God's string. Hafez's Holy Spirit is the Magian elder, who blows his Christlike breath into the poet.

> So what if the Magian elder became my spiritual leader?
> No head exists devoid of some mystery of God.[85]

Among all the well-known spiritual elders, the poet chose the Magian elder as his spiritual guide. His guide to the realm of truth has spent his life in the aberration of unbelief, in the tavern of wine worshippers and the debauched, and his aged eyes have seen much ugliness and much beauty. This "clever libertine who disregards consequences"[86] and disregards fame and notoriety has engaged in every act, has played every role, has not set his heart on any deception, and has not feared the end. He has regarded this and the next world and science and religion as naught, and he has committed every sin but one: hurting others! Indifferent to the heavenly maidens and the rivers of honey in paradise, heedless of the demons with fiery maces in hell, with a cup of wine, he has removed the rust of sorrow from the heart of the good and the bad.

In the distant past, the magi were religious leaders with esoteric knowledge of divine secrets. They knew astrology, medicine, magic, religious rites and rituals, and they were interpreters of dreams. They knew of the secrets of the sky and the body—the macrocosm and the microcosm—how to affect the lives, deaths, and good fortunes of others, how to read the roles of destiny and the future in the shape and movement of the flames of fire, the ways and customs of conversion to the religion and joining the celestial world; and since they understood the mute language of dreams, they received signs, good tidings, and warnings from the invisible world. The magi were secretive, and because of this, they helped terrestrial humans to enjoy the kindness of God and safeguarded them from the hostility of demons. But the issue of who they were—were they a tribe, a secret sect, or a class—is not very clear. Was Zoroaster himself one of the magi and their master, or did they exist before him and later convert to his creed and become leaders in the benediction of fire?

Our knowledge of the magi is sporadic, based on conjecture, and mostly by way of outsiders who at times recounted what they saw, and most often what they heard. Whatever the truth may be, however, in all pre-Islamic histories, the magi were mentioned among the religious groups, and they engaged in spiritual matters.

In the Islamic period, Muslims interpreting *magi* (*majus*) to mean "Zoroastrian" considered them to be worshippers of Hormoz, the god of light, to be fire worshippers and wine drinkers, and they avoided them. The poet chooses just such an undesirable figure as his desired ideal. He turns away from the war among the seventy-two factions,[87] each of which claims to hold the gem of truth in its own bag alone, and he turns to a lost soul, a lowly, vanquished person who cannot boast of guiding anyone.

Iranian mysticism and mystic poets in particular were cognizant of the monastery of the magi and the Magian elder, and occasionally, they toyed with this idea; but no poet other than Hafez considered the Magian elder his spiritual leader or lived as he did in the aura of the monastery of the Magi.

In that period of disarray after the Mongols, the Ilkhanids, the Atabaks, and others, when the spirit and the home of Iranians were being torn to shreds by bared swords and raw violence, the eternal memory of the Magi, which had been asleep under the cover of oblivion, was awakened in the memory of the poet. This is not to imply that, like a sociologist or a psychologist politician in a chaotic time and with a predisposed plan, he reminded the people about their cultural history so that they would not neglect their interconnectedness and unity. Rather, the fluid ancient spirit of Iranian culture worked within him secretly, lived in his soul, came into being on his tongue, and was born; and the Hafez (memorizer, protector) of secrets became the discoverer of secrets, like water that runs underground and once it reaches amenable land bubbles forth like a spring and gleams from the joy of seeing the sun. A lost memory was returning through poetry. The war and chaos of politics and the social disarray had scattered the people with their distraught consciences, and the star of poetry brought them together around the center of light.

Hafez, of course, was a child of his own time, and with the Koran that he had in his memory and with the Semitic mythology and philosophy, he lived in a Muslim world, and mysticism wove together, like warp and weft, his self-awareness and his knowledge and gave existence to his worldview. Nevertheless, from the soil of the same worldview, the plant of an ancient indigenous idea continually raised its head and created from all this a pleasant and harmonious nature. Mysticism irrigated these "plant temptresses"[88] that blossomed in the subconscious of the poet and took on a new color and hue with the language of the poet.

In Zoroaster's Gathas, there is a constant struggle between light and darkness and truthfulness and lies, with a burning desire to see the truth, to look within, and to witness the brightness of the heart's eye. In Mani's creed, every seed of light makes an arduous effort to be freed from the darkness of the body and to join in endless light. The God of Love, Izadmehr or Mithra, is born in a cave—like a spring of light—from a rock. The worshippers of Mithra, with seven ceremonies of conversion and with the help of secret sciences, worshipped this mysterious god of light in secret societies and dark Mithraea. The messenger angel, the good-news messenger of the sky who always accompanied it, gave the good tidings of its rise at dawn.

The radiance of ideas of this sort, consciously or unconsciously, infuses the entire *Divan* and bestows brightness upon it. It seems as though the foundations of the subconscious of the poet should be sought in the distant past, having reached him from memory to memory in various ways through stories, legends, anecdotes, narratives, beliefs, and superstitions, and more than all the traditions of mysticism, written and unwritten, have reached the hidden well of his memory, like internal currents of water, and have every time jetted out from that depth; and as they have come, they have also called him toward them.

The poet's turning to the Magian elder, whose name is the twin of *wine*, *fire*, and *light*, is the return of the enlightened of the past to the Koran with the generous and accepting heart of Hafez, who had opened its door to any seeker of truth. The ancient and mysterious Magian knowledge that led the way to God's secret came back to life in him.

Hence, a poet who chose an indigent beggar as his ideal spiritual leader not only escaped like a clever bird from the snare of the learned and the mystics in order to fly freely but, with the adroit wine-worshipping Magian elder, he also reached the light and rapture of inebriation and joined the old Magi, who was a mysterious reminder of old times, in order to reiterate the ancient word in a new language.

My Rose-Colored Elder . . .

After all these fears and hesitations, once I threw caution to the wind and took a few steps, again in vain and naked, and I am stuck where I was like a dried-up tree, an empty-handed man whose feet are in the chains of the earth. I see this garden, and I am bewildered as to how and on which path I should take an excursion into it. I see all its flowers with the colorful stories they compose, and all of them "no more than one tale,"[1] simultaneously calling to me; and from every image a flower garden grows in my imagination. Every ghazal is a living being whose heart beats with a mountain of memories and feelings and with colorful dreams, albeit in a cloud of ambiguity. The thoughts of the poet flow throughout this garden like a single stream with runaway branches and furrows, saturating every flower and plant. When you linger for a moment and gaze at some corner of the garden, the entire garden becomes visible in the mirror, because a halo of light and shadow surrounds every ghazal; and depending on the light that every reader shines on this crystal prism from his own thoughts and feelings, the surrounding vague halo provides a new color and aspect to the ghazal. No ghazal is an isolated, small flowerbed set aside from the magical garden of the bard's *Divan*; rather, even though it is separate, it contains a mystery and an intimation of the entire garden. The mood and atmosphere of the entire *Divan* flows throughout most of the ghazals and soaks into them like fresh water. The images of a singular idea come to life each time within the skeletal frame of a ghazal, and each time, a corner of the nocturnal sky is reflected in a colorful pond. But the stars that are reflected in the water are themselves parts of the bodies of the firmament; and if we have the face of the sky in our memory, the reflection of a few stars awakens images of the sky in our hearts. And when we want to express what we see from the radiance of the stars that we see in the mirror of the water, we must speak all at once about all the images that are before our eyes and in our memory. This agitates the water of the pond and makes everything muddied. And if we only speak of the few stars that we see unrelated to the heavenly bodies, the fear is that we will spill the blood of the ghazal and be left with merely certain euphonious but lifeless words. Yet, if the *Divan* of the poet is a mirror as wide as an ocean that reflects the entire sky of his mind, then his thoughts are a sky, every part of which is the center and circumference, every part of which is the beginning and the end. No matter on which star you are, you are at the center, and all the other stars are around you, and from wherever you begin, that place can be the end.

> There is no end to the story of me and the beloved
> That which has no beginning has no end.[2]

For instance, in creation, man is separated from God, like a drop from the ocean; but before he is separated, he is in him and unaware that he is God. In order to contemplate and to see a ray of the sun, he must first be separated from his own source; otherwise, he will be submersed in it and unable to distinguish between himself and the spring of light. As long as man is in God, he is not himself and cannot have self-awareness. Hence, inevitably, he is not aware of his nonexisting self. Thus, the creation that separates man from God connects him to God and to himself. On the other hand, the God of the mystics is in man; and once the mystic attains himself, he has attained God. Hence, when man is separated from God, in that very moment, he rejoins him. Alienation and unity are but a single moment and "identical." If thought begins with God, it reaches man and is imperceptible without imagining God; and if it begins with the created world—which is a manifestation of the face of God—it reaches the creator, who is imperceptible without man, because more than anything else, perception is a human concept, and if the perceiver does not exist, the connection between God and the world and man remains broken. In that case, the world is no more than a raw and meaningless substance, the existence of which is no different from nonexistence.

Now we will look at this "seemingly false" notion in another context.

In the continuous current of time, man is but a spark that flickers and fades. He is an instant in the eternity of God; but since the same swift meteor is a light from timeless God, he is present in the past that has no beginning and in the future that has no end; he is from preexistence and he exists for all eternity. Every timeless being, however, in order to contain all times, must be released like a "shot arrow" in time, such that as he passes through time, time also passes through him to become accepting of time and aware of time; and the knowledge of preexistence and eternity is awakened in him. Had man not fallen into the world, there would be timelessness without an awareness of time, and, therefore, he would not recognize that he is eternal, because outside the movement of the world, no time exists. Similarly, if God had not created the world with time, his eternity would not have any meaning. Hence, in order for man to be eternal, he must be mortal, and because he is mortal, he can be eternal and exist for all eternity.

Also, from a different perspective, "the worldly wise are the pivot of the compass of existence,"[3] because they are bewildered lovers; and bewildered lovers, like the prudent, are the axis of the circle of existence and are in the center of it. They so overflow with the beloved that they are oblivious to their own selves. And the otherwise self-sufficient, coquettish beloveds need the lovers and exist because of them. The lover and the beloved are "dependent on the existence of love,"[4] and in its free prison are static wanderers.

These few examples are indications of the interconnected beginning and end of the poet's thoughts. Within this circle, every point is both the center and the circumference. The revolving movement of his thinking, like a skein as immense as the firmament, simultaneously turns around itself and around another truth, a conception of God, the friend; and its fluid warp and weft with colorful images continuously float in the heart of this firmament. It is an earth that itself revolves and also revolves around the sun; and the workshop of spring and autumn imprints fresh images on its water and soil through the hands of sunlight and moonlight and flowers and plants.

The fear always exists that if someone "dissects" this revolving, evolving, and fluid firmament, the delicate balance of which hangs by a hair, its wholeness would break apart, its colorful magic would fall asunder, and the harmony of the magical music of the words would crumble like a shattered cup. "You know that the mirror cannot withstand a sigh."[5] As soon as the surgical knife that would dissect an organ descends on the solid, interconnected body of this thinking, its blood is spilled; its living, active, and effective body is transformed into a dead corpse, a test subject that has no function of its own and is now an externally drawn, passive, receptive body ready for dissection and not for anatomical study. Who is the elder and what does being a clever free-spirited libertine mean? What are honesty and hypocrisy, drunkenness and sobriety, love and reason? Is the beloved an earthly sweetheart or a celestial god; and is wine the essence of grapes or the symbol of divine blessing? Is the world a ruined caravanserai or the workshop of God's creation? What is a human being, a manifestation of Satan or the masterpiece of creation? There are many other questions. Separating each one of these concepts in the *Divan* from others and dissecting it might be useful in the study of its lexicon, but it will not constitute a way to understand the poet's thinking. Rather, ultimately, it would present the *Divan* as something like *Golshan-e Raz*,[6] which, although an excellent collection of verse for understanding theoretical mysticism, is not poetry, especially the poetry of Hafez. If the different places of rest for the travelers through the mind of the poet are separated from other places of rest, and the roads between them are cut off, each place of rest becomes a desert oasis, and the travelers lose their way and do not get anywhere.

The eager devotees of Hafez, of course, have always been satiated by his refreshing spring without the help of commentators and interpreters, even with those "inauthentic" manuscripts. A knowledge of rhetoric, prosody, meter and rhyme, and so forth is not the main requirement for experiencing and perceiving poetry. Great is the number of astronomers who are oblivious to the colorful beauty of the earth. Devoid of knowledge of the solar system, the relationship between the earth and the sun, and how and why seasons occur, no one is deprived of enjoying spring and autumn. To observe the outstretched wings of summer and the white silence of winter, one need not learn astronomy.

Of course, commentary on the terminology and interpretations of the concepts of the *Divan* undoubtedly help us understand the content of the poems; but they do not show us a way into the mystery of the insightful mind of the poet. This is not a mystery or an encryption for which someone can uncover its secret codification system, decipher it, and be done with it. Hafez's thinking is a rainbow that in the light of the eyes of every clear-sighted person presents new details and chiaroscuros. It is the magic of colorful light in the sky of the eyes of the onlookers; and every eye, within the limits of its own vision, penetrates the changing spectra of the primary colors. In that case, setting the sights of one's heart on a flight in the atmosphere of this rainbow and traveling with light might be a way into the interior of this sphere filled with images and an attempt at unraveling the mystery.

If we consider the poet's thought processes to be like a living body, instead of dissecting each organ, we must find a path to the veins and run our blood through them; then we might travel throughout this body or like a moving star traverse the firmament of the poet's thoughts. But how and via which path should we fly in the pleasant sky of this man's imagination and take an excursion through the evergreen garden of his *Divan* to gain some insight? Should we, like a breeze, pass through the claws of the trees and the disheveled hair of the grass and become drenched in the scent and color of the flowers, or should we remain in place, like the ground, to nurture the roots of the flowers and plants in our hearts? How should we find and stroll along the green paths in the garden, such that we are not deprived of the joy of perceiving in our gazing?

Not knowing what to do is precisely the source of my fear and hesitation. Even so, since our friend's rope had fallen around my neck and pulled me wherever he wished, neither could I let go and pass by, nor did I know if I stayed how to find a way to free myself from wandering. In the end, after my wanderings, I entrusted myself to the Tongue of the Invisible, Hafez, for he himself to perhaps resolve my dilemma. To undertake the task of Hafez, I made a divination of Hafez's *Divan*:

Last night the wine-seller,
    A man of great experience,
Conversed with me (and here I share
    With you his secret sense).[7]

I will not quote the entire ghazal here. You already know it, or if by chance you do not recall it, you can easily find it. You see that at the beginning, the Bard of Shiraz does not provide any answer. He only recounts the secret that his elder has revealed to him at night in private: regarding the affairs of the world, go easy on yourself, or else the world will be hard on you, will grapple with you, and you will get stuck in what you do. But what is there that this "bird of the celestial flower garden,"[8] which has fallen into the snare of this "old wolf"[9] and knows that his free heart is a slave to the world, can take easy, and how? The antidote for this wounded soul is in the healing hands of the Magian elder: wine from a cup, from the rapture of which the world—by the favor of the beauty of the beloved[10]—changes into the alley of the friend, and the stars share their cup with humans, a cup of light and truthfulness that both draws aside your dark veils before the eyes of the world and also reveals the secrets of the world before your eyes, in order for the world and man to observe each other, in order for Venus to shine from the light of your cup to say, "to your health,"[11] and for you who are drinking while watching the star of love to glow from her light. In this friendly reconciliation with the world, matters become easy for you, and you do not cry out because of life's suffering and lie that you will not cry out. You are no longer a person without pains who cannot see, know, and pass by free of care; but because of that friendship, pain no longer possesses you. You are able to hide the moaning of the wounded heart beneath the singing of smiling lips, to pour your words and ghazals like wine into the cup of the reader's soul. What a difficult albeit easy task to express darkness with the help of light, to speak joyfully about sorrow, and not to vex others. You conceal ill fortune within yourself and offer the smile of lofty aspirations to one or another, not in order not to vex others, but in order not to collapse under the burden of your own grief. If your wings for flight do not break, you will find a way to the heart of the friend, and he will not remain in his sorrowful sleep and will not wither in grief. In this way, your ear will become familiar with the whispering of the wind and the water and the sound of the sleep of the earth and the wakefulness of the sky, the internal whispering of life, and you will perceive the message. The world has something to say. When your heart becomes a mirror, observe the angel in it. He will read God's message in you. Once you are ears from head to toe and you hear, you will become intimate with the world; you will learn its secret; and your difficult task will become easy.[12] At this point, the elder's counsel with the poet concludes, and as though the poet knows that I have gone to my own Magian elder, in the tone of an elder, he says: "Heed my advice, son, be not sad about the world."[13] The poet is now speaking directly to me. He who sat listening like a follower, now, like an elder, conveys the truth to another follower; he is a link between truth and me, provided, of course, that I am not deprived of the gift of hearing and my hands deserve to care for the pearl of words.

The "world" in the language of the poet means those worries about one's possessions—being the abject servant to one's own greedy ego and being greedy to dominate the ego of others—being enamored with possessions and power. In contrast to contemplating the next world, the worldly man defends his life of "eating, sleeping, anger, and carnal desire,"[14] and in doing so, he is at war with and hostile to not only the world and the people in it, but also himself. This termite involuntarily chews its insides and outside and everything else with its tired teeth, "slowly and continuously." My elder says: Hey son, you unripe intellect, relinquish worrying about the amount of material possessions in this world, since beyond it is the realm of love. But passing from this restrictive confinement to the realm of flight is a difficult task that can be made easy if I have a cup of the wine of the wine-seller elder from which the poet drank and is now making me drink. But this ease is difficult, because here I must relinquish all my previous ways and habits and speaking and hearing, and totally devote my eyes and ears to the conversation of light. The ostentatiousness of tempting reason is to no avail and inconsequential. Face to face with an intractable, sagacious elder who disrupts the game of the imposter world if it is not to his liking, what can an empty-handed person such as I offer that would not cause me embarrassment? A wise man, even if he learns nothing from him, would not utter a word. But my gazing beauty with his open mind sees an empty-handed person like me and knows that if I drink the wine of his poem, I might speak with knowledge. That is why he does not leave me disappointed and says in the end:

> Give me wine, oh cupbearer
> For Asef, the imperial monarch,
> Who conceals sins and faults,
> Understood the libertine ways of Hafez.[15]

Hafez's thoughts, which have differing and seemingly contradictory facets, do not provide a simple, straightforward, and clear answer. Here, in an equivocal language, he says slyly that my work with him is easy yet difficult and difficult yet easy, both this and that! If I do not entrust my heart to the bright cup of poetry and do not find my way into the sanctuary of love, an easy task would become difficult for me, and if I do and find my way, I would be a lover whose task is easy. Yet, even in this case, I have a calamitous journey ahead, because without love, no way to the friend exists, and love does not exist except in "the manner of clever libertines who can withstand calamity."[16] Happy am I who at the level of my own comprehension have perceived the cleverness of my poet. I do not know who Asef is, but now I myself am an imperial monarch,[17] who has control over his good and ill fortune, and I am the ruler of my own fortune. Now I have had my divination, and my wakeful friend begins to speak from within his dark sleeping quarters to show me a clear way. In the same way that one day the Magian elder was his guide, today, he has become my "guiding star."[18]

My guiding star is now in the seclusion of the earth. He is the color of light and truthfulness, the purple color of sunrise and sunset, and as bright as midday. When the fire in his heart shines on the garden of the world, the blue mountains rest on undulating plains; the plains crawl to the shores of the green sea; the sea constantly caresses the land; and the sky descends to settle down the tumultuous sea in the cradle of its breast. Nature, with its birds that rise at dawn, permeates me like early morning light. Morning awakens the memory of the friend and entrusts it to the wind, and the wind spreads the seeds, and the silent whisper of restless grass sprouts in my ear. Spring shivers in its green body with the memory of autumn, and the wings of autumn dry up, whisper, and fall, waiting for the spring that is yet to come. The heart of the wandering cloud is sorrowful, and raindrops fall to the ground like cold stars. The soil drinks the stars, and the naked stars that have come from far away are the light of the eyes of the dark soil. And the black eyes of that wild deer in the faraway meadow are the light of my heart. "My rose-colored elder" is a colorful sun under a rock beside a garden in the soil of Shiraz; and because his light shines on my heart from that depth, my world becomes a colorful garden with happy flowers and sad flowers and "many fruits, except for sorrow and happiness."[19] In the garden of his eyes, the world is of a different design, and my eyes are the mirror of his adorned eyes; and in the mirror, I observe the passage of time that runs like blood in the veins of nature, making it bloom and wither; and its children go to sleep; and death comes as silently as snow and covers them.

What fanciful thoughts form in my elder's heart, and what notes he plays on every scale! And what pictures his image and voice create in me, and what songs he composes in me! With the landscapes that he unfolds and the songs that he composes, he teaches me to see and to hear. He shows me a different world and humankind, and he changes my relationship with them. Once this happens, I become acquainted with a different self within me that has within it the roots of a new relationship with that which is other than myself. The invisible world that was inside me now becomes visible, and I see its good and bad faces. My elder, too, like the sun, works night and day to make colorful the light and darkness of the soul. He cries and roars "inside my wounded heart,"[20] and my calm and restless heart awaits his message, to perceive that which he surmises by surmising, imagining in imagining! And yet he himself says: "Our existence is a puzzle, the solving of which is the stuff of sorcery and fable."[21] I do not intend to solve it, but I cannot abandon my heartfelt desire for fables and creating fables. The distant world of fancy is closer to me than the actual world, because I build that one as I wish and adorn it with the sense I have of beauty; but I have fallen into this one without wishing it. There I am free, but here I am captive. Since I must live dependent on the repeated and annoying necessities of nature, involuntarily I escape from this monotony to the flight of my imagination. This escape is also necessary, because it is inevitable to me; but it is not beyond my free will, since I wish for it. Even though my wish is impossible and cannot materialize, because it was galvanized in me and conquered my being, it has become possible in some way, because it has taken up existence in me, and I in it. My reality has changed, and my life here passes with the longing for there, in the imagination! Not in daydreaming that toys with one in confusing shapeless clouds of illusion and conjectures, but rather, in an imagining that creates a new picture of the world, so that I can embrace the river of existence like a riverbed, and its ugliness and beauty and its sorrow and happiness can flow in me and not keep me from myself, rather than gush over me like a flood, roll me like a stone, and drown me. In any case, I have hurled myself from here to there, and I am totally "the story of longing."[22]

Am I merely a shrub on the course of time with the sap I suck from the soil, a trunk in the shackles of time, a body in the prison of the skeletal frame? I am the flight of the free bird of my soul, a forlorn star that is separated from its light but has not forgotten its brightness.

I am a bird,
 from the flower garden of Paradise,
How can I describe separation,
 when I fell into this trap of time?

I was an angel,
 and supreme Paradise was my abode
It was Adam who brought me
 to this flourishing, ruined monastery.[23]

Still the friend contemplates within the heart of my elder, and the heart of my elder overflows with contemplation of the friend. Then my heart is the colorful garden of paradise and the enchanting beauty of the friend. He has taken up residence in me to see the manifestation of his beauty, and I take my place in the home of my heart, in the alley of the friend, to see the beauty of which I am the manifestation; and as I sit watching myself, from that lofty sight I view this place: my soul that grows on the bed of time, and death that is hidden like a seed in the soil of my body. But my body is not merely the hiding place of death and the windowless prison of darkness. This house is the home and the hippodrome of the bird of light. And as long as it has a ray of light, it is the manifestation of the creative power of that friend, and it is beautiful.

The tall stature of my friend grows like the cypress with its head toward the sun in the sky and eyes looking at remoter places, with nimble feet and happy, proud, youthful steps. A beloved who one night lit a lamp in my heart, who was my garden and gardener, and in the soil of whose body I sprouted and grew, and the tulip garden of my soul blossomed, and now like a Judas tree with bright fingers, I stand at her grave. Everyone grew from this very dustbin and took up residence in this very spring and autumn.

And now my body, the house of my soul, is right here. This spring land of autumn, the alley of the friend, is the resting place of the beloved friend, and even when I run away from it like the breeze at dawn, I yearn for it and seek it.[24] My fleeing light in that free country of the imagination is anxious about this very happy prison from which it is separated, and in these flourishing ruins,[25] seeks the happy reunion of that time and says to itself:

> I am the falcon on the wrist of the king
> Lord how could they have forgotten
> my fondness for my perch there.[26]

At the time when the soaking wet scent of green wheat wafts in the sown fields of my body, I wish not to be deprived of the dream of imagination that bestows eternity in order to be immune to the fate of the abandoned earth. Both here and there, I am neither here nor there, and in both places I am separated from my self, and I seek it. The poet is forlorn in both worlds, in the terrestrial world and in the celestial world, because always inside him another "cries and roars," and even though this other is his essence and truth, he is always unattainable and inconceivable. He always remains the "other," someone, something, an alien state! The poet is both a stranger to himself and a stranger to the friend, because even while being one with him, he is aware that he is nothing other than him, and while being one with himself, he knows that his essence and truth is something else from somewhere else. The poet is eternally forlorn and wanders with a longing for the alley of the friend. When he is here, the alley of his friend is there, and when he is there, the alley of his friend is here. He always is and is not in the alley of the friend, because he is always with and without his self and is in a state of union and separation. He is a dual oneness in the field of his soul, where the fertile seeds of light and darkness have been spread; and with his eagerness for light, he constantly tears at the curtains of darkness to gain access to his harvest of light, and in that light, he is restlessly enchanted by this light and dark picture gallery of earth. Hoping for a self that is higher and closer to himself, he constantly relinquishes his self. "But you yourself, Hafez, must draw / The veil of Self aside."[27]

When my elder removes the veil of his self, he reaches the friend, who is the luminous source and his origin. He reaches his self when he relinquishes his self. Fortunately, however, our Hafez never reaches the end of this endless path, and he cannot completely remove his self. He is the to and fro movement of a light, one who, in his attempt at release and escape to light, cannot give up darkness, and before he leaves, his eyes that see beauty yearn to observe the garden of the world. Like a static wanderer, impatient and excited, he all at once sees his entire vast colorful landscape. Even when he is resting like a dream in the nest of God's hands, the wings of this wandering swallow are spread, because precisely then, God also awakens spring from its winter sleep in the meadow of his heart: a flower garden and a stream, the smile of a cup, the shimmering of a flower, and the memory of a beloved! And a breeze brings "the fragrant scent of friendship"[28] to his soul's sense of smell, making him "enchanted by the world,"[29] and he is both enchanted by the world and known in the world for being in love. "Love, youth, and being a clever libertine are all we desire / Perhaps in the meantime, one could strike the polo ball of some pleasure."[30] Prosperous and flourishing, my elder is in search of "the bride of the world."[31] His ambitious soul, falling and rising, seeks the creator's coiffeuse to the bride and is waiting in ambush for a sign of her hands in order to find his way into her concealed dreams. The poet travels simultaneously in two seemingly separate worlds, and these two separated ones, blessed by his internal journey, regain their oneness in him. The unity of existence takes up residence in a single house of existence. He has a single existence, but a dual appearance. Having a heart set on earth and a heart beyond the firmaments causes one to be of two minds. His soul is distant from beyond the horizons, as though it is out of his own reach as well; but the roots of his body that are deep in the soil have bound him to the earth.

The bountiful generosity of love draws down the bird of his soul to the point that he involuntarily gives up the open expanse of the sky.

> The bird of my soul that sang from the Lote tree
> Was in the end trapped by the seed that is your mole.[32]

Love's long vacillation draws the human soul down from its heavenly nest to the field of seeds and snares. It is here that complete beauty, formless and inclusive of celestial love in terrestrial love, becomes possible and achievable. One can hear the sound of the footsteps of the friend, touch the warmth of her body with one's hands, and, blessed by love, forget the coldness of death. This lover-nurturing and beloved-caressing soil is more pleasing than any paradise.

> Paradise, the shade of its Tuba tree,
> and its palaces and maidens,
> I would not exchange them all
> for the dust of the alley of the friend.[33]

Imaginary palaces with their beauties and the garden of fancy with its colorful trees and indescribable streams are from the tomorrow that is yet to come, and who knows what tricks the world will play tomorrow. Better that we "not put back today's pleasures till tomorrow."[34] If the beguiling promises would not rob me of the calmness of my heart, then why "shouldn't I sell the garden of paradise for a grain of barley"[35] and vex my thirsty soul, which is satiated in the home of the friend, with the fear of the days to come? Love has brought me here to this blessed soil. How joyful is my beloved place of birth and slaughter! I want to stay here and to die here.

The beauty of the best creator sparked in the mirror of the face of the most beautiful created one a beloved, a companion of my heart, a good and a bad, like you, and the light of the friend descended into and is housed in a familiar body that is beside me and with me. Now, the creative power of God is in my arms; but alas, my arms cannot hold on. Would my provident eyes allow me to repose in today's pleasure and leave tomorrow to tomorrow? They dream of nonexistence: no arms and no bosom, no sleep and no dream! The world warns, "Wake up, for the sleep of nonexistence is imminent."[36] The time will come when my sun is no more and the spring cloud weeps for the transient life of flowers.

How joyfully and tenderly you strut, oh young spring branch,
May you not be disturbed by the turmoil of midwinter.
The kindness of the wheel of time and its ways cannot be trusted;
Woe to him who feels secure with its ruses.[37]

Time is a strange housemate who spares me the sun, takes me away from my self, and brings the debris of the earth down on my head. The revolving of days disposes not only of me but even of my children in the abyss of nonexistence. In this revolving, as it gives birth to the days, it deprives yesterdays of seeing the sun and buries them in the oblivion of the past. I abhor this dark house that devours the lover and the beloved. "Happy the day I move on from this desolate staging-post" in ruins.[38] Otherwise, soon I will be ruined, nothing will remain in the empty hands of the earth but my dead corpse, and nothing will be in my hands but the wind; and the dominion of love will be no more than an imagining.

You are from the lofty heavens and from the beloved soul of God. You do not want such an end, any end, and you cannot consent to the death of any friend.

They call you from the empyrean pinnacle
I know not what ensnares you here.[39]

Your lofty longing for ascension once again draws your high-flying ambition to the sky, so that, like Christ, you bestow light upon the sun.

Then a light splits the darkness of this appealing snare, and without ever giving up the love of the earth and terrestrial friends, hastens toward the friend. In order to stop "revolving like a compass," he hurls himself outside "the cycle of days."[40]

Like a bird, I flew out of the terrestrial cage
Hoping to be hunted by the royal falcon.[41]

Not that I would flee from love and leave the beloved in death's cage. Love drives me toward the eternal beauty of the one from whom I am and toward whom the erosion of time and the tightness of space have no path, and since the friendship of friends is from him, I reside in the house of his heart for the love of all there is to be mine.

You are not less than an atom
Do not debase yourself, make love
So that you may reach the private residence of the sun,
whirling.[42]

And when I reach the sun, once again, "the seed that is the mole"[43] of a beloved, the enchanting coquettishness of a friend, draws me to the breast of the earth. My elder is vacillating between two friends, two worlds. A ray is freed from the confinement of a particle and reaches the freedom of light, and then, like a sun, it falls into the trap of a seed. The dual movement of a singular light is the lowly and lofty fate of our Hafez. He is two souls, at every moment relinquishing his self to once again attain his self. His consistency is in this constant search that binds together, like warp and weft, the texture of his thinking.

But often the poet cries out because of this constant vacillation and wishes himself not to be, so that all would be the friend and naught else.

My body's dust is as a veil
Spread out to hide
My soul—happy that moment when
It's drawn aside![44]

If a body and heart into which eternal light has descended is not there to intervene, that light is released and rejoins the "private residence of the sun," and the bird—a fellow traveler of his internal light—takes its place in the light of light. The essence of his being reaches the essence of existence and nonexistence and becomes a timeless universality. He sets aside the burden of the prison of the body, the injustice of the world, the battle of the ego, and the hurting of others and perches on the tree branches of freedom. But how could such a nightingale open the closed doors of the cage and spread the broken wings of flight? Alas, he is grounded in this forgotten corner. What is he doing here anyway? Why has he come, and why will he go? Why does he not know, and why is he unable to break open "the shackled frame of the body" and open his wings in the celestial air?[45] If only they would remove his this-worldly existence so he would be all: "the companion, the minstrel, and the cupbearer."[46] To join with the sun is the impossible dream of our simorgh.

It is not, then, surprising for this eager bird to lament and, despite his smile and eloquence, for a fire to burn inside him. His soul is distraught, and his heart is bleeding; and the blood of this longing heart wafts in the air of the soul more fragrant than the musk pod of the Tartary deer. Bird and deer! The images that my rose-colored elder has in his imagination are mostly those of a bird and a deer, two captive runaways, two sojourners on the run: "two lonely beings, two wanderers, two who have no one."[47] Two strangers who have come from faraway lands and have ended up in the narrow alleys of lovely Shiraz. And now the bird and the deer of the poem, having just arrived, desire to leave. Each wants both; each wants this confined place of joy and pain. And a restless longing to see its place of birth reverberates in the wings in flight and the legs that run. Because it is a deer, the plain of the earth is its alley of the friend; and because it is a bird, the bosom of the sky is its alley of the friend. This dual oneness traverses the rainbow of the world like a zephyr: in the white of dawn and the red of sunset, in the darkness of night and the light of day, and in green spring and golden autumn! This colorful one is not merely the pleasant color of sight, of which we would become tired in any case after some time. He is the combination of various spiritual states and stages, and his crystal is a prism of colors the constant flowing of which is an astonishing and unending spectacle. Ugliness and beauty, fear and hope, and honesty and hypocrisy simmer together and ferment in this wine cellar. And this human-divine and two-worldly fusion is an involuntary but self-conscious tendency toward truth and light.

> You said that our Hafez reeks of hypocrisy,
> Bravo to your breathing, for you have sniffed well.[48]

Thus this enemy of hypocrites is himself a hypocrite; the lie also robs the light of his heart and tosses him from God's lap into Satan's trap. Yes, my ideal elder is not merely the pure manifestation of divine light and the unalterable albeit unattainable truth of the sky. That dear one is an amalgamation of truth and falsehood; and as he travels, he falls and rises in the twists and turns of the path. But he is not a liar; yet, if you say, oh friend, you speak with the same tongue as the lie, he will kiss your truth-telling lips. His blasphemy is not concealed under the color and glaze of piety. He says: If in one gathering I am the memorizer of the Koran, in another, I am an insatiably thirsty drinker who would not even shun the dregs. Behold me, how I dupe the creatures of God with my ruses. To tell you the truth, I, too, like that ascetic of the altar and the pulpit,[49] do the same in my secluded privacy.

> Bring wine! Qur'an reciters, clerics,
> religious spies —
> Look well at each of them, and see a man
> who lives by lies.[50]

So, be kind and "cover the eyes of cynicism, oh charitable one who covers faults,"[51] because I am no better than I am. My cunning elder comes to me with open arms and straightforward colors. He is one of us, the difference being that I am shifty and I steal and conceal my tricks and ruses, while he does not. Good and bad, he is what he is; and with his barefaced honesty, he escapes the trap of two-faced hypocrisy. He is truthful in his hypocrisy, and in darkness, he speaks the language of light.

The duality of my elder also robs him of his faith. A man who is in a covenant with and shares the cup of the celestial denizens, a man whose heart is the cup that reveals the universe and has the friend in him, "trembles like the willow tree over his faith,"[52] because in his heart, he yearns for her heathen coloration, and even though her mesmerizing beauty is a glimmer of his beauty, it makes the poet negligent in remembering God, calling to mind anything and any recollection, and grounds him in "the house of nature."[53] In "the prayer niche of the eyebrow" of the beloved, one's "presence of mind for prayers" is forgotten.[54] It would not be surprising for the bird of a soul yearning for the seed that is the mole on a face to give up the lofty garden of the sky and nest in the dustbin of the earth, if he is enamored with a "tall, coquettish, cunning beloved,"[55] to pursue the ogling eyes and capricious heart, to break his pledge of repentance and yearning for a beloved soul, to forget the beloved soul of souls, or, similar to those who "laugh at the dreg-drainers," to sacrifice his faith on the path to the tavern.[56] Rare wine, love of the body, the face of spring, and naught else! But my elder is distraught with the sorrow of separation and fears captivity in the pleasing cage of the earth. His heart's eye is worried about lost precious freedom. This perpetual preoccupation that was born with him does not release him, and the memory of companionship and amity with that king of faith rages and swells.

I am the falcon on the wrist of the king
Lord how could they have forgotten
my fondness for my perch there[57]

Now this ambitious man has reached from the absence of disbelief to the presence of faith and sits on the king's hand that sets faith into flight, once again yearning for some seed that is the mole, to seek refuge in a trap. "As they call Hafez to this threshold, they drive him away."[58]

Need and needlessness call out to our elder and also drive him away. As he gives advice to others, he also gives himself the warning that he "be not sad about the world."[59] Jamshid and Croesus do not even have one fistful of dirt from the world and their worldly possessions, since they themselves are but a fistful of dirt.

Why let the world upset you? Why, and for how long?
Drink wine, since sorrow in a wise man's heart is wrong.[60]

He yearns for the kingdom of poverty, needing God and needing nothing else. Companionship with the mendicants is gold, their wealth without decline, and the seclusion of their hearts is the flower garden of paradise. And if a man who has aspirations acquires such wealth, he is the richest of the rich, because the one whose ailment is the desire for worldly possessions, like a scorched salt desert, grows thirstier the more he drinks. Thirst does not give him respite to the point that he forgets everything, even himself. A bad state to be in, may it never happen to our Hafez! Yet after all, like everyone else, this man needs a meager piece of bread and a sip of water in order to live his frugal life, a commission from a minor prince or an unimportant vizier to provide him with a rose and some wine. Having the richness of God does not result in being absolutely without need of God's creatures. And it is this very need that, coupled with a degree of greed and excessive demands, had turned our eulogists into flattering and pretentious beggars who pompously boast of panhandling. In the same way that ineptitude and helplessness are the tools of the abject beggar's trade, being a poet is capital in the hands of these ignoble people: requests to a wealthy notable for wine and a horse and cash and credit! Our Hafez confronts a tradition of several hundred years of these eulogists of the past and the abjectness of the contemporary destitute people, and he disdains any resemblance to this beggarly crowd.

Even though covered in the dust of poverty,
    I will not shame myself,
Tarnishing my integrity by begging for the generosity
    of the spring of the sun.[61]

But the chains of need bind the owner of this celestial aspiration to the earth. After all, he as well—of course, not in their manner—is an associate of prominent notables with status and wealth, so that he can in the meantime receive some stipend. Life's necessities enslave the longing for freedom, and the light of richness is tarnished by the darkness of need. Even though he does not require much, since he must occasionally ask someone for a few dirhams and dinars for his meager living, he chides himself:

> O selfishness! Leave me, you greedy thing;
> Though a mendicant, I will live like a king.[62]

At the core of the soaring soul of the poet crouches something obstinate and hungry. The hunting claw of the greedy self has sunk into the heart of the bird, but this dagger has not immobilized him and made his enemy happy. The eyes of the bird continue to gaze anxiously at the spring of the sun, and his heart longs to fly.

> If my wounded heart has any aspirations,
> It will not ask the hard-hearted for a panacea.[63]

And the untiring aspirations of the same wounded heart and fighting the internal enemy—the greedy self—returns the soul to the "spring of the sun"[64] and washes away the dust of indigence from the wings of the bird.

The truthfulness, faith, and poverty of my rose-colored elder is of all colors, with a streak of the color of hypocrisy, blasphemy, and need running through them. But the twilight of his character has the nature of dawn, and light lifts the darkness without annihilating it. At the root of this sun that rises in the sky with every sunrise is an image of a sunset that sinks into the earth. Neither is he released into the air, nor does he remain sitting in the ashes of the earth. The revolving of this sun unifies light and darkness, high and low, and the created and the creator, and turns me within myself.

Two Hafezes, one the free bird of longing and the other the cage of life's prison, are reflected in each other and read in each other the ugly, the beautiful, the good, and the bad, and tell stories and complain about the two realms; and then another Hafez emerges, who is himself the friend and the alley of the friend and the meeting place of God, the world, and man.

> The story of longing as recorded in this book
> Is the same story without error that Hafez taught me.[65]

Now those two forlorn twins are of one voice, and the words of one are uttered by the other. One Hafez inculcates a true story in the other. That which either the messenger angel, the Holy Spirit, Gabriel, or Khezr tells him is the unmistakable truth, and the poet sings in harmony and at dawn shares the secrets with the messenger from the invisible and the voice of the friend. The truth of the man, the poet, was discovered by his nature, and he perceived the dust of the path of the cup that reveals the entire universe. The cup that reveals the entire universe, however, is all-seeing, all-knowing; and when my elder joins the friend, he knows that not only is he not all of him, but also when he looks with the eyes that reveal the universe from the earth to the heavens, he does not see himself as anything more than the twinkling of a star in this galaxy and a drop in the ocean.

Nurturing the thought of having the capacity of the sea, alas
What is in the mind of this droplet that dreams the impossible?[66]

What a difference between a colorless light and the capacity of the sun, for a shooting star to draw boundless time into itself and an insignificant droplet to embrace the expanse of the sea! Alas, my elder is in search of the impossible, and once he regains his consciousness, the wings of his imagination break and he falls from the endless flight of longing to the dust of your house and mine, and since his hope is frustrated, he prays for others: "May no one be in search of an impossible dream."[67]

The ideal elder of our Hafez is also an impossible man. I am speaking of the Magian elder: a familiar stranger and a strange acquaintance who is and is not with and in me and whom one can and cannot find; a dweller of the tavern who possesses the world and a world in the hiding place of a cave; a destitute man without needs, a fortunate indigent man, and a free captive; a man made of the essence of time, with death and nonexistence, and a man made of the timeless essence of the friend, an aspect of his thinking, eternal and the source of all beings; a secret that can be seen but not told and a riddle that can be solved but not found. This is the poet's imagined depiction of "the perfect man," a man who is infinite and hence powerful, since his heart is a companion of God's heart; and since he has now fallen into the lowly little house of nature, he is finite, and as a result, incapable of chronic but pleasing entanglements. A finite time that comprises infinite time, a passing restriction and a traveling ray. How joyful to rejoin the spring of the sun; "should the Holy Spirit help once again,"[68] the sleeper will awake, the dead will be brought back to life, and everyone will become a Magian elder and an incorporeal Christ worthy of being a cohabitant of the sun. Otherwise, he will be as dust on a road, to be toyed with by the wind.

And now this dust of the road seeks his own Holy Spirit. May Christ help and free him from the Antichrist. You are a truthful hypocrite, an innocent sinner, and a rich mendicant with delightful sorrows and worthy pains, one who tastes the bitterness of the world; but instead of drowning in the invasion of its continuous waves, like the sea, in the mirror of your breast, you look at the sky and the sun. The smile on your face is the remedy for the bleeding heart, because your pains, as they come like a breeze and blow in me, shake off the dust of decayed sorrows from my branches and leaves and entrust me to happy sorrows. With the light of your thinking, I make excursions into the garden of my emotions. I find the obscure narrow paths and the crossroads. I find my colorful flowers and poisonous weeds, the sleepers and the invisible within my being. I see and set in order the image and the design of my inner self. And with your various emotions and states, I irrigate the seeds of my thoughts. My stammering tongue yearns for the Tongue of the Invisible, Hafez, to find the mystery of your words, to reach the invisible world, the what and how of another world that is within me and that is at war with this world of mine that is all about how much I have and how much I do not, and anger and avarice. "I will endeavor to perhaps hurl myself there."[69]

Another World . . .

The abode of the beloved is there, and the abode of Hafez's beloved—existence being a manifestation of the beauty of his face—lies in the heart of the poet. He is in the friend, and the friend is in him. The lover and the beloved reside in each other. The happiness of the poet, the freedom of his soaring heart, is in reaching this "nowhere land," this friend and this alley of the friend. "The source of happiness is there."[1]

Here is the crypt of unconscious sleep, and there is the garden of conscious wakefulness; and once the gift of consciousness flashes and erases the darkness of sleep, the bud of the sun blossoms in the garden of the heart. No one goes from one place to some other place; rather, here changes into "there." That is why my rose-colored elder tries to fling himself like an arrow from his own bow to get from one state or station to another, that perchance "the demon departs and the angel arrives,"[2] so that he would make another man of himself and another world in himself, because as long as this "clever bird"[3] is here, he is a captive in his snare in this place.

> Humans cannot be found in the terrestrial world
> Another world must be built, and an Adam anew.[4]

The terrestrial world is this world of fate, need, and lack of free will, the world of revolving firmaments, passing time, the four basic elements,[5] and chaotic order. The terrestrial world is the world of being forlorn, because forces such as rage, greed, and lust are restless in me; and they have blocked my way to my self. Many things are highway robbers; and as long as I am here, I am like Adam driven away from paradise. I am confined to the ground on earth, and like a storm, the savage law of time pushes me, tossing me in every direction, and I have no opportunity to sit in seclusion alone and think about what I am, who I am, where I am from, and where I am going. Time rushes by like a flood in the riverbed of my life, and I am so entangled in killing time that I no longer have any chance to be a "knower of my time"[6] and understand it. In this condition, I remain far away not only from the world around me, but also from things and people. Nature is not my home and the focal point of my perspective, as though I will never sleep in the cradle of the earth. I do not see the carefree wandering of spring clouds, the playfulness of the light-winged wind, and the homelessness of the birds in secluded alleyways. The patient complaint of the mountain does not rest in the breast of the sky; the transparent stream does not run down the mountain slope; and the green whisper of the meadow cannot be heard in the caress of the breeze. The earth does not breathe, and the beating of the heart of the sun does not light the spirit and bestow sight on the eyes.

In the same way that humans are deprived of their natural dispositions, nature too loses its human dispositions and becomes merely possessions and the circus of our injustice, and we must gain victory over it as far as possible in order to acquire more. We are no better than this toward each other. We are a group of runners in the business arena of society. We are all running at the same time; but in this unrelenting competition in which any pause to look at a fellow runner results in falling behind, everyone runs for himself, and everyone gets out of breath in his own loneliness. In this way, I continually struggle with myself to run faster and arrive sooner. God only knows where!

In such a world, humans cannot be found. If a person wants to visit the truth of himself, like a seed made of stone, he must split the soil of his soul, and as light as air, reach free light. He must build another world within himself—a long difficult journey in the hazardous desert of the self. It is not that first another world is to be built and then another Adam created; one is not the rational consequence of the other. The creation of both occurs at the same time, because another world can only be built by another Adam, and as long as another world does not exist, an Adam cannot be found. Here the poet contemplates the simultaneous death and birth, the captivity and freedom of the soul, not the continuous journey of time and change of space. However, born at the same time as another world and another Adam, another time and space are created, another totally different space and moment that stem from the change in the quality of the soul.

The world and society have their own rules and ways. The firmament revolves and creates time, and time is the lord of our life and death. But our life and death occur within society, and as the firmament wishes. The laws of both flow in me. On a day I do not know, in a place I do not know, I was released, and I must grow "as they nurture me."[7] I am not the possessor of time and space. Life's predestination in its own ways and customs will deliver me to my final resting place. This is a design in the warp and weft of which my life passes and takes its form. Now, if I want to hurl myself from this unfree terrestrial world, I must destroy this design in my *self* and tear apart the warp and weft of the world to "hurl myself to another kingdom."[8]

Come, let us scatter flowers
  and pour wine into goblets
Split the vault of the heavens
  and make a new design.
If sorrow incites an army
  to spill the blood of lovers,
The cupbearer and I will attack it together,
  and uproot its very foundation.[9]

Now here is a sample state and mood of another world: spring scattering flowers and the light of wine in the sun of the cup and a beloved who offers wine that shows me "in the cup, the reflection of the beloved's face,"[10] so that the night assault of the army of sorrow is thwarted. And all this comes from the blessing of the crumbling of the firmament's structure that has no foundation and the cruel design of the firmament that is the source that gives birth to sorrow. Nature and love, the rapture from wine, joy, and the gift of seeing the friend erase from my heart the inevitable revolving of the firmament in the sky and its tyrannical law and save me from the confinement of this place, which is the egotistical circus of religious police, the piety of hypocrites, and the injustice of the people. Our Hafez, of course, is not a so-called "social revolutionary" who seeks to turn the foundations of the society upside down. He is neither the angry spokesman of Yamakan[11] nor the lofty eagle of Alamut.[12] But in his time, as well, the pseudopious made a business of other people's souls, and the lives of these others were playthings of petty princes and governors who came and went by way of killing and massacring; and in the course of these conflicts, injustice assaulted the life and heart of everyone. The city, which is both the center and the place of the crystallization of social life, was the most obvious scene of such unbridled chaos. The one who seeks another world must not only go beyond the world of nature, but must also split open such a cocoon.

> The city is devoid of lovers
> Would that from some direction
> A man would emerge from his ego
>   and do something.[13]

To have another Adam and another world, one must come out from among the loveless, whose hearts are dead and who are captives in the beehive of the city and under the ceiling of the sky, and free himself from this wheel and that skein. But "the blight of the revolving of the firmament in the soul and body"[14] and the calamity of the lies and injustices of the city are inside our hearts and souls. Hence, one must "emerge from his ego," or make the rules of "the terrestrial world"[15] within himself crumble and then rise from beneath his own rubble "pure and incorporeal."[16] Such a man will be liberated from the firmament of the moon, which is the first heaven, and from the evolving world, and from being annihilated, and from cause and effect, and from reason seeking cause; and like Christ, he will reach the fourth heaven, which is the firmament of the sun and the abode of light.

> If you go to the heavens,
>   like Christ, pure and incorporeal
> Your lamp will bestow
>   a hundred rays upon the sun.[17]

Like the sun and Christ, my rose-colored elder is in the fourth abode of the firmament, in the source of light and vision, in the "flower scattering"[18] site of music and song and wine and happiness, "waving hands and dancing."[19] It is as though the longing for the paradise of light and song and oneness with "the Wise Lord"[20] as promised by old Zoroaster[21] still continues to effervesce and stir in the depths of my elder. But the words of our Hafez, who says, "Come, let us throw the dust of our existence before the lord of beauties,"[22] are not addressed to just anyone; his addressee is the lover in the city of no lovers. Even though "in every head, there is some mystery of God,"[23] until this mystery is revealed, the mystery of love will not blossom in the garden of the heart, and the city will remain devoid of lovers.

In any case, the wish to emerge from the self, to be rescued from the terrestrial world, and to build another world and another Adam in a city full of lovers is not merely the wish of our Hafez; it is his message. He calls us to this strange metamorphosis that is possible only through the blessing of love.

But love is "a hidden subtlety"[24] one cannot know, because knowledge deals with things in the external world and rational relationships between human beings. Reason measures such things and relationships, discovers the connection between their cause and effect and their laws in nature and society, and utilizes them. The domain of knowledge lies within the circle of reason, within the arena of common sense and self-consciousness. Reason deduces how things are. Through logical deduction, it tells us how the laws of the world interact and, hence, how things are in the world, and vis-à-vis them, how we should behave.

The worldly wise during the time of the poet—I am not speaking about the intelligent and the truly wise—the worldly wise at that time were the scholars of religion and of the world, that is, the Koranic exegetes, the theologians, the religious jurists, the preachers, and other superficial believers who knew that a wise and powerful creator is the cause of all causes, who based on his own wisdom wanted the world to be such and created it. His wisdom is aware of that which is right for us; but our rational faculty cannot understand his wisdom. Even though he knows everything from all eternity, and no leaf can fall to the ground without his will, he has created us in order to discern what we will do through our own free will. We have come into the world to be tested; and this world is a stopping place on the journey to the next. On this path, we must travel in the way that is shown to us; and we must refrain completely from asking why or how, because, otherwise, the result will be blasphemy. Satan did not refrain and saw the result.

Such people are the organizers of the society's thoughts and beliefs, and with the organized, systematic, and limited conception that they have of the boundaries of existence, they know how human beings must organize their being to make it compatible with that conception. The answer of these worldly wise people to the human problem vis-à-vis the world and the self is easy, acceptable to the people, and practical. It frees the people from the tangled skein of inconclusive ideas and, nonetheless, shows the way to a little village, as it were. Because they solve "the puzzle of our existence,"[25] they have the prescription for our behavior in their pockets.

> The worldly wise are the pivot of the compass of existence, but
> Love knows that they are bewildered within this circle.[26]

The worldly wise are at the center of the circle of existence, because they have drawn the circumference of it themselves, or they have placed themselves inside a prescribed circle, and because they begin with themselves, no matter where they go, they revolve around themselves and are unable to come out of their selves. They have one foot in the terrestrial world that turns the other leg around itself, even though it tries to run away and even though it refuses to go. Within closed boundaries, "they are static wanderers."[27] These wanderers have one foot firmly on the ground, and they know where they are in this revolving and evolving system. They keep accounts of the revenues and expenditures of their actions, of heaven and hell, and of this and the next world, and their utilitarian prudence shows them the ways and behaviors needed to get through their lives day by day, simply this confinement of getting through their daily life! But the destiny of man is to exit this repetitive confinement and fly toward unknown horizons.

The why of things is an inherent question that arises from the hidden depths of the soul, and thus far, humans have been unable to escape it. "What is this simple high ceiling full of images?"[28] The involuntary inclination and will to know always draws us toward knowing, toward the darkness of a puzzle the answer to which "no sage in the world knows."[29] Here, reason, which is the result of and the guide to our knowledge, is itself left bewildered.

In contrast to the idea of creation in the mind of the worldly wise, regarding the divine wisdom for which we know nothing, in Hafez's thinking, beauty is the motivation behind creation. God is beautiful, the world is a manifestation of God's beauty, and love is the result of seeing this beauty: seeing with the heart's eye. Here, as well, we are dealing with how and not with why, not the profiteering and limited why of practical reason. Why is God beautiful, and why is the manifestation of this beauty inevitable? Who knows? "Thus it was as long as it was."[30] The sun is the spring of light, and a seeing eye, blessed by its light, sees the world. But why is the sun the house of light? Is it by the blessing of the sun that we see, or is it because of the gift of our vision that the sun becomes visible? God breathed in me and I became alive, or did I blow my lover's soul into the world and bring this dead thing to life?

> Speak to me of minstrels and wine
>   And less of the secret of life and fate
> For no sage has solved this riddle with wisdom
>   And no sage ever will.[31]

If the why of the world is an unsolved mystery, the dispute about the why, and perhaps even the how, of the friend might be the futile war of the seventy-two factions.[32]

Hafez might be for the most part speaking about his own moods rather than being in search of the secret of the existence of the friend, the why, and the friend's work in this workshop. When the poet speaks of his moods, however, inevitably, the mystery of the other is also expressed.

In any case, in the poet's thinking, the beauty of the creator cannot remain concealed and inevitably shines through. Existence is the manifestation of this beauty. In order to look at himself, he brings into being the already existing, albeit unseen, beauty, and that which has existed is seen;

existence happens, and existence is a mirror that reflects the beauty of his face. Among all creatures of this existence, however, his breath is blown only into man. Hence, in order to look at himself, he longs for my existence, and now I exist. "We wanted him and he was filled with desire,"[33] but his longing for us is in order to observe his own face, because the created is a mirror in which the creator sees himself. Hence, he created me because he wanted himself. I am in love with a king, the possessor of the world who is self-sufficient, who is beautiful, and who loves beauty, and since he is absolute beauty himself, he is the absolute lover of himself, and he is no longer a helpless needy being in the thinking of one such as I, who am struggling in vain in the midst of all this.

> How can one benefit from union with the beauty of a king
> Who is in love with himself for all eternity?
> The companion, the minstrel, and the cupbearer are all him.
> The illusion of water and clay is an excuse along the way.[34]

If, however, existence is a manifestation of his beauty, I too, a self-conscious being (aware of my existence), am the manifestation of the beauty of the friend, and when he expresses love for himself, he worships his own beauty, which is in me. He wants me because he sees his own beauty through me. Hence, the water and clay of my being are no more than a means and an excuse. My being is the mirror of his face and the place of the manifestation of his vision. Were there no Hafez, the friend would be a light without brightness, an unlit fire, and a soul in sleep. He would be an invisible being, without a manifestation, who could neither see nor be seen. He appears through the blessing of the existence of man. And as he can observe himself, man can also be inebriated by the pleasure of observing him. Since his manifestation, however, is not only in man but in the entire universe, the joy of seeing him profits the moon and the sun that "turn the same mirror."[35] He is the sight of my eyes and the light of the world. And with that sight and under the rays of this light, I see myself and the world, both of which come from him.

Hitherto, he was an unfound beloved and I, a searching and seeking lover. And when I found him, I perceived myself and realized that

Mansur[36] is God, and that he who is in the garb of Bayazid[37] is no other than the friend. And now, this *I* is a beloved lover, a lover who is beloved, "who is in love with himself for all eternity,"[38] but with a *self* that is in an embrace with the world and the soul of the world beyond these "four opposing unruly humors,"[39] like a drop with the sea and rain, a tree with the soil and the sun, and a man with existence and nonexistence. The world is born of love, and love is the only truth of the transient world:

> I offered both worlds to my experienced heart
> Other than love for you,
> it regarded all the rest as transient.[40]

Not only this transient world but also the everlasting world is something transient and does not have much value compared to the eternality of love.

And man has fallen from the realm of love—the safe meadows of paradise—to the hunting ground of this "old wolf,"[41] and with empty hands and tired feet but an "experienced heart,"[42] he travels in this strange desert, and his voice remains in the sky like a star in darkness, because in the same way that God was a hidden treasure who could not remain hidden, the poet as well holds a treasure of the sorrow of love in his breast that cannot remain hidden. And being in love is that which happened to man's heart, and from the beginning, his heavenly destiny was to be on earth. And being on earth is like being a stalk of straw in the clamor of the wind, a twig in a roaring river; it means instability and change.

The lover's heart, with rapturous and unconscious eagerness and leaping, yearns for the friend, so that he can fit the eternity of time within the hurricane of a short life. Obviously, any sane person would quietly laugh at such silly daydreaming. "Such false delusions, such an impossible dream!"[43] A practical intellect recognizes its limitations and would not nurture false delusions. The poet's heart, however, accepts the "burden of trust"[44] in the inebriation of madness. Where the mountain is struck by fear, the madman—the prophet, the poet, or the lover—jumps into the arena and says: Yes, you are my God, and I am your messenger on earth. Then God puts "himself in the mouth of man," and man's voice resonates like "the most pleasant reminder in this revolving dome"[45] and says "that which the master of eternal beginning said."[46] The terrestrial fate of this eloquent lover, however, is in the hands of the tribe of men of reason. During the waiting period that slowly counts the days of the poet before it robs his corpse, they drive him in whatever direction they want.

> Dark night and the desert, where can one reach,
> Unless the candle of your face lights my path?[47]

Night is the realm of silence and sleep. Alongside the twilight of sunset, oblivion comes. Like a wounded animal, the wind creeps into the caves of darkness, and the sun, like a stone that has fallen into a well, is forgotten and alone. One cannot hear the sound of the day's footsteps, and sluggishness, as heavy as the slumber of satiated sheep, approaches as slowly as a shadow. Sleep has arrived. It climbs up the toes; it comes up like the seeping out of the night from the eastern shore and the rising of water in a marsh. And the body surrenders, naked and limp like an inflamed wound, such that the closed eyes can no longer see and the tormented ears no longer hear. In the night of trying to find answers, which is so concerned about the rainy day that it has lost the now, sleep weighs heavily on the chest and sinks me into the river of darkness. Like a prison in the depths of the earth, night is closed and windowless. It is like thick congealed tar, an unfamiliar lonely dead end in the nightmares of which wolves are waiting in ambush. Grasses are bent under the burden of darkness; seeds have crawled into the heart of the soil from fear; and darkness, like oppression—heavier than lead and more unpleasant than carrion—has fallen upon the ground.

But the night of lovers is hidden wakefulness. The blades of grass stretch out through the skin of the earth looking for the lost sun; the plant sap sucks the root of the soil and comes toward the leaves; the wave of the blowing wind makes the massive hands of darkness shiver; and the night embraces the stretched-out body of the tree and runs its hands over the downslope and upslope of hills and ravines, over the bottom of the valley and the skyline of the mountain, and farther away. The wounded earth takes a breath and falls asleep to the murmuring of running water. In its sleep, the white boat of dawn sets sail, gliding toward the shore of the sky.

The night has green dreams, and the forgotten stars awaken. The night of lovers is the night of stars, the night of light.

The candle that is the face of the friend turns the falling and sleeping night of the worldly wise into the night of lovers that has a sleepless heart, such that the mad traveler with his burden of trust or the treasure of love traverses the dark loneliness of this desert and finds his way to somewhere. Love for the friend—whether that eternal beloved or this one with "disheveled hair, smiling"[48]—takes the lover from a dark night to a luminous night, and as long as he is on the path, he is immune to heavy inanimate sleep; he has a light in his eye and a light in his heart that at every moment guide him through external and internal darkness. The fiery-winged bird and the starry-eyed deer pass through the sleeping plain of night and the sluggishness of nocturnal sleep. Lovers are the travelers of this caravan, and the men of reason are those who remain behind in this caravanserai. The former are the stream and the sea, and the latter, stagnant water.

> Whosoever is not alive through love in this circle,
> even before he dies,
> Perform the prayers for the dead for him,
> on my religious decree.[49]

Because those without love in this "dark night and the desert"[50] have no light on their path, they will not find any path. In darkness, they have no path to find. They remain where they were, their "arms and legs, lifeless"; otherwise, their bodies would be alive, rather than being dead corpses requiring the ritual prayers for the dead. In the view of our bard, a person who is not in love is dead, even if he is busy with his life. Conversing, socializing, working and business, and having a wife and children, these are not signs of being alive, because body and soul without love comprise an existence without purpose. The purpose of creation is love, and a created being that lives without love is both separated from the purpose of his being and also untroubled by this separation, because all else aside, a heart without love is mere water and clay, not the house of awareness.

Of course, the lover and the unaware are both separated from their source. But one knows and seeks the time of reunion, and the other does not know and wanders about aimlessly among the thieves in this chaotic bazaar. In the beginning, when there was nothing but love for the friend, everything began with love, because the friend's enamored state of longing to see the face of the friend caused us to become the mirror. But as the mirror reflects the face of the friend, it sees both him and itself because of him. The result of this seeing is the gift of our love. Even though man's heart is the most joyful house of love—in the same way that the sun is the most joyful house of light—the whole world is burning with love, in the same way that the whole world seeks the blaze of the sun.

In the time before time began
the rays of your beauty appeared

love was made manifest
and set the whole world on fire[51]

In this ghazal as well, imagining God is coupled with fire, lightning, and brilliance, and with flame and light, as though the face of the friend comes into existence in the formless light with which the universe is overflowing. Everything is seen in light and everything, even an insignificant particle, seeks light to take form and to again attain itself.

You are not less than an atom
Do not debase yourself, make love
So that you may reach the private residence of the sun,
whirling.[52]

In this falling and rising journey, which is the desired end of being, if I settle in my darkness, I am dead and my heart has no light for the particle that is me to seek my sun, and my sun no light to accept the particle that is me. There is no effort and attraction in me. It is as though my body is the coffin of my soul, and my legs with every step are dragging a corpse to the graveyard. Such a self-centered, self-absorbed being is so enamored with observing himself that he is unable to see anything unless he measures it by the touchstone of his own profit and loss. In this way alone, he has a connection with another. He who out of his egotism only loves himself and does not know any other love has arisen in opposition to everyone and claims to own the entire world. If it is as he wishes, so be it; otherwise, be it not so! Our Hafez says: Conceal the secret of love from this pretender, "Let those who are full of themselves / die in themselves,"[53] and then he warns:

Fall in love, for if not, some day
 the affairs of this world will end
Before you are able to comprehend
 the purpose in this workshop of existence.[54]

Love is not only the motivation but also the goal of creation. The world is created from love and for love, and love is the beginning and the end. That which came "into the clime of existence from the frontier of nonexistence"[55] is setting out on the path of love, and longing for a mandrake, he does not take to heart the harshness of the thorn of the lote tree. On this love quest, this journey, if you are not of the same heart as the friend and you are not a companion of the world, you are dead in life; and if you are, in the end, you are one with the friend. Hence, you are alive even in death: "He who finds life through love will never die."[56]

Death is the offspring of time. Time—that is, the journey of time, the embodiment of this journey in the revolving of the heavens and the result of this journey and excursion—plucks the guests of the world from the banquet of the earth and hurls them into the abyss of oblivion. Hence, inevitably, the one who does not die must either be standing somewhere outside this time and space, which he is not, or if he is in the same circle, he must nonetheless hurl himself out of its circulation to uproot the undesirable fatalistic foundation and establish the foundation of a self-desired destiny: to change the natural and universal predestination to his own human free will. Union with the friend, oneness with him beyond time and space, is the elixir that saves the lover from nonexistence.

from the dawn of time until eternity's evening
love and friendship are bound by one covenant[57]

"Before that green roof and enamelled vault / were raised to the sky,"[58] the friend was the lord of my heart, and after the crumbling of this "enamelled vault," he will continue to be. Our covenant is from the time when there was no time and there was no world for space to exist. Under this azure sky, nothing remains the same. The movement of time in space, birth and death, changes everything and then destroys it, with the exception of the covenant between the friend and the friend, the agreement that said, "Am I not your Lord?" to which I responded, "You are." Then he entrusted the burden of trust to my hands and the treasure of love's sorrow to my heart and let me go on earth to retell his word. This agreement is based on "one promise and covenant," because the heart of the poet "has fallen in love for all eternity and has remained eternal in this."[59] Beyond the time and space that come, deteriorate, and go, the covenant and those who made it will continue to be valid.

In contrast to the created world that is subject to change, the human being is of a different essence. His body is also the place where disease waits in ambush and the hibernation place of death, which all of a sudden awakens and engulfs him. But "the fire that never dies is in his heart,"[60] even though at every moment the wind of calamity destroys a crop and harvest in the world.

If the wind of calamity casts chaos into both worlds,
Our eyes shall light the path of waiting for the friend.[61]

For a human being who is both on the ever-moving path of time and also unable to give up the longing to be and stay, love is the antidote to all instability and nothingness. While the world steals a sheaf from the harvest of the poet's life every day, in its place, love returns a spark of his inner fire to his sun every day.

In the darkness of the world, the lamp of his eyes is lit, and his eyes are watchful on the path of the friend. Blessed by this light, he splits that darkness. He remains neither in his own darkness nor in the darkness of the world. Hence, he remains neither alone nor without the friend. In the face of external darkness, internal light comes to the rescue. In the chaotic night of the world, the star of the eyes is the pathfinder and guide. The lamp of the lover's eyes seeks a singular sun that is the source of darkness and light, and it resides beyond the open boundaries of these two in his soul and is farther and closer to him than anything else.

With such a bright light that gives birth to the sunlight of love, the worth of the borrowed transient "harvest of the moon and the cluster of the Pleiades" is no more than a grain of barley.[62] The grandeur of the heavens and the world of existence and nonexistence is insignificant compared to a man in love, because blessed by love and unity with the beloved, he is the source of all existence. Now, the world is of man, not man of the world. "The world was created because of us, not we because of it."[63] Man is free from the world, and the world is enslaved by man. "I am the slave of love and free from both worlds."[64] Love is freedom, and it saves me from the misfortunes of both worlds, from the fear of nonexistence of the world and the yearning for the maidens of paradise in the cozy house of the next world or the painful punishment of hell, and it changes the dreaded God of the muftis and religious police to the friend of the mystics. That frowning, harsh God who, eager to punish his slaves, blew into the fire of hell is now sympathetic to human pain, is kind, and longs for man, in order to observe and find himself again in him.

in the beauty of your face   admire God's handiwork
in the mirror of my heart   behold the divine[65]

A beautiful face is a mirror that reflects God, because not only is the handiwork of God visible in this garden but also he sees the manifestation of his own face in this garden. That hidden treasure that could not remain hidden was manifested in this spring of light, in this house of exile: the friend came to the alley of the friend, and "my eye became the manifestation of his face."[66] Not only does such a garden and such a place of manifestation deserve the love of the world, but also humans and spirits are enamored by it. The lover who sought the friend now himself turns into a beloved who is being sought. A human who has lost his heart to God through him becomes a human who is a mirror that reflects God, a two-sided mirror that both reflects God's face and also is a sign of the artistry of his hands. The lover turns into a beloved, and humans, too—like God—fall in love with humans. Hence, love for the created is not only not alien to love for the creator but it is also fused with it; and inevitably, both are born from each other. Hafez's love is divine-worldly, Godly human, and celestial-terrestrial. Man and God are both lovers and beloveds.

Adam, who in supreme paradise was a cohabitant of angels, sold paradise for a grain of wheat and, in search of love, turned to this "flourishing monastery in ruins."[67]

> We saw the fresh beauty of your face and came
> From paradise in search of this mandrake.[68]

This friend, whose mandrake the poet desires, is not the eternal beloved, because he resided beside him there, and he did not need to leave paradise to reach him. But the poet has no quietude in that "refuge of pleasure."[69] His "celestial soul desires the dimple in a chin" and in order to become entangled "in the lock of the curly tresses"[70] of a beloved, he descends from that lofty height to this dirt pit, as though being with God and in God does not quench the thirst for love. Even though love for that omnipotent friend frees man from his terrestrial limitations, until it becomes physical in the being of this powerless friend, it seems to remain in the realm of imagination and does not become an actual reality. A person who has never lost his heart to one like himself, with such an afflicted body and soul, who has not experienced the suffering of waiting and has not succumbed to the hopelessness of separation and has not gained a new life in seeing someone, might know love, but he is not afflicted by it. This knowledge in him is a matter of thinking, not of living. He has thought about love and can speak about it, but since he has never been alive through love, he can never give life to love. "What pleasure can be drawn from the fruits of paradise / By anyone who has not bitten the apple of a beloved's chin?"[71] Even if everything else can be learned from a book or a teacher, love cannot be learned, because it is not learnable, like the soul of the tree, the bounteousness of the sky, the blessing of rain, the growing of the plant, like the freshness of spring, and the soul of the universe, which can neither be learned nor taught! *Being-evolving-living* love is love. It is the beating of the heart, the seeing of the eye, the flying of the wing, and the advancing of the foot, which, should it occur, does not remain concealed and inevitably shines through.

In theoretical mysticism, worldly love is a bridge to real love; in other words, human love is a path to divine love. But in Hafez, one is not the point of departure and the other the destination; one is not the road and the other the wayfarer's stopping post. They are twins; they are both real. Even though divine love is the original source, human love is also such a truth that it pulls the lover from the happy arms of God without the fear of death and dying of this land of dust.

> What is the heart's purpose
> in viewing the garden of the world?
> To pick flowers from your face
> as with the hand that is the pupil of the eye.[72]

Now that I am separated from the friend and forlorn, I am by the side of this friend because of whose being the world is no longer the "ruined monastery"[73] but the "flourishing monastery in ruins."[74] Love for a "seditious and inconstant"[75] beloved makes the ruined world flourish and transforms "this house of sleep"[76] into a garden to be viewed, from the observation of which the heart achieves its purpose.

Love makes the ruins prosper, turns ugliness to beauty, and saves the life of the lover from one lived tediously and meaninglessly. Now his heart has a purpose; it is beating intently for something: seeing the friend and having the flower of her face in the flower garden of the eye! Because the world that was created from love kept me away from that friend, it became my prison, and because it connected me with this friend, it became my house of hope. Hence, worldly love is not metaphorical in Hafez; it is a reality that transforms his view and perception of the world and gives it a different meaning. Blessed by this worldly love, the bitter hostile world becomes sweet and friendly.

Two gardens of love and friendship, in the heavens and on earth, are the abodes of the poet. Each garden is the reflection of the other, and it displays itself with the light and the mirror of the other. The two alleys of the friend are twin gardens in which the character of love is the same. And in both, love has a mysterious and unknowable nature. A spark leaps in the darkness of night from the depth of a puzzle and strikes a heart. A man imprisoned by the body and life becomes free, permeates the world, shares roots with water and soil, becomes the intimate companion of flowers and plants, and on the bed of night and day, embraces darkness and light, plunging into the soul of the universe, like a starfish in the spring of the "water of life"! He who, restless for union with the friend, says, "hoping to be hunted by the royal falcon"[77] I flew like a bird from the cage of the earth to be annihilated in him like Mansur[78] and for him to be eternal in me, now before this friend says:

Rise and display your stature, oh graceful idol,
And I will rise from my soul and the world, dancing.[79]

In both states, my elder is eager to split open the cocoon of the body and join with another. For a person to wish for death a hundred times in order to move beyond himself and attain union with a friend or to fulfill a wish is a mysterious state and stage; for a person "to rise from his soul with the good news of a union,"[80] to get out of the trap of the world, and to soar to be a companion of and harmonious with existence and nonexistence, this freedom from time and space, and presence in the time from before the dawn of creation to eternity, which is the state of lovers, is unknowable. One may be able to describe the how of it, but the why of it is a problem that cannot be solved by reason. "Debating the how and why results in headache, oh heart."[81] A lover like our Hafez describes how he feels and his state of being in love, but he does not know why he has such feelings and is in such a state. No one knows this secret:

Along the path of love, indeed,
none truly grasp the mysteries

One and all make conjectures
    based on their own fantasies.[82]

Not only love, but also the beloved cannot be fully understood: a friend closer to one than one's soul and yet farther, "in all conditions"[83] with me and I without him, invisible light and being outside existence, my created and creator! In the same way that everything can be seen by the light of the sun, but one cannot look at it due to the intensity of its brightness, everything can be understood because of the friend, except the one who is the original source of knowledge.

how can eyes see you as you truly are
everyone understands in proportion to their vision[84]

Even though every eye, depending on its ability, sees some of his beauty, since the world is overflowing with it, the essence of the friend is out of reach of our intellect. And love for an unknowable beloved is mysterious and strange by its very nature.

Since the love of the poet for the created is of the same essence and root as his love for the creator, this worldly love, like that other love, has a subtlety and a mystery to it that cannot be discovered. The allure of the beloved "is not due to her hair and slender waist."[85] "A beautiful face has no need for colors, rouges, and beauty marks."[86] It is as though beauty, which does not need all these, is an essence that is and is not all these; and in addition to these, many things—which we do not see and do not know—may pass through the depths of the beloved's soul and the privacy of her heart that make her deserving of love. In the sun, there is the fire of eagerness; in the soil, there is the pain of waiting; in the cloud, there is the weeping of rain; and in the wind, there is the restless wandering to make the earth deserving of spring.

There is an unknown but tangible magic in the friend of which our Hafez is so enamored, to the point that uncontrollably he says, "Without you, I say, I do not want life."[87] At times, the poet calls this perceptible but unknowable mystery the "gentleness and kindness that can win over men of vision,"[88] and at times, "that certain something"[89] is neither a beautiful face nor a soft and delicate body, and by no means has a name that uncovers the mystery through which the hidden meaning is revealed.

> Love arises from a hidden subtlety
> Called neither ruby lips nor rust-colored down.[90]

It defies the tongue and is unsayable. The lover is constantly in front of a window that is not fully opened, or if it is, before the eyes is a scene that extends farther and farther away the more we look. It is as though love is a foggy, unclear realm, a revolving sphere, and a changing landscape with dreamlike and colorful horizons and the rarest perception of purple, green, and blue that do not exist in the sky, land, and sea, but the image of which appears before the eyes of the imagination like the manifestation of musical melodies to a listener with closed eyes and open heart, in fluid mingled forms of innumerable colors, and in the oneness of the face, in sound, in that which is seen, and in that which is heard, in a totality of the same essence and harmony with the observer and listener. The beginning and the end of love, the lover, and the beloved are a single essence. And because love is not merely this stagnant, raw reality but, rather, is something more internal and more concealed and the substance of the soul of this external world, the person who finds his way to the city of love is he who hurls himself beyond this external world into another world, into the same place where the poet "endeavors to perhaps hurl himself."[91]

And this flight to another place requires the far-flying wings of imagination. The lover and the beloved nurture the hidden subtlety of love on seven colorful canvases of the imagination; otherwise, this real world, this stone-hearted unbeautiful law, turns every lofty desire into dust and every unruly flame into ashes. How the realist that is reason sneers at and stares at mad love!

At any rate, love is nurtured by, rather than born from, a fertile fancy that does not remain the same, and, more of a player than the world, causes chaos in the world and builds another wheel and firmament of a different form and function for itself. Reality turns into a pleasant dream. The will, which was in the prison of necessity, is now free, and when this fancy that has fled captivity imagines the darkness of the world, due to the same freedom, it constructs it as much darker and even more painful. The vacillation between captivity and freedom is one of the expanding and contracting motivations of lovers and mystics. To be in one's lofty star in the heavens at one moment and then to fall into the well of one's depths, to be turned upside down and downside up on the constant waves of happiness and adversity, and to run in heaven and hell is the resurrection of the soul; but it is not within the power of endurance and ability of just anyone.

The joy and sorrow and the ugliness and beauty of love go beyond the truth of reality, and in heaven and hell, at times in light and at times in darkness, at two extremes, the lover's condition is never the same. And so often, he might have both extremes within him at a single moment: a silent nightingale and a speaking lily that laughs in the midst of crying and wails at the moment of union. The imagination, which as fast as thought comes in new forms at every moment and passes, transforms love, like a patch of cloud in the hands of a hurricane, into another shape every time and does not leave the lover in one state: "at every moment the image of your face / blocks the road of my imaginings."[92] The essence of love has such a confusing and rapidly changing face that it constantly escapes recognition by the lover, because by the time he wants to set his heart on one face and explore it carefully, new faces come and bring about new states of mind in him. Moreover, recognition requires leisure, patience, and a little contemplation, which he lacks. The one to be recognized and the recognizer are both ever changing, and the lover only describes that which he sees, in other words, his dispositions while observing; and he knows that the unsayable and unhearable cannot be told: "to whom shall I tell the things / I see in this shadow play"?[93]

Love is the individual experience of social man. By social man, I do not have its restricted meaning in mind, that is, someone at a particular time and place from a particular group or class! I mean a human being who comes into the world among others and leaves the world among others; and in relation to them, he builds, destroys, and gives meaning to his life. In encountering the world, such a person might lose his heart to the spirit that bestows existence on the universe. Also, in encountering other human beings, he might lose his heart to one like himself who is the abode of the spirit of the universe. A person disengaged from the universe and from man, one who does not contemplate these two and is enslaved to himself alone, is deprived of the light of love, and his path to join another remains obstructed in the heavens or on earth.

The love of social man, however, is not a universal experience or a personal experience that is placed at the service of everyone. Every person must test it with his own body and soul and plunge into it with his own heart. On the one hand, the characteristic of love is that it cannot remain within one person and must find its way to another. No one is a lover without a beloved. On the other hand, the nature of love is individual, personal; every person perceives it himself. Every tree in the forest has its own rain to drink, its own springtime to wear, and its own sky to watch; and every spring bubbles up through its own body from the darkness of the earth and presents its breast to sunlight and moonlight. This is not a possession or knowledge that one can give to another or have another enjoy, something he has accumulated or learned. Love is social-antisocial, something with a dual essence and with disorderly order; and to the point that it is social and is linked to the foundation, to the psyche, and to the culture of social man, it is transferable to another; and to the point that it is individual and internal, it is not transferable, only describable. For this reason, the poet in love who inevitably needs to speak drifts back and forth between speaking and not speaking. Because he does not know of any memory more pleasant than the sound of the words of love, he always praises love; but in the same state, he always remembers: "Talk of love is not that which is uttered by the tongue."[94] Nevertheless, he cannot restrain the tongue.

The poet recreates his love through the mediation of language and thus makes his inner passion possible and brings it into the world; in this way, the painful force that was inside him and would not give him respite, that force that would explode like a storm in the air, an earthquake on land, and a volcano in the mountain, and like a seed would tear apart in the body of the soil and bloom like a rainbow in the sky and a bud into the petal of a flower, that mad and rupturing albeit beautiful force, quiets down. Every ghazal is the colorful bottle of a demon whose life depends on it. A demon is contained within the frame of an angel. In this way, my dexterous elder steals the amorous moments of life from the hands of the pilfering world and saves them from annihilation, because at least he leaves in place a memento of them under the revolving dome. Inevitably, he must come to terms with the fire he has in his breast; and the gift of poetry offers him this happy opportunity to hurl the fire outside of himself by composing the inner cries and roars.[95] That internal, mute, destructive, and destructible force turns into an external, perceptible, constructed, and polished phenomenon. In the course of this kind of creation, the poet comes out of the nocturnal whirlpool of the soul and steps onto the shore of the dawning of the soul.[96]

In the course of this private and intimate give-and-take, the Bard of Shiraz also has a conversation with us. He is not merely addressing himself; but to the extent that he is involved with the world and with humans, he is also addressing you and me and our world. Even when he has chosen seclusion in some corner and has "moist eyes in a conversation with the self,"[97] he is speaking to me, so that I can split open my closed shell and try to perhaps hurl myself to where he is,[98] to come out of my circumstances and place myself in his frame of mind, such that his conversation with himself also becomes my own conversation with myself. Nevertheless, in both instances, the poet cannot transmit to me his feeling, temperament, and experience regarding love, because everyone must test love for himself, and be tested by love. But once my social man becomes familiar with the spirit and culture of the poet, he becomes aware of his feelings and experience. Of course, in this respect, the windfall that I gain is not merely awareness. If the essence of love is in my nature, and the ability to love has a place in my heart, I will be nurtured for life beyond my prison. If I have any seeds in my soil, blessed by the rain of love, a sapling may sprout, and my flower and thorn grow as he nurtures. This gardener does not plant a seed in me; he brings the existing seed to fruitfulness.

Through reading, even the poetry of Hafez, no one will become a lover. But the fortunate reader will become open to love, "for love is a journey that requires a guide."[99] And guidance comes from the beloved who dawns like a star in the eye of the lover and shows him the alley of the friend.

> one cannot find the precious pearl alone
> it is an illusion to think this can be done
> without another's help[100]

A ray of the beloved must be reflected in the inner mirror for the beauty of a love to be manifested. According to the poet, a person seeks love who has "pure essence."[101] The magic of poetry does not make such a person a lover; rather, it awakens in him the memory of multidimensional and multifaceted love.

Not only is love, like any living phenomenon, a twin of death, but, because it has a more ecstatic and more restless life, it also embodies a more tormenting and more untimely death, untimely no matter when it arrives. Poetry cannot give life to a dead love, nor bring back a departed beloved; yet, it always brings to mind the essence and substance of being in love, and it causes the heart that is accepting of love to recreate in his creative mind and to test past and even future experiences, one's own and other people's experiences, known and unknown, clear and unclear, as well as the meaning of love. The bard's ghazals provoke the memory of the most authentic human experience, love, which is a gem with varying manifestations in every wayfarer and causes the most hidden and the deepest streams of existence to flow in the realm of the soul. The green memory of love sprouts from under the forgotten soil and spreads across our meadow before the eyes of our imagination. In us, that "pure essence" awakens, and the eye of the heart opens for us to view the garden of the universe. In this way, the reader with the light of the poem discovers an astonishing relationship with himself. His loving self emerges from between the light and dark shadows of unawareness, and he senses the truth of his own nature, a euphoric feeling that blows like fresh air in the branches and leaves of the tree of the heart. The magic of poetry that awakens an experience and the thought of love and makes us able to see it is a reminder of the path of wakefulness and insight. In the inner darkness, a sun has set and is invisible but rises and becomes visible through the blessing of poetry, emerging from the realm of darkness into light. Poetry makes of us poets of the hidden treasure we hold in our depths; and when I look inside me, I am reminded of myself.

In that time without beginning
the Sultan of Eternity
gave us the treasure-trove of sorrows of love

from the moment we turned our faces towards
this empty caravanserai[102]

Love is a divine gift. Because the friend wanted me, he wanted me to also want him. Hence, by the blessing of love, he made me fall in love. He was a hidden treasure, a manifestation that appeared at creation, and existence is the visible manifestation of his invisible being. Love is a hidden treasure that cannot remain hidden, that manifests itself outside the wishes of one person or another, that conquers our being and takes us where it wishes. We are captives of liberating love. The gift of the friend is the treasure in the ruins: light in darkness, life in death, knowing in not knowing, happiness in sorrow, and freedom in captivity! In man, love signifies God in the universe. In the same way that God is inside the universe and outside the universe, love is also a gem inside the treasure of the human heart and outside the universe;[103] it is a being in nonexistence that was entrusted to man at the dawn of creation, and the lover in the realm of union became one with the beloved. Love is alienation from the self and oneness with another. The burning passion of longing for this *other*—like the eagerness of night for day, and day for light, and light for the sun, and the sun for the sky, and the sky for the earth, and the earth for the bosom of the concealed body of the night—is rapturous. In an involuntary journey, the lover is left without his self, separated from his internal and external self; in other words, he "would give up lordship over the earth"[104] to join the truth of himself and the universe—the friend and the alley of the friend—because only in this case will he rediscover his lost self, will the lost Joseph return to Canaan, and will order come to his distracted mind.[105]

The lover who has returned to himself because of being blessed with the beloved in the state of union willingly and knowingly shares the destiny of the friend. He is with him from the dawn of creation to eternity and from shore to shore, in the same way that the path is with the star, the star with the water, and the water with the light. Two traveling companions pass through the empty desert of nonexistence and reach the tumultuous shore of existence. Man is with God in God's sorrow and happiness, and man gains God's sorrowful freedom and free will that are accountable for good and evil. Because he is with God, he is free, and because he is free, he is responsible, and because he is responsible, he has a painful destiny.

The fortune of union with the beloved is a sorrowful freedom that is gained by remembering the suffering in the world. The restless glance of a friend seeks refuge in the hands of a friend, like starlight seeks refuge in the eye and moonlight in the lake. A morning splits the shell of darkness and disappears in the eyes of day. In the perilous circumstances of union, the lover emerges from the darkness of his soul and offers his bright soul to the beloved, the dust and mass of his earthly confinement remains, and his bird flies to the home of the beloved. Something has died and something has joined another; and it is as if the lover has vanished and no longer exists. The feeling of this nonexistence causes the lover in complete union and ultimate joy to taste the bitterness of separation. The poison of loneliness runs through the veins of a person who has drunk the nectar of union. In the same way, without the tragic affliction of distance, the good fortune of closeness is not appreciated.

> I shall not lament your absence   since without it
> how would I know the pleasure of your presence[106]

The rising and setting of the lover's star of fortune passes through the twilight of dawn and sunset. The rising of the star awakens in the heart the memory of its setting, and in its setting, the memory of its rising. When the happy lover is jubilant upon seeing the beloved, his heart shudders at the days when seeing her would be impossible, because even when lovers have absolutely no anxiety of separation, "the stone thrower of separation is waiting in ambush,"[107] and one day, the pit of death will distance the hands from each other, and love will be lost in the salt desert like a dewdrop; the bird will not split the clear screen of the sky and will not make the pearly air of dawn tremble, and will not make the heavy indolent silence sit on the ground like the body of darkness; the bright smile of morning will not bloom and its early rising eyes will not open at dawn. The world is the house of the drowsy, with multitudes of sleepers. And loneliness blindly wanders on the face of the earth.

Even when a lover like our Hafez is a partner in the eternal destiny of God, he does not separate himself from his mortal fate. Some saints and spiritual people might be able to forget themselves like angels and perish in the spirit of God. The poet, however, cannot. In the ecstasy and rapture of love, he feels the river that runs rapidly and slowly through him, the untiring and incurable wayfarer. Every day, a sun from him falls into the abyss of nonexistence. Being in step with time always keeps awake the thought of tomorrow, the tomorrow when the autumn wind has blown and the green leaf of love has dried up because of the blight of fall, and no longer "is any sign left of the vine or the vine planter."[108] The poet is aware of death and knows that the passage of time makes the high granite mountain low and pulls the peak from the sky down to the ground. Even when the existing although transient beauty of the beloved can be perceived, precisely then, the ear of his heart hears the sound of the footsteps of time, like the murmuring of running water. Beyond the pleasant dream of beauty in the distant night gallery of truth, a hazy apparition can be seen that makes the heart of the lover tremble. In the face of the eternal revolving of the spheres and the tireless movement of traveling stars and the undeniable future, he cannot do anything and is helpless. He must either flee from love, to be free of the dread of separation—which is the fate of lovers—or like a straw in the wind or a twig in a flood, let go of the brightness of his star in the darkness of the night, so that perhaps one day he may emerge from "this wave and storm."[109]

The sorrow of lovers, however, is not merely about the days that have not come, a future that is standing in our path with empty hands and vacant eyes; it is about right now, and the foundation-shattering joy of union.

A nightingale was holding in its beak
the petal of a brightly colored rose
but even with this beautiful token
in its possession   was crying its heart out

I asked why   in the very eye of union
it lamented in such a way and it replied

> it is precisely because of this manifestation
> of my beloved that I am distraught[110]

The eyes of the lover do not have the fortitude to see. A sign of the beauty of the friend is a flame, a flash of light that burns. Beauty and goodness are two faces of one thing. Goodness is beautiful, and beauty is good. Perfection is harmony between goodness and beauty, the result of which facilitates creation, the ability to evolve and accept existence; and absolute perfection is absolute power: the alliance of light with light and the distraction of darkness.

In relationship to humans, as well, in the language of the poet, good is the same as beautiful; and when he speaks about the good, he is referring to the beautiful. In his delightful mind, power occurs coupled with goodness and beauty: The beloved is the sweet king, a ruler with the bow of eyebrows and arrows of eyelashes, the royal falcon of the heart of a dove in love, and the lord of his soul. The beautiful are monarchs, and the beloved is the "sovereign beauty without whom the heart begins to fail: Woe from the sorrow of loneliness!"[111]

The celestial and terrestrial friends of our Hafez are perfect. One is absolute perfection that cannot even be contained in the imagination, and the other is a desired perfection that is not only a sign, a reflected ray of the sun, but an infinite and ultimate beloved that can be held in the arms, that can be seen with the eyes, and that can be desired by the heart.

To be face-to-face with the beauty of God is terrifying. The perfection that cannot even be contained in the imagination not only stops the mind's endless wandering but also even paralyzes the power of imagination. What is godlier than God? The other side of this dead end is falling into nonexistence. Then, only the thought and illusion of his opposite and converse can cross the mind: evil, ugliness, and nonexistence, the alliance of darkness with darkness and the distraction of light.

I visit the friend with the light of a beautiful heart, but the grim face of the enemy is waiting in ambush in the dark chamber of the eye, in this dungeon of the mind. The inner eye is a pondering seer; when it sees God, it does not forget Satan, and in the bright hands of God, it takes refuge from the dark memory of Satan. Good and evil, beauty and ugliness, and life and death are runaways bound together, joined yet separated beings.

Observing the beauty of the beloved is also painful, because from extreme happiness and good fortune, the memory of suffering and misfortune is awakened in my heart, and my wakeful heart remains empty handed. How could an insignificant measuring cup drink the light of that great a sun? After all, this angry sluggish cup is as small as a bud, as thin as glass, and as fleeting as a breeze. But despite all its inability, the greedy heart wants the flowing gush of a spring that, like light, can neither be caught nor possessed; rather, like the sun, at the same time that it exists, it is transitory. The beloved has engulfed the internal and external reality and the unreal, actuality and dream, and presence and absence; and because she exists and does not exist, the lover is in her, he is and he is not. The lover who has given up his self and taken a plunge is not only defenseless in the face of the threat of an unkind future, but also, because in the happiness of the good fortune of the time of union he cannot obtain the entirety of the beloved and keep her to himself, he remains unhappy. While the greedy lover cannot contain himself due to the inebriation of beauty, he is distraught with the sorrow of the muteness of the heart. In Persian ghazals, the nightingale and the rose symbolize the lover and the beloved. One signifies lovesickness, restlessness, and the cheerful but needy sound and song of lovers, and the other signifies fleeting vulnerable beauty, the blossoming but coquettish coyness of the beloved. A nightingale with a rose petal in its beak is a happy lover who despite all things laments the manifestation of the beauty of the face of the beloved.[112]

Beauty is a painful thing, because it shows itself but for an instant and is gone; yet it robs its lover of all his being. Before this, if—like spring and nature—beauty would become perceptible in the beloved, now—like freshness, which is the nature of spring—beauty is the same as the beloved, and the beloved is the same as beauty, and this sameness creates another world in the lover and makes him a different person. It plucks him away from the world in which he is—the world of profit and loss and the good and evil of those who observe good manners and the ways and customs of the worldly wise—and hurls him beyond fame and infamy, such that he shuns fame and is famed for infamy. A human being who shares customs and habits, a tamed and trained horse in the herd, turns into a bird in the sky and a deer in the desert and becomes restive. The fact that it has been said from ancient times that some person in love with another took a plunge and became a wanderer in the desert and homeless in the mountains, that it has been said that because of his love for Shirin, Farhad complained to the silent mountain, and because of his love for Leyli, Majnun told his story to dumb animals, among other things, means that lovers do not follow the ways of others, are not one of many, and even though they are in society, they are alienated from everyday social life.[113] Either they are away from others, or their hearts are elsewhere in the presence of others. In contrast to civilized social people, they have a strange nature and character, they are wild; and from the perspective of the worldly wise, they are mad. The one who considers the dust of the alley of the friend more precious than

> the gardens of paradise
> the shade of the Tuba tree
> or the abode of the heavenly maidens[114]

is mad in the eyes of any faithful Muslim; and the one who considers his beloved to be "beyond comprehension"[115] and says, "since all existence is alive from your scent,"[116] do not take your shadow away from us, is mad in the eyes of any unfaithful atheist. To consider the one who himself like an ember shines but for a brief moment and fades in the night to be the one who gives life to all existence is pure madness. Indeed, if madness is the alteration of the mind and emotions, the disintegration of the intellect that creates order, and the loss of human self in the invisible and foggy desert of the unconsciousness of the self, then lovers are mad.

> My whole heart and being became so filled with the friend
> That thought of the self was erased from my consciousness.[117]

Not only do they not think about themselves, but thinking about themselves or their thoughts is erased from their memory and consciousness, and because they have lost themselves in themselves, they are self-alienated; they are mad!

The awareness of such lovers and poets, like that of prophets, lies in their ecstatic lack of awareness of the self, their reality in their dreams, and their truth in their imaginations. Their physical eyes are not asleep, but the eye of their heart is also awake. While on this side of seeing, they see things that are visible, they also keep an eye on the evolution of things that exist. They observe that which is standing before them, and they also contemplate that fluid essence that is occurring and evolving in that which "stands before them," that inner composer that appears in its external form. They observe the warm activity of spring in the depths of the sleeping autumn roots and the sprouting of the bud of love on the other side of the flower garden. In the hiding place of every actuality and phenomenon, another sometimes incompatible reality is hidden that longs to create its own reality: love is an ailment that has no remedy; the lover dies from the Christlike breaths of the beloved that bring the dead back to life; and one not in love who falls in love with peace of mind is a clever bird that has fallen into a trap. This is that which it appears to be; but behind this actual incident, a seemingly contradictory reality can be seen: the remedy for the lovesick heart of the lover lies in that ailment,[118] and his life is in that very death, such that by following the scent of the beloved, he splits the breast of the earth, and in poverty gains the kingdom of Solomon, and in captivity, the freedom of the sky; and he creates the truth of his own reality.

Compared to reason, which measures human behavior on the scale of prudence, those who say, "I've lined up with the libertines now, come what may,"[119] are far removed from prudence; they are mad. But the human being of lovers, poets, and prophets is not merely a rational phenomenon. Essentially, he is not one of the phenomena of nature that is merely at a higher level and a higher boundary. The human being of our Hafez is of a different creation and a different category. He is an essence in love who, when he joined the soul of the universe, became one with existence and nonexistence and rejoined himself. Reason has no path to this state, the characteristics of which I do not know. This state is out of reach of ordinary human logic; and our elder, as well, can only speak about his dispositions in this state, and pass over its why, since why does not apply, since prudent reason in the face of love "is like a dewdrop that draws a shape on an ocean."[120]

Nonetheless, the eager lovers of the alley of the friend seek another world and a different human being, and are themselves of a different essence: of the essence of not wanting the world and the human beings that exist, of the essence of wanting a world and human beings more similar to my rose-colored elder and closer to the image that he has of the friend. What he has, however, is the ability to see the beauty of an invisible friend in the world of imagination; it is a revelation by the blessing of the light of the heart's eye.

> at every moment the image of your face
> blocks the road of my imaginings
> to whom shall I tell the things
> I see in this shadow play[121]

The painter in the workshop of imagination draws a new image at every moment and brings the invisible before our eyes. The image and the painter as well are the distraught mind of the lover. Now if this changing, capricious image, this imagining of the creator, this contemplative dream in the poet's soul, finds a light greater than the sun in the sky and a darkness greater than the depths of the earth, a truth greater than life and death, if it finds a grace more pleasant than "the memory of the kind friend,"[122] more pleasant than the memory of fleeing in the mind of the captive deer, more pleasant than the memory of spring in the sleep of autumn, and a physicality more solid than the heavy height of mountains, then I, as a man of reason, would say that this elder, with a lover's temperament, is mad. And he himself apparently hears my taunting proclamation:

> Might I go mad in this passion, since from night to day
> I speak to the moon and dream of spirits?[123]

The memory of the beloved so overcomes the lover's soul that a spiritual matter (being in love) becomes more real than an external matter (the beloved), to the extent that it is as though the poet is more in harmony with the perceptible internal world than the tangible external world. For him who has reconstructed and erected in the free workshop of yearning an ugly and beautiful beloved with the most beautiful conception of beauty, the memory and imagining of the body of the real, what he has in his mind gains a more formidable gravity and reality.

Hence, there is also a deception, among other things, in love, since the lover—wittingly and unwittingly, but also by choice—worships that which he has created in his own imagination. In other words, the truth that he is seeking he has created himself. The greater the "deception" of love, the more imaginary and remote and subsequently the more unattainable will be the beloved, and the more crazed the lover. He creates and remains separated from the created. The more perfect the created one, the more complete the separation of the creator from her! The lover is powerlessly powerful and sorrowfully happy. To be emptied of oneself and to be overflowing with another, to lose one's own persona and disposition, and to live with the hope and hopelessness of another is the same madness of passion in which the lover spends his nights and days and his sleep and wakefulness. The poet in love is anxious about this passion that nurtures madness.

And, incidentally, he is mad; but he is not a madman who has lost his reason, rather, a madman who has let go of reason and left it behind! The realm of reason is the domain of fate, with the perpetual time and place, unalterable causality, and the good and bad that distinguishes and separates acts worthy of reward from sinning. A man of reason travels with cautious feet along the roads of the world of dust and adheres to its unquestionable order; he believes in the transience of life, in the inability of the body and the demonic ability in it, and he fears the end. On the other side of these impassable boundaries, the seven cities of love[124]—which I dream of—extend from horizon to horizon, and I yearn "to perhaps hurl myself there."[125] But with the wooden legs of reason,[126] one cannot flee from the land of reason; men of reason are alone at every step, no matter where they go. I am liberated by love, the frenzied flight of which makes the walls of my being crumble, to relinquish my weary soul: lonely and forlorn love in search of the alley of the friend, love of the bird for the sky and the deer for the meadow, love of the meadow for the rider and the rider for the horse and the horse for the rider in the meadow, departing love, liberating love, love of love!

> Your love will come to the rescue, if you, like Hafez,
> Recite the Koran from memory in fourteen versions.[127]

The love of the migrating bird for the times to come draws it to places worth seeing, and hoping for new lands, sends it ahead to welcome the seasons. Love demolishes time and space, such that one can pass through the dark and light curtain of night and day and be submersed in the depths of light in moonlight and sunlight.

The joy of love makes my time fly as well; it gathers together in the present the bygone pasts and the futures yet to come; and the memory of the amorous present surrounds the distant past and future and reaches the shores of eternity for a moment, as though death and life join together at their source before the dawn of creation, and the lover in an endless moment becomes one with his destiny, like one in haste who pauses in an unconscious wakefulness and conscious sleep.

The joy of love is such that the lover's soul cannot contain it, unless the container expands as wide as the endless expanse of the content and extends to before the birth and after the death of the lover, to the point that it is as though he had been present in all times and spaces and had experienced everything in an eventful life. At the dawn of creation, when beginning and end come into existence and existence and nonexistence are twin brothers, in that unmarked alley of the friend, the garden of his soul blooms. The union of lovers is a garden that in its eagerness to blossom revives the silent autumn and dries up the seeds of death: "being with you / postponed my doom."[128] For lovers, as well, like martyrs who are killed for love, leaving is a new return, and "death is not an end, it is the beginning," since love neutralizes the ruse of death. But even when it cannot awaken the lover from his heavy sleep, at least it rejuvenates the world around him and returns spring to his sleeping soil.

if ever the breeze of union with you
blows over Hafez' grave
from the earth of his corpse   tulips in profusion will grow[129]

The self of such a lover goes beyond his own reach in the expanse of time and space. This man in ecstasy lays down the burden of the sorrows of the wounded heart and the worries about having and not having more, or having less, and he lays down his contemptible narrowmindedness; he falls outside the boundaries of reason, and is plucked from limited reason. Now, the dawn of a new self overtakes the darkness of the previous self. In this amorous struggle, I, who like the morning star was observing the twilight of my existence, am now baptized in the white spring of morning.

Union with the friend makes me of the same heart as and harmonious with the world that is from him, in the same way that in my love for the universe, as well, I commingle with the eternity of he who is the eternal soul of the universe, and at the moment of immortality, I reject the hand of death! Self-desired destiny comes, and unwanted fate departs, for fatalism to turn into free will. Love is freedom from reason and death, freedom from self-consciousness, and reaches toward awareness of the heart. But the freedom of love is the "impossible dream,"[130] impossible fortune, and the untimely death of happiness.

To join the friend, one must leave one's house of nature and be freed from its walls; one must release the bird of the soul, like a far-flying—but not tamed and trained—pigeon, to sit on the roof of love. Social life and its customs and habits are those walls that, as accomplices of the erosive pressures of the world, at every moment drive the lover to the confines of reason and life, making him aware of his time and space. With those customs and habits, the desire of the heart and the free longing for love diminish; the autocratic will of the society and the tyrannical necessities of the world cast their shadow; and the lover who imagined himself to be a king realizes that he is no more than a beggar.

Purely because of his love for you, Hafez became
As rich as Solomon; and from his longing for union with you,
Like Solomon, he has nothing but wind in his hands.[131]

Not only is the poet happier being a beggar rather than being rich, but he also considers "undiminishing riches"[132] to be destitution akin to having only "wind in his hands." He is happier in this very "kingdom of poverty," the smallest domain of which is "from the moon to the fish,"[133] because the richness of my elder is not "in the form of being a master," but "in manners, like a dervish."[134] "The mark of the people of God is to be a lover,"[135] and he has the love of the friend, and the world, and the people. While the rich have a hand that is not in need and a heart that is in need, he who in the manner of dervishes possesses the world in his nature has a heart and hands less in need than the ocean. Even when he has nothing in his hands but the wind, even when he has failed in his quest, he is a Solomon, because in the same way that God had placed himself in the mouth of that king, he is also on the tongue of the poet; because this one, too, like Solomon, is the fellow traveler of the wind, shares the suffering of the deer in the desert and the bird in the sky, and speaks the same language as tongueless nature; because this one, too, like him, possesses the ring and the seal of prophets and is the messenger of the friend on earth; because this one, too, like him, has seen the light and possesses the vision, and when the darkness of separation takes over his being, still the vision of the sun flickers within his heart, and since he has "the emblem of being in love with him,"[136] when night engulfs him, still, like every night, he possesses his own morning. Hence, in the captivity of separation, as well, even though the freedom of love has been separated from the place of the manifestation of union, it has not been annihilated. The voice of the friend resonates in the ear of his heart, shows him the way, and calls him to himself.

Now the voice of the friend comes from the bottom of ancient roots, from within the expanse of the face of the earth, from distant roads, from high mountain peaks and open plains, and reaches me, like the hidden beating of the heart of the star. She names me with a silent voice, and I see her voice in her moist eyes and open lips. An invisible wave comes from the ocean of silence, and before it reaches the shore, it pours into itself; it is anxious and sad, and it speaks in the tongue of no tongues. Words grow within me, like the sprouting of green buds in the heart of the seed beneath the cold of winter, like the scent of spring! The voice of the friend, the voice of love from the distant land of forgetfulness, from between the sown fields of suffering, blowing on the sheaves of sorrow! A voice from the heart of loneliness, from empty depths, and from the settling of massive shadows, a voice that—like water from stone—springs from the depths of the heart of the friend, runs in the warp and weft of night and day, and disappears like the resonance of the ocean under the azure cup of the sky. The wakeful voice of a silent friend who is sleeping on the bed of my heart. And as I was sleeping, with her voice, I opened my eyes and looked at her hands. She named me, and I came to myself among the beings. I saw that I had risen from the body of the dust and was standing on the earth. Above my head, the eagle of longing was flying in the open wings of the sky, and under my feet, the deer of fortune had fallen asleep. My heart became acquainted with sorrow and happiness; I found my star in the heart of the night; and in darkness, I recognized my destiny. The voice of the friend was my beginning. It was the dawning and blooming, it was the whispering of the pregnant earth, the sleepy murmuring of dawn and the splitting of the horizon, and the lamp of the sun. The voice of the friend was compensation for the cold silence and the heedless absence of God, the remedy for my distraught loneliness. It was the voice of a kindred spirit that said, you are the light of my eyes, and I gave her my glance like I gave my hands and said, you are the patient earth and captive sun, you are my friend. And, oh friend, I love you in your various manifestations, because you are that friendly truth in me that has various manifestations. At times, you are Christ and Mansur,[137] at times the universe full of colorful images, at times a heart-stealing beloved, and at times, like my rose-colored elder, you are this and that, and in all cases, you are my mother, the one who gave birth to me and nurtured me. Even though you have innumerable manifestations, in your essence, you are one! In you, the essence of love is a concrete and complete oneness, like the singular sun in the sky. The flame of that hidden fire that is in your breast makes possible the manifestation of the mesmerizing beauty of the friends; and because all are seen in one light, a single light, they are all emanations from a single essence. "Since like the divine attributes / you are beyond comprehension."[138]

God was manifested in the work of his hands, in the image and character of the terrestrial Adam; and now, because this unmatched beauty is the place of the manifestation of such a creator, like him, it is beyond my ability to comprehend. The beautiful perfection of this beloved, who might be from my own alley and neighborhood and from my terrestrial family, reaches the point where it is out of reach of comprehension, because her face is the handiwork of the friend. Hence, her beauty possesses that "thing" that is beyond human limitations.

> the angel kneeling before Adam
> was in its own mind
> kissing the ground beneath your feet
> for in your beauty it found
> something better than mankind[139]

Divine beauty in human form! In the same way that, in order to pass beyond his invisible seclusion, God flees to mankind, now man, in order to pass beyond himself, has fled to God. The beloved is "a body / created of the spirit,"[140] a spiritual body and a physical spirit! The poet himself is astounded at seeing such a body, and he asks, "who ever saw"[141] such a fine body, a body made of dust but more fluid than water, lighter than fire, and more transparent than light? Such a body is not made of water and dust; it is composed of the soul, of that rare ethereal breath of the world above, or of the water and clay that blossomed from the breath of God, celestial-terrestrial, beyond the level of water and clay, beyond comprehension! The existence of the friend is where man and God join.

Such a perception of the beloved makes the lover fly between the creator and the created and sometimes makes them interdependent and conjoined twins, each of whom carries the other. The friend of the poet is sometimes God and sometimes man, and even sometimes in a single ghazal, he reaches from one to the other and speaks about both. "Hitherto you were more considerate to lovers."* The poet is addressing a terrestrial beloved from whose sweet lips at one time he had had nocturnal whisperings of amorous secrets. In this reminder of the past, the poet's free imagination reaches to before creation and eternal love, and then in a turnabout and a

* See the rest of the ghazal. [From ghazal 206; Geoffrey Squires, trans. *Hafez: Translations and Interpretations of the Ghazals* (Miami: Miami University Press, 2014), 253.]

turning, he goes back to the time after the end, the evening of eternity and the sameness of the pledge of love and the indestructability of the foundation of love! Physical love—mediated by the thought of time—calls to mind mystical love, and from thinking about humankind, the poet begins to think about God, from friend to friend, and the need and the longing of the lover and the beloved for each other—the characteristic of both of whom is love—are uttered. But after this, when he speaks about the kindness of nature and a good temperament, the "king and beggar," and that God is the provider, the thread of the ghazal seemingly breaks and it falls apart like a broken string of beads. The poet knows this and apologizes for having his hand "on the lap of the smooth-legged cupbearer." Longing for the warm body and the desirous breath of the beloved has broken his stream of consciousness and has drawn him down to earth once again, to spend the night until morning drinking with a tipsy beloved and "a cup in the wall niche." But in the closing couplet of the ghazal, the poem of the transient, terrestrial poet reverts to being about the dawn of creation and paradise: a man from here with words from there; one love, two beloveds, and a lover in between![142]

At times, elsewhere on this grave, amorous journey, without being hindered from going toward the beloved, for the moment, this man from paradise is entangled in love for young beauties. The bird of the celestial flower garden, an angel from the high heavens who suffers from the pain of separation, in the meantime has given his heart to someone's darling offspring and fallen for one or another. My elder calls God as his witness that he is with him everywhere he is, that he is with God, but at the same time, slyly, he has his eye on another, since following another couplet he says:

> Excited by the intoxicated narcissus eyes
> of a tall-statured beauty
> Holding a cup, like a tulip,
> I have fallen beside a stream.[143]

Giving his heart to a coquettish, tall-statured beauty is not a sign of his taking his heart away from or even neglecting his creator, in the same way that it is not necessarily a sign of simultaneous attention to the other.

Since the poet has seen and experienced a great deal and is a man of many colors, he has various states of mind. Sometimes his friend is God alone, and his words overflow with mystical ecstasy and rapture, and sometimes he only thinks about a friend made of Adam's clay, and that is all. But yet, Hafez's this-worldly love is not always the same. At one time, the longing for companionship with the soul of souls and observing his astonishing beauty, longing to be separated from his self and intending to reach the friend, and in this impossible dream, to be removed from his self and not find his way to the other, is expressed by the poet. Hoping for union and the reality of separation from an absent beloved who is always present in the lover—this absence and at the same time presence—is the basic substance of the magical sorrow of the love story that he tells, the story of a mood to which at times "the story of the fear of Resurrection Day"[144] is merely an allusion. This story of the joy of the sad heart, this song of happiness and suffering, is the origin and source of his love songs.

But at times, he is only eager for a beauty, "with her torn dress, singing a love song,"[145] and things that become alive and acquire a more pleasing meaning because of the presence of such a beloved: flowers, wine, and a song, a meadow and a stream! He is eager for the bounty of the world and the delightful joy of the body; he "longs to pierce a delicate pearl in the darkness of the night and to sleep with her till morning"![146] In this case, his poetry is a delicate praise of physical pleasures, or as the poet puts it himself, "cleverly libertine poetry."[147]

Even when the divine love and the worldly love of the poet appear to be distant from each other, they are not alien to each other; rather, they dawn in the lover in two states and arenas. And when they become of the same blood and the same nature in the rapture of unity, they do not annihilate each other, or one does not necessarily cause the other to be forgotten; rather, they are reflected in each other, like one image in two mirrors, and create a new image that is both a new phenomenon and also what it was.

From one perspective, the lover has a dependent life; he lives through the beloved. Love has completely engulfed him. Filled with the memory of another and empty of the memory of himself, it appears as though he is diminished and not conscious, and that he perceives the brilliant song and dark lamentation of the universe with the memory of another, and her ears and eyes. His thoughts and feelings find their way into the world by passing through the transparent mirror of the friend, from beyond this colored glass, and he contemplates and experiences her. The world, as well, permeates the garden of his mind in the same way upon imagining the creator. "The lamp of our eyes is lit / by the breeze of our beauties' hair."[148] If a breeze blows from the direction of the friend, if her glance shines on my dark house and the memory of her revives my heart, the lamp of my eye lights up like a fire; otherwise, the lamp remains unlit, and the astonishing ability of the lover to observe does not change from potential to action. But when there is an attraction from that side and the lover is able to see, he sees the universe in the face of the friend, which is like a cup that reveals the universe. "Your mole is the pivotal point of my vision."[149] The poet's glance, like a ray directed to the world, shines on the most remote and most concealed places, travels in search of the truth of realities, and explores the phenomena on the other side of the invisible. This meteor that splits and sees that which is hidden dashes with pauses and with speed, wanders, stops, and goes, but it does not separate from its root that bestows light. This ray has branches and leaves everywhere, and its root and its foundation are in the mole of the face. On this orbit and from this perspective, it observes the universe. The face of the friend is the source and the eye of the lover, the stream of light. One is spring and the other a flower garden; one is the substance of life and the other the body. "May the evil eye spare you / who are both lover and beloved."[150]

The mere fact that in our Persian language the words *janan* and *jananeh*[151] mean both "friend" and "beloved friend" shows that there is a connection between the concept of the "beloved" and the soul and life of the lover, and that the beloved is like the soul of the lover, the force that gives him life, and the meaning of his life:

> although as a *hafez* I am well-known
> to all and sundry in this town
> I am not worth one barley-corn
> unless out of loving-kindness
> you consent to be mine[152]

The lover is alive because of the beloved, and if he does not leave this lived-through-the-beloved life of his and is not annihilated, it is perhaps, among other things, because accepting the friend in the house of the soul does not mean the arrival of one and the departure of the other. It is the acceptance of light in the house of the sun. In the same way that a flower comes out of the sepal of the bud and opens in its own color, scent, and shape, also the barren garden of the soul—which is not a garden because it is barren—blooms in the presence, in the manifestation, of the beloved and becomes a garden, since it is no longer barren. Hence, the beloved does not gain access to the soul of the lover in order to invade it and for the lover who "has lost his soul" by the will of the ruler of his soul to live by the desire of someone else's heart; rather, because the beloved is the embodiment of ideal perfection and the crystallization of what the lover longs for in both worlds, by having the beloved in his soul—like a wave in fusion with movement—he becomes fused with the ultimate desired object and purpose of his life without mediation. He is suddenly distanced from everything accidental, superficial and meaningless, incidental, relative, and transient; he is one with absolute and lasting necessity, with the truth of existence, and is now at the very core of life, and its essence flows in his veins; and he, as well, like the essence of life, flows in the veins of the universe.

The existence of the beloved is the renewed life of the soul; and the revived soul is "the same" as life itself, and one is in the place of the other: soul in place of the beloved. Hence, when the poet says, "May it be forbidden for me to choose my soul over the beloved,"[153] his words are in fact the repetition of the obvious, "saying the same thing," since one can choose one thing in place of something else when they are different from each other; but when two things are "the same," choosing one in place of the other is impossible. For the poet to shun himself is futile, because even if he should want to, he would not be able to choose the soul in place of the beloved.

The beloved is the lover's soul, and everyone who possesses a soul has a length of life that is his particular time in endless time. The length of life is the movement of the soul on the bed of time in its changeable form. As life passes, the soul takes shape and changes. The beloved, who was the soul of the lover, with the passage of time becomes his life as well. The meanings of *jan* and *omr* in Persian,[154] at any rate, each call to mind the other, and the one who is the *jan* of the lover is also his *omr*.

Moreover, the lover lives within the beloved, who has engulfed all of him. In this sense, in the same way that everyone lives in his own span of life, the lover is also alive within the beloved. If the departed beloved returns, the past part of his life might return, "even though the spent arrow does not return."[155] Time is a shot arrow that is gone when it is; and if the beloved is the life of the lover, her departure, "even if she returns," is irreversible, because when the beloved is not there, it is as though life is not there: "Who counts the day of separation as a part of life?"[156] And the poet without life—without time—has an amazing life; he lives in timeless time.

The lover gains access to another concept of time that is not the "external" time that stems from the revolving of firmaments and the arrival of day and night, quantitative and measurable time—the stretched out time for us to travel and wear down its pathways like a planet or for it to travel and eat away at our fate like a termite—time stemming from young age and old age, being born and dying; it is an inner, emotional, qualitative, and immeasurable time. Compared to that independent time that has a perpetual and similar movement from present to future, this one, if one can say so, has a circular self-propelled rotation, sometimes jumbled and sometimes reversed, that stems from the disposition and mood of the lover and is dependent on the mystery and coquettishness of the beloved; it is a constant of two permanent variables.

When I am with you, a year seems a day,
When I am without you, a moment seems a year.[157]

The measure of time is related to the beloved and the lover's feeling for her. It becomes an actual issue external to the mind and loses its sequential order and continuity that stem from the movement of universal phenomena, and the lover whose eyes were enchanted by the beauty of the friend prior to the raising of "this green dome and azure ceiling" becomes present at the time when he was kneading and molding Adam's clay.[158]

Not only in relation to God but also in relation to humankind, the sequence and continuousness of time are reversed.

However old, incapable,
    And heart-sick I may be,
The moment I recall your face
    My youth's restored to me.[159]

In his memory, the poet returns from old age to youth, and his creative imagination travels contrary to that of the created world. In another mood, the poet runs out of patience: "I will draw a sigh from my despondent sinful heart / That will set ablaze the sin of Adam and Eve."[160] His fiery sigh scorches something that occurred in the past, at the dawn of creation. He applies a current sigh to that time, or he brings a sin from the most distant past to his own time and sets it ablaze, and in both cases, he disturbs the course of time.

Sometimes a moment in time, because of its quality, has a timeless effect. If the friend one day were to remove the veil from her face, "the whole world forever"[161] would be adorned, as though the phenomena of the universe at that very singular moment would forever take on the beauty of the face of the friend and bestow on time a new measure. In a ghazal in which from the start the topic is the curls of the tresses and the magical enchantment of the eyes of the beloved, suddenly the thought of the beauty of her face peaks to such a height, as if it is the beauty of the face of the eternal beloved.[162] In the imagination of the poet, something internal and specific, the effect of the beauty of the beloved's face, becomes external and universal and shines on the entire universe like the manifestation of the radiance of that friend. When the perception of the terrestrial beloved resembles the perception of the celestial beloved, the function of both those worlds also resembles a manifestation in a time, embellishing and giving meaning to the universe for all time, turning a moment into eternity! What God did at creation is now done by man in a different state.

The beloved is the soul and life of the lover. And this life is a time that only stems from human existence in which love also travels. When this existential time finds its way into universal time, the poet gains access to a new arena of the sense of time, an arena in which happiness and suffering, good and evil, the observing of existence and nonexistence, and the emergence of manifestations of nature assume another shape and meaning. Hence, when the internal and external worlds of the lover change, another human is made of the one who used to say, "another Adam must be created."[163]

The lover not only reaches another time but also another space, one apart from the land of those without love and ordinary people, and apart from geographical space in the natural world.

> Why would one who has chosen seclusion need sights to see?
> Who needs the meadow when the alley of the friend exists?[164]

Because the lover has chosen seclusion, mountains and plains are of no interest to him, since in the seclusion of the workshop of his imagination, he envisions and sees the friend and his abode. It is as though seclusion and the alley of the friend are both evoked simultaneously.

In nature, no space is of value on its own, and one can easily give away the prosperous ancient cities of Samarqand and Bokhara for a mole on a face.[165] If a space is the place of the manifestation of the friend, that space is the residence of the soul, and anywhere else is "Alexander's prison,"[166] and the poet recalls it because he is depressed by the pressure of its walls and despises its narrow dungeon.

A lover who lives within the beloved (in his own span of life and "time") is always where she is. For the forlorn poet, his city—with its starry nights and blossom-covered gardens and local coquettish girls, this place that is the city of his loves, in which he learned to observe the world and experienced death and life, which is his place of birth and his final resting place—is the familiar place, the alley of the friend. He longs to leave the "desolate staging post" in exile and, "dancing like a particle," go "to the door of the tavern, to the edge of the spring of the sun, to the kingdom of Solomon":[167] "to go to my own city and be my own sovereign."[168]

> to me   the air of my beloved's house
> is the water of life itself
>
> O send me a breeze from the good earth of Shiraz[169]

Sometimes the imagination of the lover goes further, and the bird of his soul nests in the soul and body of the beloved. His heart continues to spin like a polo ball[170] between the tip of the beloved's tresses[171] and the curve of her eyebrow.[172] On the other hand, the eyes of the lover who loves his home, the friend of the "eyes that see the world,"[173] is a lover who tries to remain close to his own vision, to the light of the world. "Happiness lies where the beloved is."[174] But what place of the beloved is better than the heart of the lover? If the heart of the lover is her home and her place of rest, then the heart of the lover is itself the alley of the friend; in particular, when the friend is a departed friend, like Mansur,[175] or "the pearl that is outside the shell of time and space,"[176] he has no place other than this home, the reaching of which is the lover's ascension to heaven. When such a lover rediscovers himself and resides inside himself, he is in the alley of the friend and united with the friend.

But when separation occurs, the soul of the lover no longer remains with him; it hovers in the air of the beloved who is away from him. He is in one place and his soul in another; he occupies a space that is of two parts: the helpless, empty physical cage and the bird of the soul seeking another nest!

Hence, space, similar to time, has a value that is dependent on the beloved and is an existential matter. In other words, the quality of it does not depend on external phenomena, on the season, perspective, and weather. Rather, it depends on the person who occupies it and the heartfelt connection of the lover with her, and the change that this connection makes in his nature; it depends on the change in his view and perception of existence and nonexistence. Space is also a constant of two permanent variables.

In the view of the faithful, paradise is the ideal place and the home of eternal happiness. The imagining of time and the disposition of time-bound humans is compatible with this space: eternity and happiness, deliverance from revolving time, and taking one's place in endless happiness. The alley of the friend is also the lover's ideal imagining of space, his soul in paradise or paradise in his soul; it is a lofty space in the external or internal world, and in both cases, its brightness, fluidity, pleasantness, and freshness effervesce from the highly fertile source of the lover's imagination.

Our Hafez is a poet who possesses the alley of the friend. In other words, in this desert of bewilderment, in this eternal workshop of existence and nonexistence, he is not wind in the hands of the storm. In this circle, he is bewildered, but bewildered with his feet firmly on the ground. He stands in a solid place; and for this reason, he can gauge himself and understand himself in relation to existence and nonexistence. In some places, he positions himself in the essence of space; in this "flood of nothingness,"[177] he has a place for himself and he is from somewhere. But for Majnun, the home of Leyli is not a solid and easy space.[178] I had said that "the poet is forlorn and a wanderer in the alley of the friend," because here is the land of being and not being, a nowhere land, nowhere and everywhere, the Canaan of the lost Joseph,[179] the homeland of forlorn strangers and the residence of wayfarers, the house of the beloved, and hence, the house of the heart of the lover; and since it passes beyond the paradise of the followers of religious law, it is itself the spring of the sun and the cup that reveals the universe, since if paradise is the place of the manifestation of God's bounty, the alley of the friend is the manifestation of God himself, and the garden of paradise compared to it is no more than a myth: "Oh you from whose alley the story of paradise is but a tale,"[180] a distant, misty, and vague story that cannot make us neglect the beguiling earth, a space as bright as the sun. "With the dust of the alley of the friend, we would not even look at paradise."[181] In this arena, the dust of the threshold is good fortune and the source of good fortune; "it is collyrium for the eyes,[182] it illuminates the eye of the heart,[183] and the illuminated eye fills with tears from ardent desire for it."[184] "To choose begging in his alley over being a king"[185] is eternal wealth. This lofty place, or this lofty perception of timeless space, is the preferred place. In this state, when the lover leaps out of the trap of universal space, his self is freed from its engulfing surroundings, and he chooses his desired place in existential space. The alley of the friend is the place of freedom, the abode of the free bird of the soul that refuses to endure the confinement of any cage. The poet who said that to create another Adam, another world must be created,[186] in this "nowhere" place, achieves union with another world.

From the House of Nature . . .

The alley of the friend is the place of freedom, that is, the place of the freedom of the soul, an arena in which the soul finds itself free. Man, however, is of the world: He comes into the world, spends time in the world, and lives within its time. His soul and body travel in the world, and the world travels within his soul and body. This human who has fallen into the world hurls himself beyond the corrosive revolving of the world to the alley of the friend in order to free himself from the enslavement of its inevitable laws. This same enslavement drives him toward freedom. Because he is in darkness, he longs for light: with the radiance of the face of the friend, he lights the lamp of his heart. Thus, since humans come together at the crossroads of this world and since they become aware of the creator through the blessing of creation, they are lovers and beloveds, whether in the world or through the world, and they rediscover each other, or better stated, each other in themselves. Man is of the world, and in order to attain the lofty and ideal space, the poet constantly measures himself in terms of actual terrestrial space; and once he has tested and perceived that space, he is more aware of his worldliness within this space.

This space, however, is not far and is near geographic lands, plains, and meadows. In epic poetry, space is expansive and "horizontal." Battles and feasting, victory and defeat, joy and sorrow occur on battlegrounds and in banquet halls, in crossing rivers and mountains, and as a result of traversing countries. The battle chronicle of the champions of the Sage of Tus[1] takes place under the sky, on land, or at sea. In epics, the life force is an ideal force, and because of its uncontrollable and restless driving force, the champion fights any obstacle to his will, including the ruggedness of nature, vast distances, the difficulties of the road, and the travails of travel.

This rebelliousness of the will in the champion, or the poet, at times gallops so far ahead that it breaks through the boundaries of any horizon and disregards the limitations of natural distances and human endurance and ability. Champions navigate at sea for forty days, charge from this end of the world to the other, and overcome the seven perilous feats.[2]

In the mystical and love ghazals, however, space is compressed and "vertical." The gaze of the Bard of Shiraz soars from observing the earth and the sky to the other side of the world, to the desert of darkness and light, to the realm of separation and union. And if he mentions a city or a clime, it is to express a mood, not to tell a story. For example, he laments the memory of the beloved and a forlorn land; yet still, in such a situation, he rarely mentions a place by name. Rather, he metaphorically expresses the mood that a place creates in him: Yazd as "Alexander's prison,"[3] a strange forlorn city, and Shiraz as the "kingdom of Solomon"[4] and the "country of the beloved."[5]

With his spiritual travel provisions, the poet of love songs flows in existing and external spaces and makes a spiritual journey in the visible, material world. He does not seek a "scientific" understanding of the external world and its empirical laws. He does not observe, but contemplates the world spiritually. His observation is internal, because, on the one hand, he entrusts the image of the physical eye to the heart's eye and sees his own world from beyond his senses; and, on the other, he is in search of the "internal" aspect of the world, its hidden meaning and mystery. He inhabits the external world, measures it within himself, and externalizes it. Hence, even external space assumes an inner hue.

Space is not an abstract concept; rather, it assumes existence in nature, or in other words, nature is the creation of space. Hence, the poet's "space" is the same as the world of creation. On the other hand, creation occurs in time and is itself the beginning of this-worldly time. Creation allows space and time to exist, and "nonexistence" becomes "existence" in time and space. Hence, the world holds within itself the unique perception and conception of nature and time and space. For this reason, the revolving dome[6] is the wheel and firmament, the turning sphere, and time, and they are represented by symbols that evoke in the mind a form of movement and an image of change.

The universe is subject to time. It is in motion, revolving; and with the traveling of its stars, with its moon and sun and sunset and dawn, it gives birth to time within itself and brings it into the world and takes it out of the world, night and day. This is universal and "external" time, since it is measurable and quantitative due to the change in the external world and alongside it; and our lives pass within its days, weeks, months, and years. "This chaotic passage"[7] is a stage or an opportunity of but the few days that the universe has given us. At "the time when time is so short," we are moving hurriedly toward "the sea of oblivion."[8] The poet anxiously observes this invisible pilferer who constantly robs his present and drives it to the past, to make him one of those who have passed away. The offspring of the world are the prey of time, because anyone who falls into the caravanserai of the world moves along with the caravan of time. Time and space are of the same essence, and rarely does one enter the mind of the poet without the other, as though space is the design and body of time, and time is the essence and soul of space.

Nevertheless, oblivious to us, the world revolves; but its revolving is our time. As it finishes its task, in fact, it is finishing us off. The denizens of the world have a unilateral, mediated, and "negative" relationship with the world: Its revolving is our fate, but our fate counts for naught in its revolving. Time finds its way in between, and its revolving becomes our fate. Without this mediator, it has no access to us. The world is unconsciously impactful, and humans are consciously impacted; and this makes the relationship negative. Since the two sides of the relationship are unequal, as a result, they are not free of each other, and because they are not free of each other, neither are they free within themselves. The world without volition has engulfed man, and man without volition has appeared in the world. Two sides that are neither of the same essence nor equal, in a relationship without volition, are entwined together, or one has fallen into the rotating mill of the other, like grain. Such a relationship is fatalistic and, from the perspective of humans (that is, the conscious side of this relationship), unjust. As it builds our time, the firmament also determines our fate, because fate in time changes from potential into actual and comes into existence, because it is the firmament that "shuts the door of free will to you and me."[9] Is it not true that everyone has a star that is born with him and dies with him? Hence, destiny descends on us from the revolving of spheres and stars from the supreme wheel. The world takes our destiny away from us, separates it from us, organizes it on the basis of its own indiscernible wish, and in this way, changes destiny to accident and chance in accordance with the ruling of fate.

The world's time, like an invisible and visible blight, destroys us and disregards our will and wishes. The poet shuns this characteristic of existence, which like a chronic and deadly disease is hidden at the core of life, and he cannot locate its cause. That is why he says, "dangerous times" and "the upturned heavens / like some bloody colander"[10] are "a vicious circle,"[11] and this adversity is contrary to reason, that is, it is blind, mad, and goes against our wishes; in other words, it is hardhearted and destructive. This vicious circle is charging in a certain direction and doing something that it should not.

From this perspective, man's unilateral relationship with the world is existential and "internal," because he views the world through the ugliness and beauty of emotions and the good and bad of ideas, from behind the colorful screen of his imagination, and expresses love and hatred for it: The time-infested world nurtures like a nanny and kills callously. Every sweet nectar and sweet smile of hers has a bitter sting and a bitter bite. She is the trap we cannot escape, the sharp-shooting hunter of our wishes, and the lasso that impedes our steps and our flight. In the complex design of the turning spheres, the death-conscious poet sees "the deceitful hag"[12] and the bride of a thousand grooms[13] that sends each and every one unaware to the bed of dust and oblivion, the frenzied game of madmen in a slumber house set in a mirage![14]

In the thinking of Hafez, society is also part of the system of the firmament, not an independent phenomenon with its own processes and procedures. His society is universal; and its good and bad not only hinge on the behavior of the people but also on the journey of the stars to the higher realm. Hence, the darkness of social life: Rule by oppression and deceit also stems from the revolving of the firmament. The auspicious and the sinister in the horoscope also affect the fate of the members of the society.

Nevertheless, this same world is born from love, and "all this colorful design is a light from the face of the cupbearer,"[15] and "the lover and beloved rediscover their own other because of it." From a general perspective, the world is a divine truth; but in the course of life, it often appears to be a reality devoid of truth and the field of death and separation.

All ideological systems that consider the good to be the source of existence become entangled in a destructive contradiction in the face of the workings of the world. If the whole world stems from the same source, then what is the purpose of this avaricious plunder that does not allow respite for anything, this pointless torment? "Oh the injustice and plunder in this trap."[16] In Hafez, as well, this incurable contradiction raises its head involuntarily. His world is at times devoid of virtue and hostile to moral values, and tyrannically does whatever it wants. It does not even treat the noble and the ignoble equally, but is often kinder to the latter. The revolving of the firmament that fosters the inferior "is the enemy of the good, is after the killing of the wise heart, and puts the reins of aspired goals in the hands of the ignorant."[17]

Shifting the blame for human ill fortune, suffering, and calamities to the heavens, to the raw material that blindly continues on its unknowable path, keeps the kind and just God safe from the inquisitive eyes and bothersome questions of the faithful. They have set up separate accounts for God and the firmament to avert any harm to their faith. But since God is almighty and has absolute knowledge, and without his will nothing is stored in the mind, the path to infiltrating the beliefs of faithful Muslims remains open, "the mystery behind the veil"[18] remains unsolved, and the seekers of secrets traverse the roads of blasphemy and faith.

In confronting such a world, a poet who has suffered oppression is conscious in the face of an unconscious oppressor, a victim of the arrow of the firmament who has sought but not found justice, and who has lost revenues and capital! The world is the valley of bewilderment, the faraway desert,[19] and the house of mirage.[20]

> No matter which way I went, my fear only increased
> Protect me from this desert, this road without end.[21]

It seems as though the pessimism of the Manicheans regarding the prison of the world and the belief of the Muslims in the transience and untrustworthiness of the world, coupled with the painful experience and observation of the poet, have crystalized as the image of the world in his mind.

The world is what it is; but that rose-colored elder in his various moods is not always what he was. I had said that he, among other things, is also "enchanted by the world."[22] After all, he is a clever libertine, not a pious ascetic, and he loves this very "trap of troubles."[23] The mere fact of being in this "illusory state"[24] and the ability to make love and hold a cup of wine should be considered a chance to take advantage, "since time has many incapacities in store beneath the ground."[25] The picture of the world in the mind of the poet is bitter and despairing, but also beautiful and heartwarming.

> arise and let us dedicate our lives
> to the pen of that great artist
> who has created all these marvelous images
> within the compass of this earthly circle[26]

The world is a colorful canvas with the "sound of the words of love"[27] and the high and low voices of lovers. Hafez laments the unkindness of the world because of the great love he has for it. If "some leisure time, a book, and the corner of a meadow"[28] were not a better state than this and the next world, why would one be sad about the transience of the world? Everything because of which the poet is overflowing with the fascination for life—in step with his this-worldly existence—in the moving chariot of the world is hastily moving toward death. He has just arrived at the beloved's stopping place and not yet shaken off the dust of the road "when every instant now the bell / Cries, 'Load up to depart!'"[29] The love of the poet for the world is the one-sided love of an unequivocal lover for an inconstant beloved who follows her own path, bewildered, and does not intend to cast a glance—not even a loveless one—at the one who needs her. In the end, the enamored lover casts his lot over to fate and washes his hands of both: of the loving heart and the beloved world! A will that cannot accept existence and go further than a failed dream, out of helplessness and anger, rises against itself to negate both the desirer and the desired.

How long shall our hearts grieve
at the passage of time

imagine   how it would be
if there were no heart   and no such thing as time[30]

Of course, the poet tries to come out from under the rubble of this contradiction—this heart-rending vacillation between wanting and not wanting, love and hatred, and affirming and negating the world—and open a window in the dead end of hopelessness, albeit not in the manner of the faithful or philosophers, not through faith and reason, but in the manner of poets and through the blessing of beauty. His salvation is in beauty (goodness). The oneness of absolute goodness and beauty annihilates absolute evil and ugliness: total light versus total darkness!

O knowing heart   how long will you have to know
the pain of this mean existence
how sad that the fair should come to love the foul[31]

Space and time are twins, and for one to come to be is dependent on the existence of the other. Dawn and evening, midday and midnight, all pass in the sleep and wakefulness of space, and they always change its perpetual soul and body. Because of time, the world is continuously the same and not the same as it was; it is a motionless runner and an eternal transient. Every cycle, every day, season, and year, permeates another change in space, confronts it with new denizens of the world and existential conditions, and transforms it into something other than it was. On the other hand, the world is always the same, and every circle returns to its beginning. Spring and autumn pass each other to reach themselves and, like the links of a chain, to be locked in themselves and in each other. Every beginning through its end and every birth through its death is on its way toward another beginning, another birth.

This repeated cycle—like earth that simultaneously revolves around itself and the sun—is also moving in some direction. But the unidirectional travel of time in the world cannot be sensed and observed, because it is so long and faraway. Only by way of science can one conceive of what the passage of innumerable times does, not with the world but with the bodies of the firmament that are its components. However, this unidirectional time of our "world" takes the denizens of the world to an end that is not followed by another beginning. It passes by the this-worldly "I" and annihilates it forever. The revolving of the world binds itself to the life of the body, which is my particular world, like a bud that can never open. "The affairs of the world are clenched like a bud."[32] They bind man with a chain the links of which are moments and hours, and man tears apart these links to find an opening in the closed cocoon of the world. Their poison finds its way into our soul through this opening. Hence, one must fly out of that same opening to prevent the arrow from piercing the heart, so that, should it cause a wound, it would not, in any case, kill at once. The antidote of time is also in time: in being "knowledgeable of one's time,"[33] seeing the passing of this rapid water flow with the eye of the heart, drinking a sip from it and wetting one's lips! The world plunders everything, even its own time. In the midst of this, a mere instant belongs to us. If we appreciate and take advantage of it, we will have taken booty from a plunderer; otherwise, we will have lost and suffered losses.

> Appreciate the preciousness of time as much as you can,
> This moment is the sum of life, dear one, if you understand.[34]

If you are not poisoned by regret for the happiness that is gone and fears that have not yet come, and if the bitter experiences of the past and preoccupations with the future have not made your present burden heavier, if you have not forgotten yourself under the rubble of daily—meddlesome but inevitable—problems, you have rescued the moment you are in, and from the world, you have demanded your "right to joyfulness."[35] Compared to the valuable life that a human being loses, being happy for a few instants or moments is neither an excessive nor a simple reward; rather, it is a claim to his right and regaining a bit of his lost destiny. A person who values a night of companionship with a soulmate has taken possession of the chance of a mere few days from infinite formless time, from universal time that flows in the endless space of the firmament, and he has become the owner of his own time. This amount of time is negligible, personal, and as a result, possible; it is fused with life's incidents and experiences, and regarding the past as memories and regarding the future as wishes and all together—*subjectively*—will become destiny. Everyone's life is his passive and active time, "his special opportunity in universal time"; however, "appreciating precious time,"[36] means getting out of the monotonous, indifferent, and overall routine of universal time, taking a part of it, shaping it, and making it exclusively one's own.

In this way, man permeates time that, tyrannical and alien to him, traverses the path of the world, and he is no longer a vessel without resolve, a helpless bed for a flood to pass over; rather, falling and rising, he himself drives along the line of time and, in the darkness of night, becomes a fellow traveler of the star of his own destiny. "As much as he can,"[37] he implements his will in time.

Since time and space, like day and light, are together and intertwined, anyone who can take advantage of time also acquires space. Any possessor of time also possesses space, or that thing in which time passes. Nature and its phenomena are the space or thing that the poet gains, because the general idea of the world becomes specific, attainable, and tangible in nature. On the other hand, the world in the phenomena of nature—in the blooming and withering of flowers and plants, in the purple Judas tree of spring and the white poplar of autumn, in the fleeing cloud and the night-prowling star, and in the poet with expectant eyes—turns into things that are the container of time. Things of this kind (that themselves possess place and space), because they possess time, acquire a common aspect with man and in revolving time become fellow travelers with him, "share the same destiny," and share his joy and sorrow. They too come into the world and depart; they grow, bloom, and wither. From this perspective, their coming and going is no longer a reality that is external to the mind, alien and independent from ours; it is also a truth that is internal to the mind, made up and created by our existence, which acquires its characteristics from our sensory thinking and thinking sense, and takes on the state and quality of our soul. "Every leaf in the meadow is a book about a different disposition."[38]

In the same way that existential time shows the way to such a space, inevitably, from existential space we reach such a time. The two sides of this current are not two lights or lines that run into each other, one of which can always be distinguished from the other, especially since nature's phenomena—each of which is the place of the linkage of time and space—eliminate the separation of the two. These phenomena shine in the two-sided mirrors of time and space, reflect in them, and take form, and those mirrors that are reflected in each other show the phenomena.

In any case, even though it seems astonishing, liberation from the world is also in the world, in nature's phenomena that are the crystallization of time and space, and from this perspective the most "universal" things in the world. Among all nature's phenomena, because of his awareness of time and space, man is himself a time in time, a space in space, and a world in the world. And liberation from the world without the help of this "phenomenon" merely by taking refuge in nature's phenomena is impossible. The friend is a this-worldly being, and friendship reconciles and acquaints us with the world that is his home and that is his place of birth and being.

I never paid attention to the workings of the world,
Your face made me see it as so beautifully adorned.[39]

The beloved bestows vision to the eyes of the lover, compels him to see beauty, changes his vision, and entrusts him to the wind with a heart that sings in unison with nature. The soul that crawled in dust from loneliness now flies in the air with the scent of the beloved.

What is the heart's purpose
    in viewing the garden of the world?
To pick flowers from your face
    as with the hand that is the pupil of the eye.[40]

The moon and the sun are the turning mirrors, and the eye of the lover, the place of the manifestation of the face of the friend; and the flower of her face transforms the world into a pleasant garden, and life into a fruitful excursion. And an eye that is the place of the manifestation of the face of love is not merely capable of seeing the external world; it also has an internal vision by which one can not only see the soul of the world, but also one's own soul, which is one with the soul of the world.

> Whenever I desire to see my soul,
> I envision the image of your beautiful face.[41]

Envisioning the image of the beloved's face means recreating it as the face that the lover nurtures in the workshop of his imagination and views with the eyes of the heart. Nonetheless, the beautiful face of the friend is both the soul and the manifestation of the world. Hence, these two, the soul and the world, come together somewhere and become one: "Your mole is the pivotal point of my vision."[42] The lover's eyes see the world from this perspective: from the mirror of the moon of the beloved's face, which is our nocturnal light under the rays of which the beauty of things becomes visible. And should a new flower appear, it "is the gift of the color and scent of her companionship."[43]

On the other hand, the world without the friend is an unlit lamp, a silent garden, a night the stars of which have dissolved in darkness, the mass of ashes of the days that have fallen heavily on the blowing wind, the flowing water, and the tired earth! In this alien desert, the forlorn poet cannot find his way, and as a result, he knows not what to do with himself: "What can I do with the rose and the rose garden without you, oh cypress in motion?"[44]

Hence, inevitably, once again we return to love. Since love is the core and the shell, the soul and the face, the center and the circle, and the sun and the sky of the thinking of that poet in love, no matter where we begin, we are in it and with it. The ultimate human salvation is in universal love: may "love come to your rescue!"[45] But human freedom within the circle of servitude, the freedom of a man seeking success who is waiting "on the shores of the sea of oblivion,"[46] taking advantage of a moment in a transient world, is dependent on this-worldly love. If there is a friend, the world is deserving of goodness and beauty, deserving of friendship; otherwise, its existence and nonexistence are one and the same. "Without the beauty of the beloved, the soul does not desire the world."[47]

Compared to that world, which is involved in its own tasks—with its seven celestial domes and nine thrones of the firmament, from the moon to the fish, unfeeling and heedless—this one is a familiar human world with life and death, and the this-worldly friend is the link that connects a person with such a world and makes both compatible and harmonious.

If one night
    you light up our seclusion with your face
I will raise my head
    like morning over the horizons of the world.[48]

All is possible with the blessing of love. Like morning, the lover dawns from the depths of himself and of the world and goes beyond both. And he bestows to the world the morning of brightness, a bright mood and disposition: In his love song as well, because the poet sees the world through his own human nature, he grants to the world the beauty of the friend and his own moods. And because nature's phenomena resemble humans more than anything else, they acquire their characteristics from the story of mankind.

Be my beloved,
    since heaven's ornaments and the world's adornment
Stem from the moon of your face
    and my Pleiades-like tears.[49]

"The loveliness of the faces of the tulip and the rose is blessed" by the beauty[50] of the beloved, and the cup is the skull of the powerful (Jamshid, Bahman, and Qobad),[51] not clay and dust. "Yearning for Shirin's lips, tulips bloom from the blood of Farhad's eyes";[52] hence, the tulip is the result of man's failing in love and, like people who have failed in love, it "never lets the cup leave its hand, from birth to death."[53] Entangled in its affairs, the bud is saddened,[54] and the nightingale, "wretched like me, is afflicted by love for a rose,"[55] the violet is happy,[56] the zephyr listens to what Hafez says and hears it from the distraught nightingale and comes "sprinkling amber to gaze at the scented florae."[57] In this way, the manifestations of nature—not as external entities, things in and of themselves and alien to us, but, rather, as external manifestations and phenomena of our thinking and inner sense—are perceived and displayed.

In this give and take, the poet also borrows the manifestations of nature to rebuild the mood and desires of his soul. He nurtures the colorful garden of his imagination with the felicitous inspiration of trees and light, fire and water, flowers and stars, plains and sky; and before nature's spring, whose involuntary witnesses we are, he creates the spring of his own life by simultaneously sprouting and withering in one place, and he paints new images in this vernal garden with magical colors and aromas.

> I uprooted the silhouette of that spruce fir
> from the garden of my sight,
> For the fruit of every flower that blossomed
> was the anguish of longing for her.[58]

He has seen a tall-statured beauty in the garden of his sight and flowers that blossom from sorrow and cause suffering! The birds of thought fly off the branches of words, and the manifestation of the face of the beloved in view is moonlight in the workshop of sleepless eyes that all night long paint the illusory image of your face.[59] The eye is a picture gallery, with more diverse moods than the picture gallery of spring. "Life is a pleasant tulip garden from the brightness of the face" of a beloved without whom the lover's soul withers.[60]

> Wish for the spring of life, oh heart,
> as, every year this meadow
> Will bring a hundred flowers like the daffodil
> and a thousand song birds, like the nightingale.[61]

He entrusts himself to nature, internalizes it, and converts it into "the spring of life"[62] in the workshop of his imagination. This spring of life, however, is the spring of the soul, not of youth, because being young in years does not come about by our wishing it, and similar to the spring of the meadow, it comes and goes on its own. That which can be wished for and gained is the spring of the soul. In the poet, nature's spring is converted to the spring of the soul. With this spring of the soul, he then returns to all the seasons of nature, and resides in the eternally spring garden of the friend.

> From the alley of the friend,
>   the spring breeze blows,
> If you ask this wind for help,
>   you can light the lamp of your heart.[63]

The spring breeze no longer blows from meadows and streams, from plains and mountains, and it does not bring fragrance to the soul; rather, it comes like a harbinger of good news from the alley of the friend and lights up the lamp of the heart that is the private place of secrets, which is the house of the friend, which is the garden of light. Any form of nature that shines on this garden and is seen in its rays is transformed into a flower garden.

In this give and take between man and nature, nature's phenomena are not passive entities that are let loose in the world unconscious and unaware, and for man to perceive and treat as he wishes. In a different arena and state of knowledge, nature's phenomena are bound together by spiritual ties and compassion. By observing, the poet contemplates their human dispositions, and finds they have the same joys, pains, unions, and separations of lovers and the good and ill fortune of humans. Not that he likens the manifestations of nature to human dispositions and then expresses this resemblance; rather, in his view, nature appears with human dispositions. In the creative imagination of the poet, nature's phenomena have human characteristics of their own. "The birds of the garden are rhyme critics and humorists."[64] The nightingale thinks of his love for the rose, and the rose engages in robbing the heart and coquettishness. Similar to us, they also engage in pleading, coquetry, generosity, munificence, and abstinence. In "the modes of composing a love song," Hafez learns eloquence from the sweet-tongued beloved with "incomparable words,"[65] similar to the nightingale, who learns language through the bounty of the rose.[66] And the poet goes "like the bud with a melancholy heart to the garden" to learn from nightingales the secret of making love.[67] Thus, the breeze shares hidden secrets with the rose[68] and is sacrificed for the face of the daffodil and the eyes of the narcissus.[69]

> The Judas tree will offer its purple cup
> to the jasmine
> and the narcissus' gaze fall on the anemone[70]

and the remedy for the tulip's wounded heart is sweet wine.[71] The nightingale who has suffered separation goes to the private pavilion of the rose in loud lament.[72] The ruby's heart bleeds because the potter's market is thriving,[73] and the unfulfilled heart of the poet is sad because "the firmament puts the reigns of aspired goals in the hands of the ignorant."[74] This unknowing nature, among other things, is also a frequent visitor to the tavern. "The tulip is the cupbearer and the narcissus is drunk, yet I am blamed for debauchery."[75] The sad cloud weeps for the short life of flowers,[76] as though someone is lamenting the shortness of sweet life.

> When the spring cloud saw
>   the world's habit of breaking promises
> It wept over the jasmine,
>   the hyacinth, and the daffodil.[77]

On the one hand, the poet attributes his own dispositions to nature, and on the other, he assumes the attributes of nature. Moreover, the phenomena in relationship to one another have human characteristics. Obviously, distancing ourselves from a poem and looking at it each time subjectively from different angles might be of some value, as long as the poem is looked at as an object before us, and we view it objectively from outside the poem. We look at the poem from outside to perceive its various components and its context and shape. We distance ourselves from the poem to get close to it. Otherwise, by its very nature, a poem is an intertwined skein the components of which we might find in unraveling it, but we will then lose its wholeness. In the bard's *Divan*, this tripartite give-and-take is like a colorful warp and weft that is interwoven and works together to create a singular image. Sometimes even in a single ghazal,* one can identify the focusing of this intertwined outlook: the beloved's eyebrow is the feast's crescent, and the new moon is the eyebrow of the feast to which the world applies woad; the breeze coming from the beloved's direction opens the robe of the rose; the rose, like morning, tears the dress off its body; and the moon of the face and the night-like dark tresses of the friend brighten the poet's dark night like day.[78] In another ghazal,† each manifestation of spring, from flowers and plants to birds and water, transforms his soul and body and creates a different disposition in him. Spring breaks one's repentance and brings joy; in other words, it affects both a person's beliefs and actions as well as his disposition. And then nature (the zephyr) does the same thing to itself (the bud) that it had done to man.[79] Free-spiritedness, which should be a characteristic of humans, can be learned from nature (the cypress). The wind robs the rose, and the "frenzied nightingale" cries out, yearning for "the bud bride and union with the rose."[80]

> With your scent, like the rose, at every moment
> I tear open my garment from top to bottom.
> It seems as if the rose, upon seeing your body in the garden,
> Like the drunkard, has torn open the garment covering its body.
> Yearning for you, I can barely save my life,
> Yet you so easily stole my heart from me.[81]

I, too, have the disposition of the rose and do exactly the same. The rose blooms in its own body with its own scent, and I open because of your scent. The rose, too, when it sees you, has the same disposition as I and does the same thing as I: it opens. And then, that which was between

* "With woad, the world drew a crescent on the eyebrow of the feast / The crescent of the feast should be seen on the eyebrow of the beloved." [From ghazal 238.]

† "Spring and the rose became joyful and repentance-breaking / With the happiness of the rose's face, uproot sorrow from your heart." [From ghazal 388.]

humans and nature and nature and humans comes back to humans and humans, to the lover giving his heart and the beloved stealing his heart.

In this love poem, without losing his singularity and wholeness, the self-conscious poet has melded with nature. Time, as it flows in him, also allows time-bound nature in him, or like a thread, interweaves the various images of man and nature. The poet does not merely observe the manifestations of the world as a stranger from outside; rather, he lives with them in a harmonious and congruent system. In other words, he joins them, changes in step with them, and shares in their destiny.

The poet places himself in the evolution, in the process of evolving, of the phenomena of nature, and by participating in their life and death, he becomes of the same heart and tongue as they. It is some sort of dialogue, born from having the same destiny, that blossoms like a bud, a spring, a dawn between them:

> At dawn, I was telling the wind the story of my longing,
> A voice alerted me that I should trust divine favors.[82]

Standing like the deer in the ephemeral realm of dawn, the poet looks into far expanses with his penetrating eyes. He tells of his longing—the fulfillment of which is too far-flung because it is a longing—to the far-flying wind, and he finds a voice, entirely hopeful good news. This dawn is not merely a place near the sun or a benefit of the turning of time. It is the field of wakefulness and the east of vision; it is the spring of light and the light of the eye; it is beauty and the mirror, the observer and the observed, that gushes from the heart of darkness, splits the earth, the boundaries, and the confinement, and spouts in the sky, far away, and in infinity. And this wind is not a vagrant hubbub, but the good tidings of union, the message from the friend, and a messenger from him.

> From the alley of the friend,
> the spring breeze blows,
> If you ask this wind for help,
> you can light the lamp of your heart.[83]

This wind does not come from mountains and mountainous regions, from the traveling seasons and from beyond distant bare lands. This wind comes from the alley of the friend, from the spring of the soul.

Dawn and the wind, the rose and the nightingale, the cloud and spring, these comprise the nature with which the poet is in harmony; and because he is in it, he finds his way to "that which is beyond nature"—and as a result becomes in harmony with himself. It is a sublime nature, the manifestations of which are things beyond and more uncommon than external objects or symbols and signs; they are various parts of a singular soul, a unity that has assumed existence in plurality.

To be in such a dawn, telling the story of longing to such a breeze, takes the poet beyond nature and returns him to the house of the heart, to "good fortune"![84] To speak the same language as this nature is lofty; it links the conversation to the true lofty position that is within the soul and outside the field of vision of the earth and the firmament.

In a give-and-take between himself and nature, the poet "humanizes" nature; and on this journey, he is able to speak the same language as and share the heart of lofty nature. Hence, a human being who constantly goes beyond himself and further in the other direction of reaching the truth of himself, in the stages of his relationship with a nature that opens a path, attains a new perfection. "He abandons the house of nature to pass through the alley of the spiritual way."[85] And once the world, which is the cage of the soul, changes into the sky for the flight of the soul and captivity changes to freedom, nature becomes an ideal, perfection, in which and by which the poet lives; and as he lives, an ideal, perfection, comes into existence, like a plant that in the process of growing awakens the sleeping soil and brings forth its colors. This ideal nature is the utopia of love in which the wayfarer lover finds the alley of the friend.

❋ Hafez's nature, before it is put into words, is nurtured and changed in his soul, and it then begins to flow in language's river of ideas. Ferdowsi's nature, by way of contrast, is neither the alley of the friend nor a manifestation of his face; rather, it is the chronicle of the work of "the Lord of the soul and the intellect."[86] As a chronicler of the world, he sets his eyes on the external world, which he describes through perceiving it and coloring it with his own perceptions and thoughts. For him, nature (similar to the world) stands before him without mediation, both friendly and hostile, and he sets in motion language's river of ideas within its phenomena and links them together.

Our *qasideh*[87] versifiers, since they are chroniclers of the "external" world, and since with two or three exceptions they are all eulogists, are not among the true chroniclers of the world. Among them, a poet like Manuchehri[88] is so enamored with life and nature that at times he achieves the status of poet and explains some portion of the world.* In his poetry, nature is the amazing workshop of a master magician, who has provided various things with a certain intent, and with an astonishing order and arrangement. The fundamental relationship is between cause and effect, between God and things, and as a result, it is unidirectional: God is the impactor and things are the impacted, one is the will and the other where that will materializes. Things in the world do not have an open path to the being of the creator, their existence is accidental, and ultimately they are merely signs of his omnipotent being: images painted by a skillful painter, the connection of which is mediated and only through the painter. Here, we do not see unmediated human relations among the phenomena of nature. The poet sees the flowers color by color, drinks the wine of sorrow sip by sip, and perceives the moments of love. Things of the world are beneficial, and they have been created for the benefit of man. In this case, the poet pursues God's work: he has given me the world, like wine, as a gift, and by enjoying it, I do as he wishes. Existence is not the singular truth of the same essence and harmoniousness, such that God, man, and man's world belong together. The mystics' unity of existence here is by degrees, from the earth to the heavens, from below to above, one belonging to another.

Since the existence of things in the world is not inherent but the result of the will of another, the universal system and law of their lives is an external matter that—based on some unknown wisdom—has been bestowed

* Moreover, his understanding of nature is meaningful and is a representative of a certain period and the perception of a group of our poets regarding nature. The approaches of the Bard of Shiraz and Manuchehri regarding nature are so different that comparing them can reveal some signs of two different worldviews in Persian poetry.

on the world; another has destined it for the world. This world does not have the same fate as God and man; but on the basis of some external—not inherent—fate, it is God's dominion and a realm in which a connected set of unique rarities are placed side by side or follow one another. Flowers in spring, birds in autumn, and fruits in summer; horses and fire; clusters of grapes and the daughter of the vine; and wine, the same wine of compassion that is described at the beginning of most of Manuchehri-Damghani's qasidehs. And the use of the simile is the same method that is generally used for description. In other words, something is shown through its similarity to other things: autumn leaves are likened to dyers' shirts; the color of the face of the sick lover to the marigold; breasts to lemons, oranges, the silver plate of the scale, pears, or a bird chick with its head dropped down; the night to a black woman and Bizhan's well;[89] and the Persian New Year to Mani's book![90] In one qasideh,* the raindrop is likened to and described as a gem, a precious pearl, an egg-shaped clump of camphor, rosewater, the nipple of the breast, a fever blister, a teardrop, mercury, wine, a drop of ceruse, an extinguished ember, the Pleiades, and a drop of sweat. Things are measured and illustrated with the help of other things. They are the means for identifying one another. The imagination of the poet illustrates the external world through the external world. In observing nature, he arranges its manifestations side by side like an exhibition; he spreads them before the eyes and explains the body of nature by gathering and reconnecting its organs.

The organs of nature, however, do not have an organic relationship among them and are not alive contingent on one another. Since the poet mostly uses similes to help him explain an object or disposition, the relationship between the objects is mostly unidirectional and unequal: Something functions as the main source and origin, and an aura of secondary things, as fleeting images, surrounds it! These peripheral things come to the poet's mind and are mentioned not because of themselves, but to

* "It is springtime, and the world, like a thorn bush / Rise, oh thorn bush, and bring the rose with no thorns." Cited from the *Divan* of Manuchehri, edited by Mohammad Dabir-Siyaqi [(Tehran: Zavvar, 1984); From qasideh 29.]

enhance the central point. We just witnessed the things to which a drop of rain is likened. Elsewhere, a horse is likened to a bird, a snake, a partridge, a whale, a leopard, a crane, a peacock, and a duck; or every component of the beautiful face of the beloved is likened to many things, and so on.

In his mind, nature is a balanced set of phenomena, a colorful mass of things that are pleasing to the eye and the heart. The world is no other reality and totality than this set. The spring garden consists of the color and scent of flowers and the singing of the birds, with the characteristics and beauty of each, rather than a garden that emerged from these things and beyond all of these: a spiritual and universal garden in the poet's life force and soul. The beauty of the beloved lies in the features of the face, eyes, eyelashes, lips, teeth, hair, and waist, not in "that" other thing; and the character of wine is in the moods that it creates in us. Regarding the concept of the world, the principle consists of these components (things), not a sublime totality. Things exist for us, not in and of themselves. They are special because they are especially for us, not in and of themselves, and their sublime value is the extent to which they benefit us.

According to the chronicler poet, time and space, as well, rarely attain universal and abstract meanings. To Manuchehri, time merely means spring and autumn, the Persian New Year,[91] the feast of Mehregan in autumn, and the feast of Sadeh in winter, or sleeping and being awake, last night's wine and tomorrow's hangover, young age and youth. Instead of considering the abstract concept of time, he mostly thinks about the vessel of time: about a season of the year or a feast and the celebration of it. Time acquires a specific meaning and quality or is about a period of life, such as young age, which is full of vitality, about moments of drunkenness and making love! Hence, the "space" of his time involves the phenomena of nature and society or is within man—in other words, in the actual world. His perception of space is also devoid of imagination and abstract images; it is the same Balkh and Bokhara and Basra and Baghdad, the same battlefield and hunting ground of the patrons he eulogizes, the same banquet halls of princes and poets, the same plains and meadows of everyone, the same wine house and wine cellar. Hence, time and space for Manuchehri—in contrast to those of Hafez—remain within the boundaries of the world and do not extend beyond that.

The world itself, however—as if separate from nature—for Manuchehri has a different meaning. He sees that the world, beyond man and facing man, is always that which it is: nature and time and space, the components that make up the world, are constant. On the other hand, he knows that this constancy and continuity is contingent on a law. The truth and spirit of the law of the world, however, is the unknowable wisdom of the creator.* That which the limited intellect of the poet seeks in the world is precisely the opposite of what he finds: injustice and maniacal chaos, which is neither from God nor from nature nor the rulers whom he eulogizes and who are the good or bad officials in charge of the society. Hence, the evil of life that engulfs us, like the world, is there like the world, is from the world, from the strange and mysterious unknowable world within us and beyond us.†

Despite all this frustration at the vexing world, however, because Manuchehri loves life, and because living means "to be in the world," he asks for impossible kindness from the same unkind world:

No matter how heinously you treat us,
We will treat you with more kindness.
Do you not know that we are lovers who have lost our hearts?
You are the slender, tall-statured beloved of us lovers.[92]

* In Hafez's thinking, as well, the wisdom of the "firmamental architect" is an unknowable puzzle [from ghazal 299]; but love liberates man from the trap of any puzzle.

† Oh world, how unkind and ill-tempered you are,
You are like the chaotic bazaar of tradesmen.
By every means that I tested you,
You are all deception, you are all injurious.
You ruin our affairs every day,
You are not afraid that you will be ruined one day.
This is all the work of madmen.
Are you mad intentionally or unknowingly?
(From the *Divan* of Manuchehri)

[These couplets seem to be chosen randomly from a qasideh in praise of Ali ebn Omran.]

In Manuchehri's thinking, existence is not a single and consistent concept. "The world and all that is in it"[93] is created by God. The existence of the creator is inherent, absolute, and eternal; and the existence of the created is accidental, relative, and transient. In essence, the creator and the created are separate in the same way that, because of knowing God, man is inherently separate from the world. Because of this separation in existence, God, the servant, and the world cannot share one another's destiny, since when they are melded in the destiny of another, they are no longer themselves. If the servant joins God, his existence is no longer accidental, relative, and transitory; he is no longer the servant. The same is true of God, and of the world.

The same diversity and plurality also exist in the world. Time and space and nature's phenomena are placed in a revolving sphere; and the law that connects them stems from the will of the creator, not the result of an inherent need in them. And God has created the world with a purpose. He has created it from nonexistence to carry out his purpose. Hence, the law and the purpose of the world have been given to it willfully from outside, since God is free and superior to the world.

To the extent that Manuchehri is the creator of his own incomplete world, we see the same worldview in the creation and in the form and substance of his poetry. He is a composer of qasidehs and, like others, he composes poetry in order to receive a reward. He wants to have possessions, a high position, or something. The purpose of the qasideh—even when, for instance, it is composed with the intention of giving advice and counsel, elegizing, expressing the disloyalty of the world, giving a didactic lesson, and so on—does not arise of its own accord. Rather, it is imposed on it intentionally, from outside, and at the hands of the poet.

The form of the qasideh, too, is not self-motivated, and it does not—like a living body—stem from necessity and the workings of its internal elements; rather, its separate pieces have been arranged side by side. For example, in a qasideh in praise of Khajeh Taher,* these things have been

* Ibid., 122.

arranged one after the other: the beauty of the beloved, praise for the patron, description of a horse, and once again, praise and prayers. Neither are the content and themes employed out of necessity, nor is there any logical arrangement in them. One can compose a complete qasideh without speaking about the beloved, or a horse, as many have; or one can shift the position of the praised patron and the horse and lead from the latter to the former, as Manuchehri has done in another qasideh. But in most qasidehs, through rhetorical sleight of hand and poetic acrobatics, the composer takes the reader from the beloved, spring, and wine to horses, princes, and viziers and back, and finishes the job.

This is the form of arbitrary and autocratic poetry; since, based on some subjective agreement, the two hemistiches of the opening couplet must rhyme, and the poem must exceed sixteen couplets, first must come recollections about young age or about love, then praise for the patron, and so on and so forth. But it is autocratic, because such agreements have been implemented without any poetic or aesthetic necessity. Hence, the purpose and form of Manuchehri's poetry (similar to his world) are external and diverse, not internal and singular. The qasideh is an aggregate disarray that has no form, only the appearance of form.

Now, regarding the substance of the qasideh, he reports on man and the world, and he has nothing to do with anything beyond these. He is engulfed internally and externally by the undeniable self-evidence of the tree and the star, the fervor and disposition from wine and love, and the exhilarating joy of living. Nature and man are the main two topics for his senses and his thinking, and in the same way that his outlook regarding nature is partial, his report on man is also incomplete and is about a part of man. Manuchehri's man, the beloved or the praised patron, is social, not universal, and as a result, partial and incomplete. To Manuchehri, love is consciously a social bond. The lover and the beloved, or at least the lover—as far as we know, from the words of the poet—are aware of his and the beloved's social standing, and he does not forget their differences: the lover is a free man who is a crony of the monarchical and ministerial establishment, and the beloved is a slave girl or slave boy who, evidently and practically, is of a lower rank and perhaps in need of the lover, because she or he is the property of and belongs to the master "lover," even if the beloved is a free woman, again, according to religious beliefs and in social life—in other words, from the perspective of religion and the world. Flaunting his wealth, the poet tells her:[94]

> I will gently soften your heart, and in the end,
> I will soften it with dirhams, if gentleness does not work.*

A qasideh composer who has enjoyed the taste of a patron's reward knows well that if gold is placed on the top of a stone, the stone will melt. The amorous need of such a wealthy lover is of course for the joy of union, not out of the passion and pain of those who lose their hearts. "Anyone who yearns for you will get the fruits from you."[95] It is not for naught that in the mind of the poet, "playing at love is like playing chess,"[96] a two-directional battle with pawns and knights, the tactics and strategies of fighting, castling and breaking through the castle, attacking, and check and checkmate! The lover who seeks gratification is wealthy, can provide shelter, and is able to provide for the needs of the beloved and make her safe; and the beloved, with her beauty and heart-robbing coquetry, is able to conquer the heart of the lover and gratify him.

In the fever and heat of this game, the winner is the lover who can capture the beloved, like wine, the garden, and the lamp, like a fruitful sown field, and harvest her; because in an unequal relationship, the beloved ultimately is the source of pleasure and for the comfort of the body and the

* Farrokhi's beloved is "dearer than life, and more beautiful than the beauties of Turkestan, drinks wine and offers wine, and gives kisses and takes kisses."

> If God will it, I will buy an idol
> With a gift from the king, and in time give my heart to her.

The Divan of Ali ebn Julugh Farrokhi-Sistani, edited by Ali Abdolrasuli (Tehran: Matba'eh-ye Majles, 1932), 440. [The couplet is from qasideh 48 in praise of Mohammad ebn Mahmud ebn Nasereddin.]

soul of the lover,* a divine gift that God has bestowed upon him, which must be of use to the possessor, like anything else.

> Since you do not make more of an effort to serve me,
> Even though you are mine, in fact, you are not mine.[97]

Since the lover wants a beloved to serve him, he desires and seeks that which pleases him, not oneness with another. He seeks someone in whom he can find what he desires, and through her, to reconnect with himself. In the same way that in Manuchehri, nature does not have a path to that which is beyond nature, love as well does not go beyond the level of natural and physical exhilaration, and means and portends nothing more than the joyful pleasure of the body. And the poet who lacks the flight and union of love remains in the happy house of his own soul. A lover and a beloved, each of whom has a separate status and role, will not achieve union in the bazaar of love. This profiteering give and take, in which one is free and the other a captive, one is the buyer and the other the seller,† this ownership and submission, remains in the trap of limited social relationships, and only a minor aspect of love comes to be.

Love for Manuchehri is partial, plural, and profiteering, and fundamentally and generally, it is no different from his poetry and his world. This poet does not understand mystical and lyrical love. His physical love, however, is not at all similar to the perception of the Bard of Shiraz regarding that same love. Hafez understands pure physical love with a different sense. Even though Hafez's beloveds are also evidently and practically at a

* If you love me, oh Turk with the beautiful face,
You must want me more than you do.
I entrusted my heart to you so that you could measure my entanglement,
I entrusted my heart to you so that you would do right by me.
(From the *Divan* of Manuchehri-Damghani, edited by Mohammad Dabir-Siyaqi [Tehran: Pakatchi, 1947])

[The couplets are from Manuchehri's qasideh 60 in praise of Sultan Mas'ud Ghaznavi.]

† If the beloved is a slave girl or boy, she or he is not even a seller. Rather, she or he is bought and sold.

lower rank than he, a reality regarding which the poet is also aware, he pays no attention to this awareness; he does not look at the beloved through this glass and never makes any mention of the beloved being a slave girl or slave boy. In a relationship based on feelings and emotion, the passion for union replaces a social relationship, and at least in the seclusion of lovers, love is an antidote to such social inequalities and regains its powers. Here, the thought of taking advantage of one's abilities and the limitations of the other occurs accidentally and very rarely.* In this manner, he pushes back "awareness" and drives away the logic of reality from the sanctuary of the heart. Undoubtedly, the social reality continues to be in place, and its logic objects to and questions the affairs of love. The effect of such logic—any profit and loss and social acceptance and rejection—on love, however, is not by the lover's choice but rather, despite what he wants. Hence, the social treatment of the beloved by Manuchehri is precisely the opposite of that of Hafez. One knowingly allows the logic of social life to interfere in the domain of love, and the other shuts the gates of the city of love to such intrusion. One employs social relations, and the other disregards them.

In Hafez's ghazals, the emotional relationship of the lover with the beloved, even in pure physical love, is the reverse of the relationship between them in Manuchehri's qasidehs. The need of the beloved turns into the lover's coquettishness, and the bewilderment of the lover into need.

> There is a vast difference between the lover and the beloved,
> When the beloved displays her coquettishness,
>   you show your need.[98]

In contrast to Manuchehri and his rich-man's arrogance toward the beloved as a result of his wealth and social status, the composer of love songs from Shiraz—not in a mystical or lyrical ghazal but, rather, in a poem he himself categorizes as "cleverly libertine," the entirety of which concerns his desire for physical intimacy—says:

* Throughout the *Divan*, only in a few instances, mentions of this sort are found: "You must pay all you have in your purse full of gold and silver / For your covetousness of beautiful bodies." [From ghazal 450].

To use the lashes of my eyes, for honor's sake,
To sweep the dust before your gate
is what I long for.[99]

In the heart of hearts of the lyrical poet, even a beloved who is praised for the pleasure of the body has such a status. The intensity of his inner feelings forces the poet in the opposite direction, and sometimes, toward negating reality to the point that love's subconscious passion and disposition erases it from conscious "logic" and law. In Manuchehri, the love relationship—an internal and spiritual matter—is compatible with social reality. Love for him is "external." In Hafez, this compatibility does not exist, even regarding physical love. Even his external love is "internalized."

Beloveds and praised patrons are two groups to whom the composers of the qasideh essentially pay attention. Others, even if they occasionally appear in a qasideh, are not of concern in the profession of such poets. Regarding the praised patron, since he must have the ability to fulfill the wishes and needs of the poet, he is inevitably chosen from among the rulers or the wealthy, in other words, those with higher social status. This very limited choice makes the so-called poem paltry, because these characters do not shed their class-based shell and do not go beyond the roles they play in their actual lives. Here, as well, they are the same ruler, prince, or master they are in their daily lives.* And since the purpose of this choice is not poetic, the poem becomes devoid of its truth. In dealing with nature, in contrast to many qasideh composers, Manuchehri expresses his personal emotional experiences and feelings, not the usual clichés of the literati. In eulogies, however, because truth is pushed aside from the very start and because personal experience is replaced with personal expedience, his words, as well, similar to those of others, are mundane, not personal. In

* The champions in *Book of Kings* (with the exception of Kaveh) are also from among the leaders and notables of the society. Sometimes, however, those such as Rostam and Piran play a national role, and their heroic acts are tied to the fate of their people, and sometimes those such as Siyavosh and Keykhosrow play a universal role, and the fate of the world is dependent on their actions. In any case, their lives break apart the narrow class, social, and on occasions national molds.

qasidehs, the patron is usually praised for his bravery, religious faith, justice, generosity, joyous drinking, unrestrained lovemaking and pleasure seeking, even his merciless killing of enemies and opponents, and things of this sort, with which we are familiar. The model for these composers in fabricating these characteristics is the usual "ethics of the aristocracy"[100] and their motivation, the usual pursuit of profit. The law of ethics, which must be universal and acceptable to all, is replaced with a profit-seeking and private "rule" as a result of which the composer praises the patron in an unethical manner since, heedless of the truth, the poet attributes to him the characteristics that he should have, and not those he has.

The one praised by the poet is not a real man with good and evil in his soul and the dark and light of Satan and God. He is a bagful of "admirable" and often incompatible attributes bestowed upon him by someone else, attributes that are not inherent but are external and fortuitous. The poet wants to create an image of a perfect human being, but without intending to, he places side by side torn-off pieces and fragments of perfect human virtues. As a result, the human he creates is lifeless, and the qasideh, alien to the reader, disintegrates on its own. The so-called poem loses its wholeness, and in the best case, drops to the level of a historical literary source of information. The whole becomes a part. With a poem the form and content of which are incomplete, Manuchehri provides an incomplete report on the world. In his poetry, his contact with the society is through the praised patrons. Of the entire body of the society, he can only see the leaders and rulers, and for that matter, in the way we have seen. His report on the society and social man is so superficial and profit-driven that it is not of much use. Similar to his cohorts, he does not see the possibility of deliverance from the cocoon of the society, of going higher, of the rise and flight of aspiration; he does not see the essence of the universal man in the specific man. He keeps the beloved and the praised patron in the same confinement of the society, where they are like prey in a trap, and he uses them.

Precisely contrary to Manuchehri, Hafez changes the social individual to a universal man. We know that he rarely mentions the social status of his praised patrons, the prince, the vizier, the ruler, and so forth; rather, he mostly refers to them as the companion, beloved, friend, king of the beauties, and so on. For instance, in celebrating the return of Shah Shoja' to Shiraz,[101] he does not call him a king with specific attributes, but "the beloved king, beauty, musk-scented deer, and friend."* Hence, while Manuchehri places each person within a social confinement to speak about him, in Hafez's thinking, such restrictive social boundaries are broken open before he speaks. With the strategy of disregarding the social status of the patron and mentioning him as a beloved one, a poem composed because of a specific incident or about a specific person becomes a universal poem. On the morrow, when that incident or that person, Khajeh X or Y, is forgotten, since love remains, the poem also remains. Moreover, with this strategy, a social relationship contaminated by calculations of a practical life is transformed into an emotional bond. The beloved replaces the praised patron, and the bond with the beloved (in contrast to that with the patron) is not merely a social relationship, because even though love is a social matter and belongs to social man, in its essence, it passes beyond both the boundaries and shackles of the society as well as the lover and the beloved! In this manner, a poet who elevates the praised patron to the status of the beloved pulls him out of his humble social shell and releases him in the arena of the world. Since love changes man's relationship not merely with the society but also with existence, the lover and the beloved are no longer merely social individuals; they are universal human beings. And he who changes the praised patron to the beloved elevates the social individual to the status of a universal human being. Moreover, by making the subject matter of the poem universal, he frees it from collapsing into nothingness, the certain fate of the qasideh.

This strategy of the Bard of Shiraz is not a poetic technique or even a magical sleight of hand. This long flight from particular to universal and from below to above is the result of the singular worldview and the product of the power of a love that perceives existence as an interconnected and harmonious whole. To lyrical poets, especially our Hafez, since nature

* "At dawn, my good fortune came to my bedside / And told me, arise, the beloved king has come." [From ghazal 176.] Also see Qasem Ghani, *Bahs dar Asar va Afkar va Ahval-e Hafez* (Tehran: Zavvar, 1961), 242.

and man are present in each other, any discussion about one may wind up with the other. Nature is not the tool for the poet's work and a prelude to addressing the issue of man; rather, it comes to the mind of the composer on its own terms and by its own credence. Since in its essence, however, this nature is not separate from man and the supernatural, it is not only of mankind and sublime, but it also has in it the potential for human existence and the supernatural. In the same way that the consequence of the limited nature of the composers of the qasideh is the limited (social) man, Hafez's universal nature inevitably is coupled with the universal man. The same perception of man also influences the relationship of the poet with the praised patron, to the extent that the poet sees the human and universal essence of the praised patron, not his particular social status.

In eulogizing, as well, similar to love, in contrast to the qasideh composer who is inclined to "externalize," our ghazal composer is inclined to "internalize," because the reality of the praised patron is his social status, and usually universal characteristics—love and friendship, or justice and honesty—fade in the encounter. The social status of the praised patron, based on its own law, usually nurtures and utilizes his nature and behavior. He is a slave to his social status, and for the most part, he is no more than a limited individual. The poet who is present in the alley of the friend, however, shines his light on things in the world, including the praised patron, and sees them again reflected in the mirror of his own heart. In exchange for what he receives from the praised patron, the poet bestows upon him something else, friendship. The shortchanged poet sees the praised patron as friendly to this extent when he views him from the alley of the friend; otherwise, when he is not in this mood and disposition, when receiving a reward is the motivation for speaking, the praised patron is that same prince and vizier of the qasideh composers, and the words of the poet deteriorate. Hafez has merely a few ghazals and three or four qasidehs that were composed with the sole intention of praising patrons. In these, because the poet wants to profit from his encounter with an individual, on the one hand, he has broken apart the universal man and merely deals with a part of him, and on the other, he has lost his oneness with the universe and has stood outside the alley of the friend. In this case, Hafez is no longer the poet of love songs whose story of the universe and the story of his self are the same, because the universe is no longer within his soul, and he is standing outside the universe, beside it, and in front of it. Hence, inevitably, he reports to some other audience on the phenomena of the universe and man as external and alien things, with the same hollow descriptions and distasteful hyperboles.* The world is perceived through a different sort of worldview. The change in the perception of the poet regarding man (or the world) not only changes the subject matter, but his poetic method as well. The poet has lost himself; and consequently, we are also deprived of benefitting from him. He has fallen outside the alley of the friend.

❋ But where is the alley of the friend outside of my rose-colored elder? The alley of the friend is he himself. A poet who breaks asunder the social structure of the praised patron and releases him outside so that he can be the beloved and not the praised patron is also himself in facing the world and things in it, a bird and a deer, flying and fleeing. In passing beyond things and perceiving their further truth, he journeys through the house

* See the qasidehs in the *Divan* and the following ghazals: "Last night a messenger of good tidings came from His Excellency Asef / His Holiness Solomon issued a decree for feasting." [From ghazal 171.]

The standard of the prince of flowers
has been raised at the edge of the field
O Lord, may his arrival
bring blessings to cypress and jasmine.

[From ghazal 390; the translation is from Geoffrey Squires, trans. *Hafez: Translations and Interpretations of the Ghazals* (Miami: Miami University Press, 2014), 176.] "How fitting is the royal robe on your tall figure, / Your lofty essence is adornment for crowns and signets." [From ghazal 410.] "The radiance of kingship is visible on your face, / Your mind conceals a hundred divine words of wisdom." [From ghazal 489.]

Sometimes Hafez employs a different method: A ghazal is composed to the end with poetic purpose, and then the poet makes a digression and somehow patches the name of the patron into the ghazal. In such cases, the attaching of the closing couplet of the ghazal to the rest of it seems forced. For example, see the following ghazals in the *Divan* of Hafez, edited by Qazvini and Ghani [(Tehran: Zarrin-o Simin Books, 2002)], 11, 48, 49, 112, 130, and 355.

of nature in order to be able to pass beyond his own nature and perceive a truth loftier than himself: going beyond and loftiness!

> but if you are not prepared
> to abandon the house of nature
> how can you embark on the spiritual way[102]

The person who remains in the small house of his nature, in the same "four opposing humors,"[103] is no more than the discordant composition of blood, yellow bile, phlegm, and black bile. Such a person in the great house of nature is a blind knot of entanglement in a sealed prison and muddy water at the bottom of a well.* May he dawn and rise from an east.

> Even though the affairs of the world are clenched like a bud
> Like the wind in spring, be an opener of knotted buds.[104]

And the bud longs for a wind that would undo entanglements, a wind that thrusts its spread talons into the air like a fountain, and wanders halfway up the slope of the mountain, on the breast of the plain, and on the shivering body of water. The wind that would undo entanglements: the breeze, the whirlwind, the storm, slippery, whirling, uprooting! A

* "Clean and purify yourself and climb out of the well of nature / For muddy water provides no refreshing pleasure." [From ghazal 423; Squires translates the couplet as follows:

> purify yourself
> climb out of nature's deep well
> for foul water will not make you clean.
> (Squires, *Hafez*, 93)

Bly and Lewisohn translate the couplet as:

> Become clean and pure; come up
> Out of nature's well! How could purity ever
> Be found in well water stained with mud?
> (Robert Bly and Leonard Lewisohn, trans. *The Angels Knocking at the Door: Thirty Poems of Hafez* [New York: HarperCollins Publishers, 2008], 6.)]

willful stray vagrant that comes from some strange place and moves on to somewhere else far away. A homeless traveler in the seasons of earth that is exploring the heat and cold playfully drops the wings and feathers of autumn, awakens the empty-handed soil, and takes the scattered color and scent of spring to remote and isolated roads and crossroads; it pulls the rose petals open from the entanglement of the bud. The spring wind is the messenger of blossoming and growth. It comes with an open, liberated body to unfold the intertwined and hibernating organs of nature.

It has been said that the zephyr is a celestial wind, and that it blows at dawn from beneath the heavens or from the opening of the Pleiades. It has been said that this wind is divine breath that comes from the spiritual east.* In the world of the poet's imagination, however, the wind is the flowing spirit of nature; it is the "messenger of the sanctuary of secrets"[105] of lovers, and a liaison between entities in the world.

> At dawn, the nightingale told the zephyr the story
> Of all that love for the rose's face has done to him.[106]

The blowing of the zephyr is the message of one friend to another that brings the "fragrant scent of friendship,"[107] brings fragrance to the soul,[108] and plants the tree of friendship.[109] For this reason, "in bringing good news, the zephyr is Solomon's hoopoe."[110] And the zephyr [*saba*] brings to mind the land of Sheba[111] and Solomon, King Solomon, prosperous Solomon, by whose command the wind blew and whose command blew in the world like the wind. In the domain of a poet in which Solomon is the realm of light, there is a connection between the zephyr and dawn, the wind and morning, the breeze and morning. Dawn blossoms like a rose, and the wind opens the bud like dawn. The morning breeze removes the veil of the rose, and the tresses of the hyacinth are the remedy for the pain of vigil keepers, because the "breeze of the morning of happiness"[112] is coupled with light, coupled with freedom.

* *Loghatnameh-ye Dehkhoda* [Ali Akbar Dehkhoda, *Loghatnameh*, vol. 10, eds. Mohammad Mo'in and Ja'far Shahidi (Tehran: Loghatnameh-ye Dehkhoda Institute, 1966), 14838–14839], see under "saba."

O morning breeze, abet me now, tonight, because
To blossom as dawn lies in wait
is what I long for.[113]

The musk-releasing wind that releases the color and scent of spring from the prison of the soil, and when it passes over the tomb of Hafez, "a hundred thousand tulips" bloom, is the "zephyr Christ," it has the breath of Christ.[114] It comes from the alley of the friend, blows in the friendly natural world, and brings the scent of the voice of the lover nightingale—that recounts the voice of the poet—to the colorful fragrant beloved and, like a lover, "destitute, inept, wandering" and intoxicated by the scent of the friend's tresses,[115] continues falling and rising. The plain and the meadow, the flowers and plants, the nightingale and the poet, all have much to tell this globetrotting messenger. "I have many tales of the heart to tell the morning breeze."[116] Oh wind, longing for "a breath of air removed from the dust of the road or a subtle point that refreshes the soul, a letter of good tidings from the secret world, and a waft of the breath of my friend,"[117] oh spreader of sorrow and harbinger of the good news of seeing, come and

give my futile heart the elixir it craves
what I mean is
bring me a trace of the dust from my loved one's door.[118]

The heart-to-heart conversation of my elder with the zephyr is the "story of longing":[119] now that I have remained in place in the heaviness of my own body, now that heartless and without a sign I know not of the friend's house, oh free one, oh light-winged one who is passing by like a moving soul, bring me some good news to make my closed soul blossom.

On the one hand, the Bard of Shiraz is eager for the union of man and nature, and on the other, as a part of nature, he is himself entangled in all its natural limitations. He is a restless soul and, nonetheless, a rested body. The "shackled frame of the body"[120] does not give him respite to test man and nature with his soul, as he so longs to do, nor to live. Heaviness, immobility, and the needs of the body are the dreadful walls between him and that which he longs for; and he can only pass over them on the wings of his imagination. He entrusts his imagination to the wind to attain what he longs for. Among the pleasing phenomena of nature, it is only the wind that is free, and the free and liberating spring wind frees the bird from sleep and liberates the voice from the silence of winter. In his journey of longing, the poet seats his long-flying imagination on the wings of this same free wind that is unencumbered by time and space; and aided by it, the poet forgets the limitations of the body momentarily. Accompanied by it, he rages like a river on the riverbed of nature, entrusts himself to the various currents of "being and becoming," and finds his way through the darkness of the hypocritically pious to wine, truth, and light. The free movement of the wind that not only cannot be contained in any cage but also opens the doors of any cage is the symbol of freedom and a reflection of the desire of the poet regarding nature: to be the undoer of entanglements, like the spring wind, to be free of time and space, to be the breeze that is the zephyr!

Strive to Be Truthful . . .

The wind is the disentangling soul of nature, and the poet is the disentangling soul of the universe. One opens the shell of nature's phenomena—winter, soil, clouds, and vegetation—and the other opens the closed doors of the universe: the firmament and the times. Since the world is pregnant with the soul of the poet, it breathes with the pulse of the poet's soul and opens with its flight; and once the world is open, it no longer remains the prison of the soul, but becomes the garden of freedom. In order to pass through nature, the wind must leave behind itself. The poet, as well, in his journey through the universe, as he passes beyond himself and is uplifted within himself, also uplifts the universe within himself, and if he dawns within himself, he has opened the universe, like morning.

> If you go to the heavens,
>   like Christ, pure and incorporeal
> Your lamp will bestow
>   a hundred rays upon the sun.[1]

Your lamp is the spring of your heart, which is the house of light. The water from this spring irrigates the sown field of the sky and nurtures the tree of light in the stars. The brightness of the world is "from this hidden fire"[2] of the friend in whose breast is the breath of God.

Christ and the sun are both in the fourth heaven and are both lights of the world, and the brightness of the soul and body of one comes from the light of the other. But the person who can bestow on the sun his own happiness is he who is as pure as "the son of mankind," like Mansur, a person who can bring the dead to life with his Christlike breath, like Shams,[3] a person like our Hafez who blows the message of the Magian elder into our autumn in order for our spring to grow, like the zephyr! If man is a sign of the friend and a manifestation of his beauty, then the more pure and the more incorporeal, the more visible and the clearer the image of the friend in him! In man's journey toward God's perfection, as well, he will become more complete and more beautiful, like the world. The breath of those who are willing to risk everything blows like dawn into the darkness of the soul, and like true dawn, it is accompanied by a sunrise.

> Strive to be truthful
>   and the sun will be born from your breath,
> For the false dawn's face
>   was blackened from falsehood.[4]

It is as though the breath of the truthful is an ocean from the heart of which the smile of the sun opens wide, as though it is the deep mystery of water and the sublime serenity of the sky. Truthfulness is light, and since things that exist are seen in its rays, truthfulness is the visible manifestation of the world and its creation. The world is illuminated by the light of man, and man's lamp is born from his truthfulness. In contrast, falsehood is darkness; even morning that is the source and place of the soaring of light is darkened by falsehood. Since the first morning[5] is false dawn, it remains in darkness, or contrariwise, since it remains in darkness, it has been considered to be false. Falsehood and darkness are twins. In the darkness of the world, things lose their visible form and are lost and vanish in one another. Thus, in darkness, falsehood cannot distinguish its soul from itself and others; it cannot see the angel and the demon. In darkness, there is no sun; hence, there is no sight and no insight; corruption is all there is. If falsehood is the substance of darkness, then with falsehood man makes the world dark and as a result, corrupt. "The contamination of the robe means the corruption of the world,"[6] and a contaminated robe, from Hafez's perspective, is the robe of the pseudopious, the hypocrites, and the two-faced: the robe of falsifiers.

In the beliefs of religious scholars—who on the basis of religious law ran the affairs of the world and whom the poet refers to as muftis, sheikhs, religious jurists, ascetics, and preachers—God measures the good and bad deeds of his servants on the scales of justice, and places them in paradise or in hell. And the criteria for good and bad are what religious law allows and disallows. As for this world, it is a caravanserai in which one must pack up for the next world; one must pray and find reward. The perception of such faithful people regarding religion is very this-worldly. The connection between the creator and the created, similar to that of a king and his subjects, is based on fear and hope: if you are obedient, you shall be rewarded, and if you are not, you will be punished. And, "What is it the Creator's clemency / And mercy signify?"[7] They signify exacting and unforgiving accounting and accountability. Man's connection with the world, which like an expansive banquet summons the hungry and constantly tempts us to sin, is akin to an unarmed man traveling through a mountain pass where robbers are waiting in ambush. "The world is a paradise for infidels, and hell for the faithful."[8] In this deadly predicament with that kind of God and this world, man has a terrified relationship with himself, because his sinful self is always waiting in ambush for his repenting self, and he worships with the hope of salvation in the next world, and he "serves for wages, like a beggar."[9]

The fear that exists in helpless mankind in connection with the Almighty has also found its way into man's approach to the world as well as to himself. This formidable fear in facing divine glory stems not from awe of an unknowable and "totally other" absolute, and it is not spiritual; it is something akin to fearing a despotic ruler from whose wrath one might be spared by being unquestioningly obedient, a fear stemming from social life that has infiltrated and spilled its poison onto spiritual life.

Fear was the foundation of knowledge and the method of instruction. From the early years of his life, a child would be raised with terrifying fables of demons, jinn, and spirits. If the pupil in a primary or Koranic school or in a shop or workshop was not afraid of the teacher or the master, he would not learn anything. The motto was, "better a master's cruelty than a father's affection," since students whose teacher was lenient "would play leapfrog in the marketplace."[10] Domination by the father and fear of him would guarantee the health and prosperity of the family, and fear of the first night in the grave, the endless day of resurrection, and the fiery ball of the sun on top of one's head would bridle the unruliness and lack of restraint of concupiscence. Man would open his eyes to the world in the light of fear, traverse the paths of fear, and depart on the journey to the next world with his knapsack filled with fears.

Those who instituted man's relationship to both worlds on the foundation of fear were in fact the interpreters of social reality and the unwitting spokesmen of the powerful, not the harbingers of divine mercy. The social structure and relations had so subjugated the minds of these clerics that they constructed the celestial world based on the model of our dreaded world. In this version of religion, the invasion of fear left no room for reliance on and trust in God, and deprived the "faithful" of the peace of mind of the trusting.

The understanding of our Hafez, however, regarding existence is completely different. According to his thinking, God is the lover, and no judgment exists between the lover and the beloved. And when there is no judgment, there is neither punishment nor fear. God is the friend, the friend who is all forgiveness and benevolence. Hence, to make him appear to be an unforgiving judge and to consider the world to be a laboratory and man a test subject is to extract the essence of truth and offer the appearance of its opposite. Both that understanding of existence and the fear stemming from it are falsehoods. And now, the dark pit of falsehood comes between and causes separation. Because man turns not to existence but to its altered version, not to the truth but to its opposite appearance, he has nothing in his hands but the shell, which he mistakes for the substance, and he falls into the web of his own illusions. Thus, he is left disconnected from the source.

Even if the religious scholars and agents believe in such an assumption of existence—which they often do—they are merely like "the ascetic who is a slave to appearances."[11] They are truthful in their worshipping of the appearance, and they are ignorant of the truth. From the Sufi path, they turn to the path of religion, and even sometimes merely to religious rules and protocols. Even though every step they take stems from truthfulness, they are the wayfarers of the realm of illusion. They are unaware of the "false" space in which they breathe; but they are aware of breathing truthfully in this space. They are the truthful of the domain of falsehood, and despite all their truthfulness, they are considered superficial and incomplete from the perspective of those kindred spirits who follow their own hearts.

But those whose contaminated robes corrupt the world[12] are of a different type. They believe in nothing but the belief of others, which is the capital for their trade. They utilize the beliefs of others and pretend to believe like others. They pretend to have something that they do not have. Hence, inevitably, they are two-faced, and hypocrites. They make such a show of pulpit piety and act in a totally different way when no one is there to see![13] The "sellers of piety"[14] and the "blue attired"[15] knowingly engage in falsehood in religion and the Sufi profession so that they can be owners of mosques and monasteries and, in all cases, shepherds of the people's beliefs.

In our Islamic history, we can see another social group whose deeds were contrary to their words. The caliphs were theoretically the successors to the prophet, since the government was a theocracy. Even though the local kings and rulers seized local governments, they received orders from the caliph, in order to rule on his behalf and be representatives of the deputy to the prophet. Even after the caliphate system came to an end, government was not separated from religion, and the next world was not separated from this world. Theoretically, support for Islam was the primary duty of Muslim kings. In practice, however, their primary duty was to hold onto the government. In appearance, the government was at the service of religion; but in reality, religion was at the service of the government. If the rulers were to admit this contradiction between the theory and their deeds and words, the government would lose its "spiritual" foundation and justification. This contradiction was itself a sign of a falsehood in the social structure and its political and governmental organization that would not go unnoticed by the intelligent.

Hafez pays little attention to this social reality, and for reasons that we understand, he mentions it far less, with occasional exceptions, and for that matter, in masked allusions. Similar to the people of his time, he regards the good and the bad of the government—in contrast to the ways of the world and fate as they are related to human beings—to be an individual matter stemming from the nature and behavior of the rulers rather than from the political and social system. But he does not neglect for a moment another individual and collective falsehood that has contaminated the entire society of his time—similar to many other periods—that is, the falsehood of the clerics and Sufis. These tradesmen of religion and mysticism steer the conscience of the people, but are negligent of their own consciences. Profiteering is the basic motivation for their words and deeds. Pursuing their own profit, they view everything from this orbit, and "self-absorption" and egotism are their "guiding star."[16] With such behavior, they often appoint God to serve their Lucifer. They are loveless sham lovers and slaves of the body who call themselves free spirits; but they engage in injustice in the name of justice, pretend that their enmity toward the people is friendship, and practice corruption on earth, because they have replaced virtue with vice; and since they make falsehood appear to be truthfulness, everything turns upside down and acquires a different meaning. The connection between the tongue and the heart is broken, and then when someone says, "Oh friend," his voice falls to the ground, since neither does he know what he is saying nor does the addressee know what he is hearing. Neighbors have drifted apart, and only the ostentatious understand each other's language when they speak about "human dignity." Falsehood is black, and it slays Sohrab, Siavosh, and Esfandiar; eliminates Rostam[17] through ruses; buries Mazdak,[18] Mansur[19], and Babak[20] under the rubble of calumny and slander; and falsehood kills Farhad, drags heroism, love, and any beautiful ideal down into black ashes, and imparts Anushirvan-like justice.[21]

The lofty royal falcon of the soul crawls on ashes with its wings bound and ruminates on the seeds of fear. Because I was born from dissimulation and denial, and I am the offspring of expedient lies, fearing that the truth will cause sedition,[22] I hide in the bunker of falsehood. Since we have not been secure in our beliefs, and since we have not had the opportunity nor the heart to face the truth, throughout the course of long periods of history, we have justified our actions by dissimulation and denial in religious terms and expedient lies in ethical terms, and at least in order to escape to an end with peace of mind, we have found a way to flee from the truth.

Dissimulating and falsifying is a method of behaving toward others and exonerating oneself; but once this behavior is firmly entrenched in my nature, then I begin to dissimulate with myself; I stealthily conceal what

I do with my hands from my eyes, saying to myself, "God willing, it is the cat," and using every pretext, lull my negligent conscience to sleep so that it will not see what I think and what I do. For every profitable lie, I find an expedient justification—which is the same as profitability—and I conceal from myself: one with two faces, both the one I show and the one I do not show, such that I can no longer find myself. In playing games with others, I have advanced so far that I too have been trapped in the net I have spread out; I am no longer anything but an endless game of futility. When falsehood finds its way into the religion and government of a people, no one remains immune to its harm, because falsehood becomes the way of life, and like the cane of the blind, it is both an instrument for advancing and also a security blanket. If not only with its help, at least very easily with its help, one can save one's own skin and have a seat at the banquet. Moreover, in a despotic government, the social individual treads his path not as he wants but as he is shown, and behaving contrary to what he wishes, he is other than he pretends to be. He has a two-faced life. In this case, falsehood is also a defensive shield, and one can take shelter behind it. In a gathering of the ferocious and the deceitful—where the henna of the honest and pure of heart has no color—truthfulness is the sunlight at the edge of the roof that does not warm anyone's hands and heart; it is a counterfeit coin that has no buyers.

Now this falsehood stands before us like summer's dry dagger, like oppression and futile hope, like a nightmare in the imagination, torment in the soul, weeds in the heart, poison in the cup, a bullet in the mouth, and a face-to-face insult! It stands in this manner and flaunts its presence before us. And even though we know that the liar is the enemy of God, in enmity toward God, we continue to blacken ourselves and the world. That rose-colored elder says, in the same way that the breath of the truthful exhales light, darkness is born from this falsehood. One gives light to the sun, and the other blackens the morning, and many a time destroys the world. Ethics, the effect of which goes beyond man and his society and in this way finds its way into nature and the world, is not merely a social phenomenon; rather, it is an overall universal truth.

Our sages considered ethical concerns such as domestic economy and civic policy to be part of practical philosophy, the ultimate goal of which is well-being through acquiring virtues and disposing of vices. The domain of practical philosophy is human society. Hence, ethics (and its ultimate goal, such as household management and civic policy) is perceived, measured, and utilized in social relations with others, and since it does not have a loftier origin and purpose, it is merely a social phenomenon, and its character *indirectly* and *ultimately* depends on the function of the laws of the society that determines its value system. In the Islamic period of our history, the internal structure and external form of the society had an invisible, quiet process and appeared more or less stagnant. Only shocking external incidents, such as the arrival of the Turks and the Mongol invasion, would create certain changes in it. The ethical values of such a society were also more or less uniform and consistent. During all these periods, however, the rulers of the society were constantly changing, and the government went from hand to hand within various dynasties or the members of one dynasty.

In the type of ethics the goal of which would merely be a social matter, at least the prosperity of the government officials, who deal with the autocratic rulers directly, would depend on the type of relationship they have with them; and with the change of rulers, the well-being of the government officials would also be subject to change. Well-being is the goal of ethics, and virtue is the means. Change in the goal inevitably changes the means. As a result, when rulers change, the system of the ethical values of most of them falls apart, to the point that in order to achieve the goal, by shifting the places of truth and falsehood, beautiful and ugly, and good and evil, and based on expediency, they make one appear to be the other. In contrast to the static ethics of the citizens, the ethics of government officials, who mostly consist of bureaucrats, military men, the wealthy, the intellectuals, and the poets, is "dynamic" and takes on a different hue from time to time.*

* Khajeh Nasir Tusi is of the Isma'ili faith, and in the government of an Isma'ili ruler, on his order and in his name, he compiles a book on ethics (Khajeh Nasireddin Tusi, *Akhlaq-e Naseri* [Tehran: Kharazmi, 1990]. This book was translated as *The Nasirean Ethics* by G. M. Wickens [New York: Routledge, 2011]). Once the table turns and a Mongol chieftain puts an end to the reign of that Isma'ili ruler, Khajeh Nasir converts back to his

In his long life, Salman Savaji was a eulogist and enjoyed the patronage of the Jalayirid dynasty. When Shah Shoja' conquered Tabriz and the Jalayirid sultan fled, the old eulogist expressed joy in a qasideh stating that "water returned to the stream of the country," regarding the defeated and departed friend as "the Gog of calamity and sedition," and the victorious enemy who had arrived as "the second Alexander," and he did not consider his own head to be deserving of his threshold and, employing demeaning flattery, he said, Saturn descends from the sky to be your doorman, the cat that is nurtured by you can fight a lion, and other lies like these.* When Shah Shoja' went back, and the Jalayirid king returned to Tabriz, Salman composed a new qasideh in praise of the former eulogized patron, in order for the water that had left the stream to return.

At a time when, because of belief in the next world and its eternity, many of the material and spiritual foundations of life in this world were also imagined to be eternal, a set of ethics theoretically based on such a weak social foundation and that in practice would reach such a point could not be a solid guide for human behavior.

Practical ethics, of course, since it shows us the way to behave toward others, is inherently a social matter. Perhaps for this reason, our sages have considered it theoretically and in practice to be social. Our Hafez's ethics, however, is theoretically other-worldly and, in practice, this-worldly. Such ethics is rooted in his understanding of existence and his worldview; as a result, it extends well beyond the historical and social framework of

---

previous faith (Twelver Shi'ite), shifts his loyalty to the new ruler, and adds a new preface to the book, stating that even though the Isma'ilis "oppose the beliefs and contradict the path of the followers of religious law and tradition," there was no other choice, and "in order to save my life," I wrote an introduction to their liking. (See the introduction to *Akhlaq-e Naseri* [*Naseri Ethics*]). In short, he practiced dissimulation and denial and wrote something in which he did not believe. Now here is a book on ethics with an introduction contrary to ethics!

How could one be certain that in the court of Hulagu, the enemy of the Isma'ilis, turning away from and avoiding the Isma'ili faith was not another dissimulation and denial? Perhaps God only knows what was in Khajeh Nasir's heart!

* The *Divan* of Salman Savaji, the following qasidehs: "How fortunate because of the royal bird of good fortune" and "When words describing his face cross my mind."

fourteenth-century chaotic Shiraz and is contemplated as a general universal truth. Since in the poet's mind social life does not have its own particular law apart from the law of the universe, the universal rules of ethics also apply to the society, as well, and they indicate the manner of human behavior toward others. In this worldview, because man accepted the burden of trust and made an agreement, he became God's deputy; and when he unburdened himself of that trust and broke the agreement, he acted with enmity toward the friend and became the agent of Satan. The original source of man's good and evil is in trust or treason, in fulfilling the promise or failing to fulfill the promise. The more a human being is truthful in accepting the trust, the more he is one with the divine essence and the more Godlike he is, and as a result, he brings into existence God's will in this world. That is why Hafez says, "Strive to be truthful and the sun will be born from your breath."[23] Because it is God's breath that comes out of the breast of the truthful, and since God's breath blew in what was truthful, they became the owners of a breast brighter than the sun. Hence, truthfulness, in addition to oneness with the self and with God, ignites "the flame of the sun from this hidden fire within my breast"[24] and the brightness of the world.

But not everyone's "destiny from the dawn of creation"[25] is the same. Every person has his own burden of trust, and not everyone has the good fortune of lovers and poets. After all, Adam, man, is none other than he who is enamored of Eve and wants the fruit of the tree of knowledge and the paradise of earth, which is full of hardship, the same fusion of the angel and Satan. But since "no head exists devoid of some mystery of God,"[26] then everyone, every haunter of the tavern and every clever libertine, has some portion of the friend; he has been entrusted with as much of the burden of trust as befits him and is in keeping with his aspirations, and in this way his relationship with God, and as a result his relationship with himself and the world, his relationship with existence, is determined. This trust is "man's divine destiny," and for this reason, the nature of his existence. Man's behavior toward others, that is, his practical ethics, is one of the emergent aspects and manifestations of this nature. Our destiny has been decided "without our presence."[27] "We did not exist, thus our request did not exist."[28] But now we exist, and in any case, we have something of the friend in us in trust, so that blessed with it, we may find a way to his heart.

Truthfulness in trust is *man's human destiny.* Even though man has no choice in fate, he does have choice concerning his destiny. Understanding one's own destiny, accepting it as it is, and being truthful with oneself and the world, or for some ill intention or purpose presenting oneself to be something else and playing dishonestly with oneself and the world, is the destiny of our free will. Our truthfulness or untruthfulness is in our own hands. If you are truthful in your untruthfulness and one-faced in your two-facedness and unhypocritically admit that you are hypocritical, if you reveal your concealed self, you are someone, a great someone; otherwise, you have smeared with blackness love, words, and knowledge through falsehood,* and the fire of your hypocrisy "will burn the harvest / religion reaped."[29]

Truthfulness and falsehood, honesty and hypocrisy, are a paradise and hell that create our Hafez's world of ethics. The same darkness and light that comprise the nature of man are also the substance of his ethics. Man is an inclination from Ahriman to Yazdan;[30] hence, he is a wayfarer moving away from falsehood and reaching toward truth. The ultimate goal of such ethics is union with the friend and being in his alley: oneness with existence. Similar to other virtues, truthfulness is a means of achieving this goal. In this ethical system, however, the "means" itself has absolute value, because in the same way that oneness is impossible without truthfulness, it is impossible for truthfulness to exist and oneness not to exist, for the means to exist and the goal not to exist. In the circle of ethics, the goal is like the center that is surrounded by the means as the circumference, and the circumference and the center are the reason and the requirement of each other's existence. Truthfulness moves forward within itself, both as the path and as the traveler; it constantly goes beyond itself and is constantly within itself, but each time in a different stage and state.

* "Drink wine, for a hundred sins concealed from others / Are better than worshipping hypocritically in front of others" [from ghazal 196]. This is conveyed in many other couplets.

It is the wayfarer, not the one who has arrived; like the sun, it rises from its setting and travels toward its own light. Happiness is in the same wayfaring; in other words, the goal is in the same means, and these two are so fused together that in practice we cannot separate one from the other. As long as they are separated, the trap that is calculation and the ethics of expedient thinking is set, and the possibility constantly exists that an impermissible means will be utilized for a permissible goal; but when they become inseparable, one cannot destroy one in the interests of the other. And this is itself the reason why the ethics of the bard—despite all the contradictions in the field of practice—would never result in anti-ethics in the theoretical realm, and its universal rules remain compatible and constant.

Being honest in trust, accepting the high and the low and the beautiful and the ugly of one's own nature, is the essence and touchstone of truthfulness; and truthfulness is itself salvation. But man's trust is in the hands of another.

> I did not fall from the mosque into the tavern on my own,
> This lot befell me from the dawn of creation.[31]

And the responsibility also belongs to him. At the dawn of creation, when man undertook the responsibility of being the messenger of God, in accepting the burden of trust, he became accountable for the destiny of the creator and his created ones *in this world*. But the friend who conferred on us the burden of trust and let us go on our own to face existence also became responsible for our fate *in both worlds*. Both of us must appreciate friendship, since the happiness and unhappiness of friends belongs each to the other. If I am fated to sin, if something in my creation exists without my will, then, either no sin exists in me or God is also a sinner in my sinning, because if no transgression existed, it would not find its way into me, the transgressor. I want to and I strive to avoid sinning, "if fate should agree with my resolve."[32] But if this does not happen, I will not be abandoned to the vengeful hands of sin.

> Our elder said that the creator's pen made no error,
> Praise to his error-covering eyes.[33]

To be a poet is to be aware. It is impossible for a poet not to feel the injustice and oppression that twists inside us like a whirlwind and not to writhe within himself because of this unwarranted suffering. Some error must have been made somewhere and must have run through the veins of the world "that there are all these hidden wounds and no chance for a sigh."[34] But our elder—because of love—conceals errors, and because he has some vestige of the friend, he is not deprived of the friend's loving forgiveness. Similarly, our elder himself "with his divine generosity conceals errors."[35] It seems as though in this story of existence the created and the creator have suffered injustice, such that, with commiseration and compassion, both forgive each other's error. With this mutual forgiveness, the day-to-day accounting seems futile, the rational method of religion that promises paradise to the pious worshippers and hell to sinners is of no use, and the faith of the poet, from the viewpoint of the guardians of religious law, raises its head in the dark desert of heathenism. In this ethical system, essentially, not much attention is paid to nor is much mention made of hell, because religion's hell belongs to the God of limited wisdom, the God of the morals police, muftis, and politicians, the God of calculators and tradesmen, not the God of universal love, not the generous and merciful friend whose "servants have sinned and he is ashamed."[36] Otherwise, what of love and what of generosity? The generosity and magnanimity of the friend come into existence vis-à-vis the ingratitude of the other.* In the relationship between friends, if one of them has made sinning part of man's fate, he has also destined forgiveness for him, to the point that not only does the reward and punishment system fall apart, but it is totally turned upside down, and paradise is achieved by sinning.

O Hafez, on the last day, if you bear
    A wine-cup in your hand,
You'll go straight into heaven from the street
    Of drunkenness and shame.[37]

* "Paradise is for us, go away oh pious worshipper / Those who deserve generosity are the sinners." [From ghazal 195.] "Even though paradise is not the place for sinners / Bring wine, since I am backed by his magnanimity." [From ghazal 405.]

In the end, there is the cup and light, drunkenness and truthfulness! Wine is the source of total honesty, and sinning out of truthfulness "is better than displaying piety in pretense and hypocrisy."[38]

If the system of reward and punishment falls apart, and the scales of "justice" are set aside, there no longer remains any sin that would obliterate man's salvation, since our sinning, like ourselves, has boundaries, but the kindness of the friend, like him, is boundless. Our finiteness fades in his infinitude. "God's kindness exceeds our transgressions."[39] According to this thinking, apparently the sin of those who "carry out so much fraud and deception with regard to the Judge's affairs"[40] will also be forgiven, insomuch as it concerns the Judge. Their darkness in contrast to his light is like a drop in the ocean. But if they engage in deception regarding the affairs of the people, the sin is not erased, and the sinner is doomed.

> Do what you want, but do not pursue hurting others
> For in our religion, no other sin exists but this.[41]

Even though sinning, to the extent that it concerns the creator, is a religious and cosmic matter and to the extent that it concerns others, is an ethical and social issue, since in the thinking of our Hafez, hurting other people is the only sin and naught else, sinning is a social and not a cosmic matter, and it occurs regarding man's relationship with others, not man's relationship with God. From Hafez's perspective, Adam's "sin" at the dawn of creation is neither a sin nor deserving of punishment, since neither does man have free will in this connection nor can one commit a sin that is even greater than the kindness of the friend that would result in punishment.

Moreover, who knows whether at the threshold of the friend who has no needs the clerics and the pious would be more favored than the clever libertines and the haunters of the tavern? "The pious and the mischievous" open their hands and offer their goods; "who knows what will be accepted and what will catch the eye,"[42] because no one knows what the friend wants, and anyone who claims to know is ignorant of "the secrets of love and drunkenness" and is entangled in "the ailment of egotism."[43] The muftis, who have measured every action on the scales of this and the next world and who already know about the friend's attitude toward this person or that person, gallop with the flickering lamp of learning in the nocturnal gallery of reason, negligent of the fact that the logic of love differs from bazaar-style trade.

The fear of sinning and punishment and the greed for good deeds in order to obtain reward do not exist in such love ethics; neither does the dreadful whirlpool of hell have its mouth open, nor does the garden of lustful pleasures of paradise await. As a result, not committing sin is not the result of fear or being immune to punishment, nor of expediency and hoping for future times of pleasure. In this state, the purpose of ethics is not *another* promise or threat, and the goal of one's deeds is not to escape to *another place* and gain access to *another thing*. The motivation for "ethics" is in man's nature, and for this reason, it is free from external autocratic conditions.

In the mystic perception of man, being free from external fear and hope and achieving inner freedom, is not simpleminded optimism. Man is God's house. Even though Satan finds his way into this house, he is not its owner, unless he runs God's house. Hence, evil is accidental, and it finds its way into us from outside, and unjustly. Goodness, however, is internal and inherent in us, and the ability of man to traverse its horizons is infinite. Mysticism, in particular the mysticism of love—because of its perception of man—is necessarily "optimistic," and it mostly sees the whiteness, the purity, of the heart that is the place of the manifestation of the beloved rather than the blackness, the impurity, of the hand that becomes the instrument of Satan. The eyes of mystical thinking are focused on the flight of the soul in the air of union, on the feet of those who walk the path of liberation.

Attention to the helplessness of the needy soul, to anger, to greed, and to abjectness and wretchedness is for the most part reactive, and that is why harmful characteristics stop the wayfarers from continuing on the path, and man himself becomes the veil hiding himself.[44] The mystic looks at man's divine manifestations, at perfect man or human perfection, and if he scrutinizes the demonic aspects and the evil of our self, it is with the hope of emerging from the internal and external whirlpool more quickly and purely.

In the face of the external wave and storm, in facing a society that "is the army of tyranny from shore to shore,"[45] the poet longs to be free of "anything that takes on the hue of attachment under the turquoise dome."[46] The goal of the practical ethics of our elder is to be a free spirit, which one can achieve by breaking away from the world and then joining the world. The world from which one must break away is the "terrestrial world" in which humanity cannot be found.[47] From the perspective of ethics, the terrestrial world is the world of attachments, since "attachments" are confining: attachment to gold and attachment to power, both of which are the means for dominating others and are twins that complement each other. In the world of attachments, good fortune depends on wealth and power, on "gold engraved with the king's name and Yemeni tempered metal,"[48] on money and the sword! And falsehood that is at their service in its various forms, such as flattery, ruses, and hypocrisy, each time both titivates in a new color and also presents them in a deceptive shape. But when only a few among the greedy and hasty enchanted ones reach the promised prosperity, they become enslaved to their new situation, spending a lifetime on maintaining and serving this "good fortune," and for its sake, they do not hesitate to engage in lying and oppression. They present their greed and domination of the people as serving the people; they call their own cravings that which the people wish and that which is in the interests of the people; in their egotism, they speak of loving others, and with this lie, they oppress everyone. In this manner, people hurt one another for these "attachments"; like a group of prisoners in a confined prison, they make the place more confined for each other; they chew on each other's flesh and skin; like bats in the sunset of the soul, they parade themselves and restlessly bump into doors and walls.

When those who seek attachments become accustomed to falsehood and injustice and rest easy in them, they betray divine trust and do injustice to human destiny. After all, our elder believes that man came into existence for truthfulness and love. A person who adheres to attachments is a falsifier and oppressor, and falsehood and oppression occur when one finds its way into the other. Both of these are inherently aggressors. Hence, a man who accepts attachments is inevitably a person who hurts others. A greedy human being is the hungriest beast in the world, and like a wolf, even when full, for no reason, he rips and tears apart in order to have more and to dominate the world and those in it. He slashes the insides of the ocean, the land, and the sky, and as he extracts the essence of nature, he destroys himself with a stony heart, because in the marketplace of the society, he has treated himself the same as a natural phenomenon. At one time, man was an entity in line with the cow, land, seeds, and water, and in another society and economy, he was another instrument of production. The hurtful actions of those who have attachments leave nothing unscathed, and hurting is the one true sin. Hence, abandoning attachments means liberation from sinning, "for eternal salvation means not hurting others."[49] In order to acquire some morsel, a piece of bread, those enamored with the world have spoken so much falsehood in praise of denouncing worldly positions and possessions that no one any longer believes them. But the truth is that happiness, needing nothing, contentment, and mendicancy, or abandoning "attachments," are the sources of freedom.

no one profits from the market of life
except the dervish who wants nothing

O God enrich me with poverty
and make me content with humility[50]

Sa'di's merchant on his way to Turkistan, India, China, Rome, Persia, and Yemen is a wandering phantom following a mirage, in his mind the image of water and in his eyes a delusional ruse,[51] with no peace of mind and no time left to live!

Abandoning attachments means breaking away from the world in order to join the world: breaking away from predestination, from the inhumane worldly characteristics that stem from within and outside man, that ruin his oneness with existence and, as a result, alienate him from himself. In addition, such abandonment means freely belonging to the world and voluntarily choosing it. In facing an unknown next world in an insecure world, "some time for leisure, a book, and the corner of a meadow,"[52] human friendship and harmony with nature, refreshing wine and "a spring and a stream"[53] are the antidotes to human anguish in the society and anxiety in confronting the world. These phenomena are the "human" manifestations of the world, and perceiving them means joining the "humanity" of the world. Our elder travels in the garden of friendship and nature that is transient like running water, in the wine that is light, and in a book that is knowledge, in order to find momentary repose from the darkness and ignorance of the "drunken world."[54]

The ultimate goal of the practical (or social) ethics of our Hafez is freedom through abandoning attachments, and the ultimate goal of his theoretical ethics is union with the friend through truthfulness. Each of these two goals necessarily leads to the other: until you are free, you will not achieve union, and until you achieve union, you will not be free. But in a city like Shiraz at that time, when it breathed in the air of oppression and falsehood, how could one not be tormented and not torment others; how could one be free? This may be the source of the contradiction in the poet's ethics. He is both in the society and longing to stay removed from its blights. On the one hand, in order to live, wittingly or unwittingly, he deals with those who seek attachments, with rulers and the rich, and on the other, not only does he wish but he also strives to be separated from them. He is caught in the struggle between attachment and relinquishment, and he continues his effort to climb out of the whirlpool of need and reach the shore of freedom from need; but the wave of daily bread and water tosses him back into the previous predicament.

Moreover, the lone star of freedom flickers dimly. The God of religion is autocratic, like the rulers of the world, and those in charge of religion and government are the agents of this autocracy, which they implement and impose on the society. The warp and weft of despotism have entangled this and the next world for the free-spirited, and any plan for destiny that they make takes shape on this canvas. Our elder longs to be free, but he cannot be. And the shameless tumult of falsehood spirals like a whirlwind in the morning of truthfulness and disturbs the truthful voice of the poet. Under the tyrannical government of the Mozaffarids, the exacting and ignorant upstarts wreak havoc and depredation; preachers who act in a wholly different way[55] and mercenaries who proselytize repentance are busy excommunicating the people; the market of posturing and prejudice is thriving; they have no mercy on the old and the young; and "they rob love of its honor and lovers of their chance to flourish."[56] In this chaos in which the tongue of virtue is sealed and the mouth of vice is open, a defenseless man longs to speak truthfully. How could one live in such a place without falsifying? The sharp eyes of the morals police search the back rooms of houses and hearts. "Do not drink wine to the sound of the lyre, for the ears of the morals police are sharp."[57] But is truthfulness indeed the cause of annihilation? Is it only possible to find a window to truthfulness through twisted and crooked hands and the labyrinth of the branches and leaves of lies? By hiding secrets and not speaking of the mystery, is he also engaged in dissimulation and concealment in his own way? "For those who do know are never heard from again."[58] The story of Mansur hangs before the eyes of the insightful.[59] Despite all this, however, my rose-colored elder often risks his life, and a voice of truthfulness resonates under the dome of the sky:

> Not only today do we drink wine
> to the music of the harp,
> So many times the firmament
> has heard this melodic sound.[60]

At times, however, his inner and personal truth cannot escape the domination of external realities and the society; hence, inevitably, he utters the truth indirectly and allusively, and secretly gains access to forbidden wine, love, and beauty. Covertly, he commits "sin," and to achieve his purpose, he engages in ruses.

> I drink from the decanter secretly,
> and the people think I am lost in a book,
> Astonishingly, the fire of such hypocrisy
> does not set the book ablaze.[61]

And he is not only ashamed of his innocent ruse, but regards such "knowledge and skill" as the source of sleight of hand and trickery, and he speaks about himself as if in scolding terms:

I am ashamed of my soiled robe
That I have patched with a hundred tricks.[62]

In any case, even though the theoretical and practical ethics of our Hafez are in harmony and consistent, when his practical ethics leads to behavior, it is ripped in two and signifies the disconnect between free longing and tied hands, the ambition of the human individual and the heaviness of social life, and is a sign of the bewilderment of truthful steps in the labyrinth of the alleyways of the city. He is unable to be without need, to be free, and to be truthful, as he wishes. His "ethical" effort is on the path of closing the gap that has been created between his thinking and actions in order to surmount this paradox and regain his harmony.

On this path, every one of his steps falls into the trap of habits and customs, the rules and laws of social life. Once again, the same oppression and the same falsehood, and once again, the same crooked ways and customs. And since he is neither able to change all this nor to set his hopes on such change, he regards happiness as shunning the society, or better stated, shunning the pomp and power of and involvement in the society, the system of which is no less stonyhearted than the revolving firmament. He distances himself from the tumult of the collective and collects himself within himself, and hoping for a "collected mind,"[63] he turns away from the thought of discord. May he become less in need and as free from attachments as possible.

But love mysticism, as well—that on the one hand does not accept other-worldly despotism and, on the other, remedies this-worldly despotism *for itself* with internal, subjective, freedom—calls the poet from "without" to "within." In this manner, both behavior and thinking turn the practical and social ethics of our elder into an individual and non-social issue. Since a man like him *ethically* is adept in terms of his inner self and is inept in the face of the ethics of the society, he can neither accept it nor eradicate it. Hence, he does not nurture the idea of the ethical change of the society by means of a social program, through improving the organizations, the laws, and so forth. He leaves the task of reforms to the reformists. Instead, the self-motivated ethical principles that gush forth from his nature come into existence within him, and his "ethical" behavior blows like a breeze in the stifling air of the society.

Where superficial traditions, hollow values, and rigid customs dominate, the path to the freedom of ethics for those who do not want to be of the same hue as others is closed. In this case, in addition to the behavior and the thinking of the individual, the society as well drives man's practical and social ethics on an individual and nonsocial path, inward. The poet who is aware of his practical inability in the face of the workings of the society and its practiced ethics, and whose ethical behavior suffers from a painful paradox in the turning of its wheels, consciously turns inward, to himself, in order to overcome the paradox within the domain that is under his own command and to regain his own harmony. But he realizes that he cannot. One must either, like Naser Khosrow,[64] have a social life and ethics in opposition to the society and in harmony with oneself, or like Onsori,[65] have a life and ethics with the coloring of the group of which we are a part. Living with one's own particular ways and customs in a society with different ways and customs is undoubtedly a source of suffering, since it disrupts both thinking and action.

Since ethics materializes in connection with others, it is a social matter, and since it is a social issue, it changes according to the common methods of prophets, martyrs, and the like: On the one hand, prophets address everyone, and on the other, they turn all beliefs in everything over and upside down, and the field is cleared for everything, including ethics. They uproot the foundation to establish a new foundation. Prophets are victorious over the spirit of the world, and the world is victorious over the life of martyrs. If they are unable to change things and make the foundation of ethics crumble, at least they have already changed themselves, have uprooted their own foundations, and have been liberated from the contradiction in ethics. Martyrs are victorious over their own souls. Society's ethics can be affected and modified by individual methods, but they cannot be changed or toppled; they remain more or less in place, and the individual who is his own creed becomes entangled in contradiction with them, and such contradiction often finds its way inside him and settles there.

The poet, however, who is standing and waiting at the crossroads of the ugly and the beautiful of the world and is a fellow traveler of its good and evil, uproots neither the foundation of the world nor his own foundation; he is neither a prophet nor a martyr, and at the same time, similar to them, he constantly demolishes and builds the foundations of both. Since he lets go of the world and of himself, he is neither in this one nor that one; and since this "letting go" always happens within himself and the world, then he is in both that one and this one. Even though our elder, like prophets, martyrs, and others, does not remain trapped in ethical contradictions, like poets, artists, and so on, he is not free of them; the paradox in him is a stationary marcher who never reaches his destination. On the other hand, the poet is aware of being on the move. Hence, his practical and social ethics are inclined toward freedom, albeit without becoming free and achieving tranquility.

I am slave to he
whose spiritual vocation
is untainted by any lingering attachments
under these wheeling heavens
the velvet blue of the night-sky[66]

Not only is he not free, but he is a slave, a slave to the high-flying aspirations of the free! He is bound by flight and a captive of freedom, because he is free within himself, not in others. This freedom does not have a social existence: A free-spirited man can neither live within it nor make it fly into the air like a pigeon and release it among others as a phenomenon founded on his own inner self. He is pregnant with an offspring that cannot be born, that remains in the uterus of the soul; and free-spiritedness, which is the actualization of freedom in the soul and is an internal state and condition, takes the place of freedom, which is a social matter. This free-spiritedness is largely an individual matter, and similar to harmlessness, means removing oneself from the chaos of the world and its denizens and drinking "water that is pure of heart"[67] and learning "truthfulness from the cypress and the meadow."[68] In the same way that the cypress has its roots in the earth and its head in the sky, free-spirited man has his feet rooted in the people and his head in the lofty air of the heavens and, from foot to head, he is as straight and true as the cypress.

Like a cypress, gleefully,
I will raise my head above the crowd,
If it is possible for me
to leave this world behind.[69]

If only one could turn one's eyes away from the enchanting temptations of the world! If only one could part with "bitter wine"[70] and "love of youth and beauty"![71] If only repentance were a remedy for any ailment and "spring that breaks repentances"[72] would not arrive and its breeze would not fan the fire of one's sinful nature . . . Love of the joyful pleasures of this house of colorful images roars like floodwater over the delicate mirror of the soul.

How could we claim to be without sin in a place
Where Adam was struck by the lightning of rebellion?[73]

My rose-colored elder, who like the earth thirsty for rain drinks truthfulness and without hypocrisy pours out his thorns and flowers, neither claims to be innocent nor claims to be truthful and devoid of hypocrisy. He is a crossroads, a filter, a wine cellar through whom all the sweet human inabilities have passed, and have been filtered and fermented. And since he is without hypocrisy, his hands are open and his secret is there to see.

I am a lover, a libertine, an admirer of beauty,
and I say it oh so candidly
So that you might one day comprehend
I am endowed with such ability.[74]

A free spirit who could not plant the sapling of freedom among the people and live under its shadow does not relinquish the "negative" albeit proud freedom of not wanting and not accepting. If he does not like something, even if it seems desirable and acceptable, even if it is the dangerous belief of the public and the deceivers of the public, he rejects it and tosses it back like an insult. And now we hear that familiar voice that poisons the heart of falsehood by opposing the devious and vexing ethics of the society. This man so disdains the Islamic mandates of enjoining others to do good deeds and preventing them from engaging in prohibited acts, as well as fatherly advice and sagacious preaching. He neither listens to anyone's advice, other than the old wine seller—who summons him to wine and drunkenness—nor does he give advice to anyone. Merely on a few occasions, and for amusement, as "the wise elder," he "gives advice dearer than life itself to the young fortunate ones":[75]

> Speak to me of minstrels and wine
> And less of the secret of life and fate
> For no sage has solved this riddle with wisdom
> And no sage ever will.[76]

Advice against advice givers and their ethics! The goal of his advice is not to show the high road to salvation; rather, he wants to ruin the advice of the experts of the path, the straight path of the preachers. In any case, the social and practical ethics of Hafez evolve and are shaped in opposition to the ethics of the society and the "ethical" behavior of the people of the society, and for this reason—similar to his concept of freedom—in principle, they are passive.

> Oh Hafez, drink wine, be a clever libertine, and rejoice, but
> Do not use the Koran like others as a trap of deception.[77]

By observing others who not only act hypocritically but do so by exploiting the Koran, he arrives at not being hypocritical and not setting traps, at drinking joyfully and being joyful, in order to not use truthfulness for the exploits of falsehood. Unlike the "moralists," he does not have clear-cut and easily acceptable principles. Moreover, unlike philosophers, he does not have an ethical system. With his penetrating eyes, however, he scrutinizes the behavior of men in the government and religious establishments; he is disgusted by their deceitfulness and hypocrisy; and he establishes the foundations of his own ethical and behavioral ways and manners in opposition to all of them. "He learns politeness from the impolite"[78] and indirectly finds his own path through the wrong path of others. He does not follow their path, and he warns the kindred spirits against doing so. In this arena, he rarely knows what should be done, and he mostly knows what should not be done. In the matter of ethics, he possesses neither the strict certainty of Naser Khosrow[79] nor the easygoing capriciousness of the most revered sage[80] in *Golestan*. The former walks with the steps of the men of faith, and it is natural for him to call on others to follow his path. The latter occasionally treads on paths that should not be trodden and becomes involved in things that should not be done; slyly, he visits every place and returns. Hence, it is not surprising that with his model of behavior, he advises others to take various paths and to return, like him, if they do. Why be afraid?

But how could a man who is entangled in serious doubt tell others to follow his path, the path of a man who has no path? Not only does he not show a path, but he always worries about his own transgressions, about "wine, beautiful beloveds, and being a clever libertine"[81] and about "bewilderment,"[82] "negligence,"[83] "pledge breaking,"[84] not "being a Muslim,"[85] and "being deceitful,"[86] which he uses here and there as touchstones to assess himself. "There is no hope for Hafez's deliverance from vice."[87] Before he decides to teach something to someone, he "takes a look at himself, who is so sinful,"[88] and repentance does not solve any problem for him. With this strategy, he descends to our level and remains by our side, in sympathy. In exchange, we too overhear his whispering to himself, and we take a sip from this stream. Hence, that which he says, wittingly or unwittingly, nests in our hearts more than advice from advice givers.

In giving advice, the assumption is that one person knows something that the other does not; hence, the former places himself as a knower before an ignorant person. With every bit of advice, there is a distance between the speaker and the listener that causes them to hear each other with difficulty; and often they do not understand each other's language, because one is acting as the teacher and the other as the pupil, one is mature and the other immature, one is experienced and the other inexperienced. The only time that the words of the advice giver nest in the heart is when he shows that he himself does exactly what he suggests and asks the other to do.

Our didactic literature is not very appealing, especially since much of what it teaches is outmoded and does not apply to our lives today. If the qasidehs of Naser Khosrow and the didactic work of a few others—in addition to their use of language and their knowledge, which are useful for the learned—still provide some inspiration for the reader, it is not because of the advice they impart or taking the paths that have already been trodden, rather, it is because of the truthfulness or the enduring ethical principles that emanate from beyond their advice. Hence, today, a significant part of our true didactic literature is exhausted and cannot keep in step with the times, not to mention the false didacticism that was dead before it was born.

The words of our poet, however, even when they fall into the arena of practical ethics, are far removed from being didactic literature, because he neither places himself as a teacher in front of pupils, nor does he speak to anyone for the purpose of teaching him something. Besides, as I have said earlier in this chapter, "such ethics is rooted in his understanding of existence and his worldview; as a result, it extends well beyond the historical and social framework of fourteenth-century chaotic Shiraz and is contemplated as a general universal truth." Hence, such ethics is neither burdened with serving as practical guidance to others, nor does it remain futile within the framework of any specific time or space. The ethical approach of the poet to any occurrence extends beyond its historical and social base.

The poet's tongue-lashing targets falsehood and oppression more than anything else, and the falsifier and the oppressor are either the cleric, the mufti, the morals police, the Sufi who has followers, or the ruler, the vizier, the autocrat, the bureaucrat, the chief of police, and the like. Both groups possess social positions and status with the help of which they can utilize falsehood and oppression among the people. Hence, falsification and oppression are social realities, not universal ones, and they have a specific and human time and space. In facing them, the poet arrives at a nonsocial (albeit not antisocial) ultimate conclusion: freedom through the abandonment of attachments! To set out on this path and to reach that destination, one must "leave this world behind" and, like the cypress, free himself from the people.[89] The means and the goal of social ethics tend to be individual and nonsocial; moreover, since man has longed for and sought freedom and the abandoning of attachments in some form and language everywhere and in every age, they have split open their one-time and one-place confinement and no longer remain within the boundaries of the specific society of the poet.

From this perspective, our Hafez is not the true representative of the ethics of his own time. Of course, in terms of good and evil and driving out the demon and beckoning the angel in order to achieve union with freedom and freedom of union, he begins with his own society; but at every stop and in every stage of this journey, he leaves behind his own social boundaries, flies further, and reaches our time, and his ethical ideals continue to be ours. His ethics splits apart his own social framework and emerges from it. As a result, the picture is not the same size as the original, because it shows something more and beyond his own era as well.

Perhaps such notable figures as Obeyd Zakani[90] and Salman Savaji[91] are clearer and more complete mirrors in reflecting the ethics of the Bard of Shiraz's time. One of them wriggles in the chaotic bazaar of moral values; he observes every type of debauchery and corruption; he tests every group and clan, from the bureaucrats and the clerics to all sorts of pederasts and catamites; and without becoming one of them, he mingles with all and with a stinging sneer shows their baseness and depravity and reminds them of the kind of cesspool in which they are so deeply steeped. And in the midst of all this, he himself struggles in vain and laughs bitingly. It is as though this mendicant is the sinning, surrendered conscience of his time. On the other hand, Salman is another example of the intellectuals of the bard's era; and in terms of ethics, he represents the same group on whom he is dependent and on whom he sponges. Eulogizing is his trade, and sycophancy his duty. He is a flatterer and a devoted crony; and like most qasideh composers, for the sake of worldly possessions, he extends his needy hand not only to every ruler and vizier, but also to their harems, their cronies, and their servants. He does not concern himself with the good and evil of things. He is the conscienceless conscience of his own time. The likes of him, intentionally or unintentionally, knead with their hands the corruption that comes out of the mouth of Obeyd Zakani.

These two, each from a different perspective, are true reflectors and examples of the ethics of their own societies, and they appear like a picture in this frame. In contrast to Obeyd Zakani, who is an astute and sharp-sighted critic, who touches each and every one of the unethical values with his scrutinizing eyes, like the edge of a sharp blade, cuts them open and scoffs at them, our Hafez has a universal outlook. Even though the rays of his eyes shine on every ethical phenomenon, his vision, like the spring of the sun, is universal. His "passive" ethical plan appears in the general texture of existence, in the relationship of man with the creator of the world and with the world (and society). For this reason, it does not remain limited merely to one person's treatment of another; rather, it is *fundamentally* an existential (*existentiel*) matter, and it is dependent on how our ideals materialize and are actualized in the world, on how we live. Because of this universality, even the practical ethics of our elder has existed everywhere and in every time for us Persians, and its essence has manifested itself brightly each time with a different face in every society of our history and inspired similar ideals. In the same way that falsehood and oppression have always existed, the longing to be free of attachments and for freedom do not belong to yesterday or today. As a result of this perpetuity, even regarding the social ethics of our elder, there is an inclination to make it an existential and "suprasocietal" matter.

❃ The practical ethics of our bard shuns the society and has a "passive," individual, and nonsocial approach, because he lived during an era in which, as soon as any noble free spirit saw the criminal face of the society, he would flee from it and take refuge in his own seclusion.

> A pair of clever companions, and of old wine, a couple of stones,
> Some leisure time, a book, and the corner of a meadow.
>
> These I would not trade for this world or the next,
> Even if at every moment I am mocked by some assembly.
>
> The tumultuous storm of events have left us unable to see
> Whether this meadow ever had a jasmine or a rose.

Observe in the mirror of the cup the images drawn by the unseen
For no one can recall such strange times as these.

With all the scorching winds that have passed through the garden,
It is a wonder that some scent of a rose
and the color of a daffodil remain.[92]

Hafez's life was spent during one of the darkest periods of our history. In the thirteenth and fourteenth centuries alone, at least seventeen clans ruled our country, that is, the lands that we today call Iran.* The emergence and departure of these rulers was always accompanied by war and slaughter, with soldiers who had no income except from plundering and who would risk their life and limb in hopes of spoils. They came like a flood, and they were uprooted when they faced a more dreadful flood. All that remained was a bunch of drunken plunderers and a half-alive plundered heap, poverty, disease, and death, in addition to the decline of religion, the degeneration of ethics, and the kingdom of corruption! The chaos and storms one after another tore all asunder.

Look at these conditions, I said
to an astute man, who laughed and replied,
Such hard times, such strange affairs, such a chaotic world.[93]

The people of the bard's time had seen and were cognizant of the fact that Shah Shoja' had blinded his father so that he himself would not be blinded on the orders of his father, and later on, did the same thing to his own son. Inevitably, he feared that his son would do to him what he had done to his own father. Brothers were thirsty for each other's blood

* Genghis Khan came in the early thirteenth century and Tamerlane later, in the fourteenth century. In the meantime, the following clans also ruled: the Ilkhanids, the Solghori Atabaks, the Atabaks of Yazd, the Atabaks of Lorestan, the House of the Inju, the House of the Kurt, the Shabankareh dynasty, the Mozaffarids, the Ilkhanids (Jalayerids), the Chupanids, the Sarbedars, the Togha Timurids, the Ruyan and Rostamdar dynasty, the Mazandaran dynasty, and Mir Qavamoddin Mar'ashi and his sons.

and killed each other over the monarchy, and within the confines of the harems, deceptions and conspiracies were plotted and carried out. The wife of one prince had an affair going on with one of her husband's commanders. The husband, who had no knowledge of this affair, threw the lover into prison for some other reason. The wife thought that the husband had learned about the secret affair. Hence, she colluded with a few of her confidant ladies in waiting and, at night in the bed chamber, they grabbed the husband and with their delicate female hands, they squeezed his testicles so hard that he died, and then the cronies of the prince tortured and killed the wife, tore her body to pieces, and ate them. The wife of Shah Mahmud was an ally of the brother of her husband (Shah Shoja') and conspired to have her husband overthrown. The brothers were enemies. Shah Mahmud found out and strangled his own wife; but then, regretting what he had done, he began to yell and beat himself and went mad. This madman had another wife, who was so jealous that she unearthed the corpse of the beloved wife who had been involved in the conspiracy and burned it. The wife of Pahlavan Asad, the rebel governor of Kerman, agreed to kill her husband in order for Shah Shoja' to take control of Kerman. The condition was that the victorious ruler would marry her after his victory. Shah Shoja' agreed, wrote a letter to the wife in which he pledged his consent, and swore by the souls of the prophets and saints that he would keep his promise. Apparently, this brave prince, in order to break through the walls of cities, would first bravely invade the strong walls of the harems of the rivals.

The governors and leaders of various regions were mostly thieves, adventurers, and conspirators. Prior to becoming the governor of Soltaniyeh, Adel Aqa was a highway robber, and Pahlavan Asad had killed so many people that when they found his body, the people tore it to pieces and took them away as a symbol of good luck. Indulging in pleasure, drinking, brawling in drunkenness, and lasciviousness were in their character and nature; and the plunder of cities and villages was the profession of the viziers, tax collectors, agents, governors, and commanders, who were all engaged in conspiracies against one another to get rid of rivals and pretenders and in order to remain in their positions and protect themselves.* I will refrain from speaking about the clerics, the pseudo-Sufis, and the qasideh composers.

Everyone's life was a plaything in the hands of a bunch of such despicable characters. The continuous wars in Fars, Isfahan, and Kerman; the devastation of agriculture and commerce; and the constant plunder had ruined the territories of the Mozaffarids and had brought indigence and chaos to the people. The wolf of oppression howled on the expanse of the earth, showed its teeth, and flaunted its power. No one was secure regarding his life and possessions, and everyone sacrificed ethical values to save his life and property. Hence, instead of friendship and truthfulness, in the depressing twilit air, fear and lies had descended like a nightmare, scattering abasement and abjectness like dust over the heads and faces of a people already covered in dust.

What kind of sugar is there in this city
    that the royal falcons
Of the path of truth
    are content to act like flies?[94]

In the twilight of this haze of dust, the brightness of faces cannot be seen. It is as though everyone has changed. The times in the heart of which the poet lives are appalling, and rarely do the ups and downs and the visible and invisible aspects of events escape the poet's eyes that see all that is hidden. From within him, a window is open to the outside and beyond. Though preoccupied with matters of the heart, as he observes the mayhem, he constantly keeps an eye on the perpetrators of the mayhem.

On the other hand, since the society and the world—or as the poet says, the times—are a unified body and inseparable, all the organs and parts are interconnected with all of this whole. Hence, every social man is inevitably also a universal man. No one is seen merely as an individual among other individuals. Such a person is constantly face-to-face with the

* For more, see Qasem Ghani, *Bahs dar Asar va Afkar va Ahval-e Hafez*, vol. 1 (Tehran: Zavvar, 1961).

world. His emotions and dispositions are not merely "social." He is dependent on all things and further phenomena, on the world and the creator of the world, and he originates from somewhere farther and closer. Naturally, such a perception finds its way into the substance of the bard's words. His social thinking and feeling is perceived and expressed in the open circle of the revolving times. For this reason, in some ghazals, the social and the personal, the worldly and the divine, the rational and the mystical, and so on, are comingled and become one, to the extent that to separate them would result in nothing but the breaking asunder of a poem that is unified in its form and content.

The perception of a man such as Naser Khosrow regarding the religious society is ethical and "sociological": The world is created by a wise God, hence, everything—including the creation of man—has a reason that can be understood through the blessings of religion. The straight path of religion not only reveals the motivation and purpose of the creation of man, but through its laws and ethics, it also shows the way for him to live in this world and among others in the society. Hence, his religious-ethical poetry is inevitably also social; in fact, it is like a travel guide and provisions for the road. Thus, in poetry, as well, he expounds ideas as he does in his *Safarnameh* [*Book of Travels*] and *Zad al-Mosaferin* [Pilgrim's Provisions],[95] and in each, he explains some aspect of religion. Not only do we arrive at the world (and society) from religion, but we also arrive at religion from the world. We must understand the world and know how to treat others and find our own way among them in order not to become victims of concupiscence, the worldly self, and not to err in religious terms. In this way, that sage must understand worldly phenomena in order for his words to be religious. On the other hand, the perception of someone like Anvari[96] about the society is not religious but "ethical" and sociological. However, since his ethics are for profit, the outcome is anti-ethics. To live his daily life, he must pay attention to the social base of others. Hence, in order to live, he must inevitably have an "understanding" of the society. I explained earlier what his understanding is, which resembles that of those whom he resembles.

Hafez, as well, sees and understands the scattered and connected phenomena of the society from the affairs and the people to their social bases;

but he does not target each in order to understand and then use the results with the intention of giving guidance, receiving a reward, or any other worldly purpose. His perception of the society is not "sociological," it is universal. The poet has a view of the world that finds its way into things even without his will, and he connects them together in a systematic and organic whole: He gives unity to the world's plurality and brings together and gives order to its dispersion. The eye of the sun, even when it flows in the river of night, sees the spring of the water of life, the waves of the seven seas,[97] and the soil of the seven climes;[98] it sees Simorgh on the peak of Qaf Mountain[99] and Joseph at the bottom of the well;[100] it sees the secret and the openness of the earth and the sky, the sunset and the sunrise. The seven-colored canvas of a glance that is cast from the workshop of the imagination of the poet views things simultaneously, together, united and yet distinct, in becoming and in being. By this analogy, in the shoreless horizon of his vision, no design—divine or worldly—remains in and of itself, separate and individual; rather, it forms and appears in the warp and weft of other things.

Now we will give an example of the two social phenomena that are mentioned in two ghazals about the falsehood and oppression of Prince Mobarezoddin Mohammad Mozaffari and the truthfulness and freedom regarding the rule of his son, Shah Shoja'. That prince was an authoritarian hypocrite and one who killed with ease, who used religious law as a pretext for persecution and bloodshed. The poet remembers "pleasurable wine, the breeze soaked in roses, the music of the harp" and the friendship of the companion* that are hidden under a heavy, grim-faced sky, like hiding "a wine cup in the sleeve."[101] Unless the quiet and secretive ways of reason come to the rescue, the sharp eyes of the times will be waiting in ambush. In the hothouse of hypocrisy and abstinence, we also wash the wine-tainted garb with the water of the eye and the stain of wine with the tears of repentance, because the reverse turning of the sphere from whose

* See the following ghazal [41]: "Even though wine is delightful and the wind scatters flowers / Do not drink wine to the sound of the lyre, for the ears of the morals police are sharp."

trap the powerful and the tyrants cannot escape undoubtedly has shut the door of joyfulness to you and me. Even though the domain of the injustice of that prince is also the land of the kingship of Hafez's poetry, the poet wishes to hurl himself somewhere outside the confinement, into a space in another time.[102] In this way, the social falsehood and oppression of a man with a social base is fused with the characteristics of the phenomena of nature—with love and practical wisdom, with the cleverness of a captive people eager to live, with the unrelenting injustice of the world, and with the visible threat of death and escaping it—and creates a singular self-organized picture.

During the rule of a free-spirited king, however, the liberation of the people of the heart from the previous prince's dark house of fear and silence is accompanied by the unsealing of silent lips and closed hearts, and the telling of concealed stories, with words, with gushing, gusting, seed-sowing words, with words that like the neighing of a horse resonate in the tranquil breast of the plain, and that, like a flowing spring, open in the undulating thirst of the desert and, like the season of spring, in the harsh sleep of the stone, and gush forth like poetry in the soul.* At one time, words had fled into the back room of silence and "homemade wine, afraid of the morals police,"[103] had taken shelter in the cellar. But now that the morals police are not hypocritical, the words and the wine are both free. Words rise to "the sound of the harp,"[104] "the sun of wine"[105] rises in the east of the face of the beloved, and "cheers of 'to your health'"[106] resonate under the sky. Now, even the former hypocrites, like the prayer leader cleric of the city, have turned toward truthfulness and inebriation.[107] After all, "in the era of the king who forgives errors and conceals offenses," the Sufis sit by the vats of wine while "the mufti drinks from the cup."[108] They have turned away from displaying

* See the following ghazal [283]:

At dawn the mysterious voice
whispered the good news in my ear

Shah Shoja''s time has come   drink without fear.
[Geoffrey Squires, trans. *Hafez: Translations and Interpretations of the Ghazals* (Miami: Miami University Press, 2014), 180.]

pseudopiety; they have abandoned "attachment"; and as a result, they have ended their harassment. What a great thing is "good guidance"; what a great thing is "the path to salvation"![109]

From the very opening of the ghazal, the good tidings of boldness and fearlessness, the good tidings of liberation from fear and falsehood, come at dawn from "the messenger of the invisible realm," from another world, and settle in the ear of the heart of a monarch who is "intimate with the message of the messenger angel."[110] "The king's luminous decision is where light is manifested."[111] God's light shines on the paths of his thinking. It teaches him "the secrets to the wellbeing of the kingdom"[112] and makes liberation possible.

This prosperity in truthfulness and freedom, this liberation from fear and lies, is not only comingled with this-worldly and social things—with music, wine, and joyfulness, with the truthfulness and salvation of others and the justice of the king—but both at the beginning and at the end is connected to the invisible realm and "the message of the messenger angel," and that is where he receives his knowledge.

I will now provide examples of two other social events mentioned in two ghazals. One event is the return of Shah Shoja', and the other, the death of another eulogized patron.

The first ghazal addresses the return of Shah Shoja' to lost, bygone Shiraz, the good tidings of a messenger, an unexpected friend from a faraway land,* wine, freedom from sorrow, good fortune, the fragrant breeze, happiness and gazing at the meadow, the compassion of the cloud, unison with the nightingale and the excursion of the observing wind, the kingship of the indigent lover, the wakefulness of sleepy fortune, and the victory of love.

The second ghazal revolves around the other event, the killing of a friend by the enemy and an elegy about the happy, bygone times:† in the

* See the following ghazal [176]: "At dawn, my good fortune came to my bedside / And told me, arise, the beloved king has come." [This paragraph consists of phrases that summarize the entire above-cited ghazal.]

† The death of Sheikh Abu Eshaq Inju at the hand of Prince Mobarezeddin Mohammad in the following ghazal [207]: "I remember, when living on your alleyway /

compassionate gathering of the circle of friends, one's words expressed the secrets of the other's heart and both were of the same heart and spoke the same words; "It was in my heart that I would never be without my friend";[113] living under the rays of love, in the alley of the friend, on the bright dust; "so often, wishes turn into dust"; the injustice of the times, the robbing trap of the world, the undying bitterness of separation in the soul, and the futility of man's effort that like a vat of wine remains with "blood in its heart and feet in the mud"! I am a weak and negligent bird when suddenly "the claws of the hawk of fate" descend, without my knowing why.[114] "I searched at length to find the cause of separation's pain / The mufti of reason was totally ignorant about this matter."[115] Yearning for the happiness of the one who died before his time, bewildered by the injustice of the world, and the settling of unjust suffering!*

In each of the examples cited, a social phenomenon or event in the poem goes beyond its own boundaries, comingles with other phenomena of the society or of nature, and comes alive and is felt in relation to them. In addition to this, however, a social issue has a longer and more diverse reach, and it extends from this world to beyond the world: from this world to the next, from the terrestrial to the celestial, from man to God! Every terrestrial incident contains a celestial secret, and is dependent not only on human enterprise, but on divine fate.

My eyes lit up at the dust beside your door." [My translation. See also Dick Davis, trans. *Faces of Love: Hafez and the Poets of Shiraz* (New York: Penguin, 2013), 58; and Squires, *Hafez*, 189.]

* Despite our insignificant knowledge about the poet's life, one can cite other examples when a poem is composed due to a social event but goes far beyond the limitations of a social incident. For example, the following two poems, one of which is a response to a ghazal by Shah Ne'matollah Vali [a fourteenth- and fifteenth-century Sufi master and poet], and the other is apparently a reference to Emad Faqih [known as Faqih-Kermani, a Sufi poet and contemporary of Hafez] and the "piety" of his cat. "For those who turn dust into gold with a glance / To turn the corner of their eyes on me, is there any chance?" [From ghazal 196.] "The Sufi set up a trap and opened his box of tricks. / He began to play tricks on the firmament, the trickster." [From ghazal 133; Squires translates the couplet as: "the Sufi who plays tricks / and engages in sleight of hand / as if he could outsmart the conjuring heavens." Squires, *Hafez*, 310.]

No friendship is seen in anyone
    What happened to my dear friend?
What became of all my friends?
    When did friendship end?

The Water of Life turned cloudy
    From the stem of the rose blood drained
Auspicious Khezr,[116] where is he?
    No hint of the spring breeze remained

Now no one ever says
    that a friend has the right to friendship
But what has befallen those who once knew
    the privilege of true friendship?

From the mine of magnanimity
    Not a ruby in years were we to gain
What happened to the shining of the sun
    and the endeavors of the wind and rain?

This place had been the city of friends
    and the soil of the kindhearted,
What became of this city of friends
    that kindness has become blind-hearted?

They have tossed onto the polo field
    the ball of success and veracity
No one has come onto the field
    Where could all the riders be?

Flowers have bloomed by the thousands
    yet the birds exist to no avail
What has become of the songbirds,
    and the cherished sound of the nightingale?

Poor Venus, now her lyre has burned,
    she plays no happy tune

No one yearns for drunkenness
Why are no wine drinkers here to swoon?

Silence, Hafez! No one knows
the secrets of the Divine
Whom do you ask concerning the events
of this revolving time?[117]

The previous examples were about significant social events: the rule of a despotic sultan or a just king, the arrival of a friendly king or the departure of another king and friend. This ghazal, however, is not about any specific event; it is a glance cast by the poet at the entire society, and he sees the saddening change in the city and the citizens and their relationships: friends, kindred spirits, the riders, and the reveling drinkers have left, and there is no trace of the city of lovers; there is no friend, nor alley of the friend! Here, there is a continuous vacillation, a departure and return, between the characteristics and dispositions of people and the phenomena of nature, between friendship, benevolence, and inebriation and the rose, the spring breeze, the sun, the rain, and the stars. Both man and nature have the same destiny; together, they are headed toward the house of oblivion, and they are traveling to the shores of the world, to the hiding place of the water of life, which is light. But it is as though light has died and the lamp of salvation has gone out; the foundations of the world are in disarray.

When the poet contemplates the world, he rarely speaks in the language of the hopeful and joyful. But the world is not abandoned, left on its own. Creation is not in vain, and the turning of the affairs of the world is not without purpose. Since the problem-solving hand of the friend is behind the veil of this irrational and baffling puzzle, undoubtedly, hopelessness will come to an end someday. At the end of a totally despairing ghazal, the poet says to himself: "Silence, Hafez, since no one knows / The secret ways that heaven goes."[118] Not knowing the secret is not a sign of disloyalty of the friend and the abandonment of the ship in "the flood of nothingness." Do not forget Noah, who guides your ship![119]

Hark! Do not despair,
as you know not of the secrets of the unknown

Hidden games are behind the curtain,
do not lament."[120]

Like a star in the bosom of darkness, a ray of light twinkles from behind the veil of despair and hopelessness in order for lost Joseph to find his way and return to his Canaan.*

This very hope of being spared from misfortune is evident not only in the face of the mysterious and inaccessible "world," but also in the face of rulers and those who have power over people's lives.

to spend time in the company
of those in authority
is like the longest of long nights

pray for the light of the sun
that it may rise again[121]

The darkness of the night of the winter solstice, the longest of long nights, falls heavily and remains for a long time, as though it intends not to be lifted. The sun is awaiting and, stalling time with its heavy sleep, has blocked the roads, and the sun continues to wait. The night is long, and in that nocturnal era of religious orders and prohibitions by the oppressors, it is not followed by a dawn. Since socializing, cooperating, and associating with these people blackens one's heart, the poet turns away from this evil bunch and their debased circle, turning toward the pure sun in the open sky. But they who have grabbed the earth with their claws have left no place with prosperity:

The army of tyranny rules from shore to shore, but
From the dawn of eternity to the end of time
is the chance for mendicants.[122]

* O you my amorous nightingale
pray for longevity for eventually
the garden will turn green again
and the rose tree bloom in spring.
[From ghazal 232; Squires, *Hafez*, 207]

"The army of tyranny" had destroyed the cities, scorched the fields, and killed innumerable people. The army of tyranny and aggression by outsiders and insiders was the unhappiness, lamentation, and death that had camped in the hearts of everyone. "From shore to shore" on earth means the destruction of the world. But the possibility of the liberation of the kindred spirits from the tyrants is boundless; it is from the dawn of eternity to the end of time, that is, from the "time" when there was no space to the "time" when space no longer exists. In the same way that that ancient time surrounds created space from beginning to end, the chance of mendicants also extends beyond the faraway shore of injustice and surrounds it.

When the doors of the society open to the world and the doors of this poet open to the creator of the world, his worldview drives him from social hopelessness into the bosom of hope beyond the society. This hope is a truth that our elder not only feels in his mind but is also aware of in his heart, and he "lives" it. But hopelessness is an unmediated, indisputable, and ever-present reality that continuously gushes out like bitter sap from the heart of the stone of the times. From the times to the creator and from the self to the friend, hopelessness and hope traverse in him faster than a meteor. But when he is in the alley of the friend, he goes beyond both, and he is in a different arena and station. Here, social and nonsocial poetry come together and become one.

In addition, since in the creative imagination of the poet, existence is a single existence and the world is the thousand-imaged face of a single soul, and since various phenomena are saplings that stem from the same root and are ultimately of the same essence, naturally, individual, social and universal, terrestrial and divine are all fused and acquire another singular order, such that the distinction between social and nonsocial poetry is erased, such that it is neither this nor that and both this and that.*

* For instance, see the following ghazals: "Lost Joseph will return to Canaan again / —do not despair" [ghazal 255; Davis, *Faces of Love*, 29] and "Come so that we can scatter flowers / and fill the glass with wine." [ghazal 374; Davis, 22.]

No One Like Hafez . . .

The sun is a flame of the fire hidden in the breast, an ever-wakeful fire, never dying, Magian, amorous. The sun is born from the breath of my rose-colored elder. It brightens the world with colorful light. "God is the light of the heavens and earth."[1] The world becomes perceptible from the blessing of his light. The faces of things that were submerged in the uniformity and ambiguity of darkness blossom like morning. The body of darkness splits open, and dawn radiates like water, like the water lily, and like air from the skin of the night. As existence becomes visible, perception also occurs. Hence, light is the origin of images, of faces, because like a secret, it has them concealed within its core. Once it manifested itself, the faces appeared and the distinction of one entity from another—and the unveiling of their essence—became possible. Without light, creation would have remained chaotic and entangled, because nothing can be seen without it. Hence, the created can also be seen and perceived through the creator. God unveils the creation of the world through light.

The words of light, however, are thought, and its veils can be lifted. God said, "Let there be," and it was. His thoughts for the creation of the world, as soon as he willed it, materialized in time, and beings came into existence. God's words revealed his thought, the void of pre-existence overflowed with the world, and nothingness was filled with existence. The words of God open his thought, and the world is the face of his thought. That which the word does to thought is the same as that which light does to the world, because the thoughts of the friend are revealed in his divine word; and through the rays of this word, we observe the sun, and the original spring of knowledge opens within us.

The world is the face of God's thought and the manifestation of the face of the friend; it is a mirror for seeing him and an image of his face, a timeless time; it is a place from nowhere and a trace of his untraceable sign that leaves within our shallow vision an image, a mirage, a memory, not the essence of his soul and the truth of his essence. Neither is it complete, nor do we completely perceive its incompleteness. That is why it has been said that the world is the house of slumber, the land of parting, and the realm of the invisible. It has uprooted me from the time of union and, like an exposed seed, abandoned me in the sown field of life and death, and the sky has descended like a blanket over the branches and leaves that rise toward the sun. After all, the world is the face of God's thought, not God's thought itself. The essence of his thought—like the soul in the body—rests in the heart of this face. Despite all perceptibility, the friend is hidden behind the mirror of his face and is a secret behind the labyrinth of the world's veil. The function of poetry is to unveil the mystery:

> since poets first used their pens
> to comb the tresses of speech
> no one like Hafez has unveiled
> the complexion of our minds[2]

God revealed his thought with words, and this revelation is itself the creation of the world. My rose-colored elder, blessed with words, also draws aside the veil from the face of thought and releases it—like the turning orb of the sun in the field of the sky—on the green field[3] of speech. The "bird of thought / that took off from the branches of words"[4] sits on the walls and doors of the eagerly expectant.

Thought is thought with words, like the star in the sky, the green in the plant, and the Judas tree that unfolds in a blaze. Words are the place of thought. Morning is born in dawning, the rose in blooming, and thought in speech. In order for thought to come into existence, the thinker needs to speak it, internally or externally, to put it into words; otherwise, thought remains a buried seed and an invisible entity: sleep without dreaming. In the subtle imagination of our poet, the image is a thought that dawns from the invisible realm and comes into the world like a beloved with a this-worldly soul and body, those of a beautiful woman. With the comb of the pen, he untangles and arranges the tresses of the words that are thick, unkempt, and disheveled; that are black, entangled, and obscured; that are mysterious, ambiguous, and dark; and he braids them like a string of pearls and pushes them to one side for the bright face of thought to dawn. The bride of thought emerges from the nocturnal gallery of words, a spring from the heart of the earth and a secret from the invisible realm! And the poet is a luminous seeker searching for a secret along dark paths.

A person who through the mediation of a religion, a philosophical system, or a social theory—in other words, through an ideology—thinks that he knows the ins and outs of existence and the ups and downs of things is deprived of the poets' gem of "ignorance," and his "being a poet" is merely the repeat of what we have known and observed in his "knowing" tongue—in which also inevitably there is no secret or mystery, and that ultimately does not exceed the intricacies of esthetics. A godless poet who does not seek the secret of that friend also thinks about a secret to uncover: the mystery of man and the world, the mystery of existence and love! To him, being a poet also means revealing mysteries. However, for a poet like our elder, not only is the world a riddle that cannot be solved through philosophy, but our own existence, as well, is a puzzle, "the solving of which is the stuff of sorcery and fable."[5] Moreover, the mystery of God is hidden behind the invisible veil.

Poets are like prophets, because if "God places himself in the mouths of prophets" so that they can bring the message of the heavens to earth, the poet, too, from behind the mirror, says "that which the master of eternal beginning said."[6] He is the messenger angel of the invisible world, the sun-winged, sky-flying hoopoe of Solomon bringing good news. Moreover, the words of the poet, like divine words, open up the mystery of thought, and for this reason, he is a creator. Contemplating the world means "creating" the world, because by contemplating the world, man separates himself from it and places himself before it. In this separation and confrontation, the thinker can observe, measure, know, and perceive "that which has been contemplated" in order to be liberated from his inevitable dependence and enslavement, to become independent and free, to be able, of his own volition and knowingly, to reconnect with it, and for harmony to replace separation. The uncontemplated world is inconceivable, unknowable, and imperceptible, as though it did not exist at all.

The poet contemplates the static concept of God, which is the hidden, potential, and possible essence of existence; and once the created contemplated the idea of the creator, he spurred it on, made it materialize, and brought it into existence; he brought it from the invisible world into the visible world. Our Hafez is the Tongue of the Invisible. Everyone's thought, however, is concealed behind his veil of appearances. Even though the color of the face reveals some indication of the inner secret[7] and some sign of God is evident in visible things, the spirit of his thought cannot be found in the world, which is a manifestation of his face or a form of his thought in the visible world. God is himself a mystery, and his thinking is the mystery of all mysteries, the invisible of the invisible world. And our Hafez, like a "droplet that dreams the impossible,"[8] nurtures in his mind the dream of reaching the hidden of the hidden of this shoreless ocean:

> Drunkenly, let us remove the veil
> from the face of God's secret,
> secluded in the tent of the invisible.[9]

God's secret is he himself. God's attributes are not considered separate from his essence. He is one and the same as his thoughts, words, and deeds. Hence, the poet, by opening the tent of the invisible, simultaneously brings God and his thought out of isolation. God revealed his thoughts in the word, and the poet as well expresses his thought in words: in poetry. His creation, as well, like that of the creator, is in words, and creation is the uncovering, the removing of the veil from the face, the revealing of the invisible, and the bestowing of another ray of light to the world and the offering of another vision to the denizens of the world. And every uncovering is another creation. Hence, the work of such revealers as mystics, philosophers, and sages is similar to the incantation of poets.

Every time that the poet draws aside the veil from the face of thought, a new light of its brightness shines on the prism of the world and gives it another hue, a new dawn buds, and things like the water lily that rises from a marsh emerge from another slumber to see and to be seen. The magic of the imagination of my rose-colored elder creates a new image in the workshop of creation and awakens a more novel design—such as the anticipation of seasons within the heart of nature—that was dormant in the mind of God. The poet's God is a more alert and more aware God; he thinks more about himself and his handiwork. As a result, he is a preoccupied thinker rather than being almighty and tranquil of heart. He continuously contemplates himself, constantly reveals another manifestation of himself, and in this way, creates a more complete world. In the bosom of such a God and world, such a human being is born in whose creative imagination lives a God who is aware of his heart: the God of poets. God, the world, and man shine on one another, and each bestows perfection on the image of the others in the mirror of his own existence.

In this manner, poetry creates a design of existence. At one time, a poet prophet contemplated the light of God's goodness and brought it into the arena of visibility from behind the veil of invisibility, and the dark lamp of thought was lit. In the light of this newly appeared goodness, hope for the departure of evil dawned in man, hope for salvation dawned in the heart of the world, and man became a twin and companion of Ahura Mazda. At another time, a poet contemplated God's friendship—or the friendship in God—and when friendship in God was contemplated, it reached another site and acquired divine dimensions: it became absolute and infinite. Hence, love wove together the warp and weft of existence and nonexistence. God, the lover, the beloved, and the world became a manifestation of his beautiful face. From the Koran to Hafez, the memorizer of the Koran, is a long way. Our Hafez removed the veil from the mystery, and in this way, creation, man, love, the world, ethics, and behavior acquired different meanings, and as a result, living and dying changed. He split open the azure shell of the firmament and created the image of a loftier sky, a more open earth, and a greater arena than the mirror of the eye; he steered the restive steed of destiny onto untrodden paths and created a new design.

But this new design is a masterful ruse, a mirage that appears to be an ocean, and a dream that appears to be reality; it is the soaring rainbow flung by the vagrant, wandering wind.

> Hafez, talk of your delightfully deceptive magic
> has reached as far as Egypt and China
> and near to Rome and Rey.[10]

Poetry is the birthplace and the body of thought; together, they are like body and soul. In the poet, even though thought, words, and creation are not the same, they are born together. He creates a unique novel design with these three. And his creation is the poetry that is the face and expression of his thought; and because of its connection with thought, his poetry is "delightfully deceptive magic," since the thought of magic, sleight of hand, is delightful, for it is done in the dark; but it is the source of light, for it is itself unknown yet the source of knowing—a bird that, even though in our cage, always makes us chase after it as it flies away. And poetry, in particular, makes this characteristic of thought pronounced, not in terms of systemizing, which is characteristic of philosophy, or its theoretical and practical necessity, which appears in logic, mathematics, and sciences. Contrary to these, thought in poetry constantly rips up its own laws, tears its own skin, and plants its own seed in order to grow with a different form in "a new design." A self-witnessing destroyer and a dying newborn giving birth, a constant dawning and blooming, a nocturnal firework display in which suddenly a handful of lamps and luminous lights pour out like a bush aflame and sink into the forest of darkness. And poetry is a breath of light and an untimely morning, the clever game of an involuntary player and a chess-playing poet on the chessboard of the world of existence with chess pieces such as the galaxy of stars, the moon and the sun, the earth and the sky, spring and autumn, truth and falsehood, justice and injustice, and fortune and destiny. He not only scatters the prearranged chess pieces, but he also changes the rules and the arrangement and role of the pieces. The unarmed pawn is not the shield against calamity; the rook does not hide behind the scene of battle; the queen does not gallop in any direction she wants; and the knight and the bishop can be used for purposes other than attacking and killing.[11] In this manner, the poet turns the set upside down, and with this endless game of thought in time and space, he finds a new situation. Moreover, by changing the function of the pieces that help him and are his partners in the game, he also alters his own nature and destiny.

But poetry is deception because it is a game, not actual reality; it takes a trace of things that exist, then changes their laws and function and makes them pronouncedly displayed in a novel form. That which has occurred in the workshop of creation recurs in the workshop of the poet's imagination. The world of poetry is a theatrical play of the world, however, with the script, the setting, and the players that the poet has chosen himself and processed in the world of his imagination; and then he has cast their roles on the screen of the actual world and bestowed on the reality of the world an appearance and luster of his own choosing. He has instilled the present but inaccessible imagined truth into the body of things and "physical perceptions"—perceptions such as blind faith and ignorant prejudice, which are so rooted and firmly planted in us that it seems as though they have infiltrated our body with their bodies—and he has toyed with their stern, firm physicality.

Poetry is the obverse albeit magical "mimesis" of phenomena, such that not only does it turn the imitation copy into the original, but it also makes us negligent of the "original," of that which actually exists—and as it exists—and sends us in search of "another world and another Adam."[12] Mimesis in poetry, however, is not for the purpose of imitation. The poet himself is in the midst of the predicament. He plays with his destiny in the gambling house of the world, and once he risks it, he is playing with his own fate. He does not go on stage like an actor to play a role for others who have come as spectators; rather, he pulls out the apparitions from within himself—from demons to spirits—and in them, he plays his role in the script of his own life. Children do not play for the purpose of imitation; rather, they live through playing, but they borrow the structure of the play from their surroundings and those around them. When they ride a stick or toss a piece of paper on water, they are not imitating horseback riding or sailing; rather, free from the limitations of horseback riding and captaincy, they are living as autonomous riders and captains. They are not testing land and water; rather, they are making their own land and water materialize and reconstructing the world in their own imagination. And when they fly a kite, they have the end of the string of the bird, the flight, and the sky in their hands. Through playing, life is repeated in children; the world enacts its script in them, and in this way evolves in them. A playful child is pregnant with the same world that the actor poet brings into the world.

In any case, in the same way that the thoughts and words of the poet reflect God's thoughts and words, his novel creation is also an "imitation" of the building of the world and the flourishing ruins of existence.[13] And playing, imitation, is deception, because it is the product of thought in the world of imagination, not a mountain, a sorrow, or an outcry standing there on the ground before us.

Poetry is deception; but it is delightful deception, since poetry is freedom, and man is eternally enamored with freedom. This freedom comes into existence in the game of poetry, and man flees from falsehood, oppression, and death, from the narrow confinement of space and the rapid velocity of time, from prison. The moth splits open the cocoon, and the star does not remain in the pit. Every time that man takes another look at his own existential condition, every time he tests his inabilities and his confined boundaries, he returns from unconsciousness to consciousness and from deception to reality, and he falls from the sky of freedom into the abyss of need. But this deception is delightful; it cannot be removed from one's heart. By the blessing of poetry, this fallen enamored man rises every time from the hardship and travail of the actual world, from the salt desert of making a living and its ensnaring tedium, and begins another game on the world stage, with his own pieces, his own friends, and his own methods and rules. The creation of this scene changes the perspective of the previous scene and spreads another landscape before the eyes of the "enamored," driving them toward another "snare of deception." Hence, poetry is the constant vacillation between the abyss and the sky and the continuous relinquishment of the need for freedom.

But in order not to think that poetry is an easy and cheap deception, I say that it is not the same as the deception of the magician. In the case of sleight of hand, the game is based on the dexterousness and agility of one side and the gullibility and blindness of the other. If the latter knows and sees, the game is over and the magician's hand is exposed. In this situation, all that occurs is in the appearance and "pretense" of things, not in their reality and "actuality." There is neither a "novel design" nor is there any change in any destiny. The causes of necessity and the misery of the soul are stubbornly in place, and ultimately from the artfulness of the hands of the Samarian, there is nothing more than the "mooing of a calf."[14] This is not Moses's "white hand."[15]

Poetry is the white hand and the "true magic" that nullifies the magic and sorcery of the imposters, splits apart the sea and drowns the false claimant, observes God in the burning bush, and speaks to him. And this poetry, like the word of God, is "legitimate magic,"[16] because like the season of spring that grows in the body of nature, its magic appears in the infinite expanse of language. And words are the link that connects the branch of mankind to the eternal tree, the link between mortality and immortality; they make God, with the words he speaks to us, human, and they make man, in the words we hear from him, divine. Words are the source of empathy and amity, since from the words of the friend, one can learn about his thoughts, and thus blessed, one can sing in unison with "the sound of the words of love."[17] A friend is not chosen without being known or recognized. The greatest of the prophets who have a book, in other words, those who have words, are like poets, because they too are kings of the realm of words, that is, gods of knowledge. And the magic of poetry, because it lights the lamp of thought and makes the "tree of knowledge" in the garden of words fruitful, is of the same foundation and nature as the miracles of the prophets.

> I am that magical poet
> who with his incantations
> draws all the sweetness from the reed of his pen[18]

Whereas the sorcerers of the pharaoh turned staffs into serpents, the magic of the poet turns the reed into sugarcane, and whereas the magic of the former was to prove the divinity of the pharaoh, the magic of the latter is at least a sweetening.

Hence, poetry is the "delightfully deceptive magic"[19] that "draws aside the veil of thought"[20] and reveals its face. The concept of poetry contains an assumption of uncovering, of removing veils and showing the face, of bringing forth and making visible some secret or mystery from its hiding place, an assumption of seeing. The idea of poetry is "seeing." Unlike philosophy, logic, and mathematics—which, based on their necessary and inevitable rules, are self-processed and expand within their own systems and procedures—poetic thought is not nurtured merely in the mind. This thought is seen as an image in the mirror of the heart:

> each night all night
> I stand guard at the sanctuary of my heart
> letting in only my thoughts of you[21]

In the nocturnal darkness, poetic thought is guarded in the sanctuary of the heart. The heart is the abode of love, that is, the place of the manifestation of beauty; and in the concept of beauty, an assumption of a form exists, because until beauty becomes manifest it does not exist, and once "manifestation" is located in something, a place or a condition, the "one that can be manifested" takes form. For this reason, in mysticism in which God is beauty, inevitably, he does not remain hidden and he has a manifestation, such as creation. In any case, beauty cannot escape form, and until thought finds its way into the heart, it remains at various levels of awareness, but it does not become "poetic."

In awareness—in science, knowledge, and all that can be known—the "form" of thought is the same as the structure and skeleton, the linkage of laws and conventions and systems that connect the components together and rotate this skein like a wheel, or, at a higher level, turn it into life, like a body. In every case, conscious thought has "form," since thinking is the same as giving form to thought. But in addition to this, as the warp and weft of poetic thought intertwine, they also weave an image into their texture. This thought is pictorial.

Moreover, poetry is the uncovering of thought through words, and as a result, it is the imitation of God's work and a repetition of his creation. The poet, however, borrows the material for his creation from existing creation, from the world that is the manifestation of the face and the form of God's thought. Hence, he recontemplates and re-creates the manifestation of the face and the form of thought, and the re-creation of the face and the form is necessarily not without form. That is why poetic thought is inevitably more formable than any other thought, to the point that the abstract soul has a face of its own, the seeing of which the poet longs for, provided his "body's dust is not as a veil spread out to hide his soul."[22] Invisible things become visible in the light of this thought, and the poet is constantly involved in the workshop of the eyes and in the imagination that shines on the seven-colored canvas, the image of existence in the painting gallery of this prism.

Poetic thought forms in the realm of the imagination, which is the poet's workshop of creation. In this place that can be contemplated and sensed but cannot be found, thought is sensed with its blowing breath, swaying body, and continuous flights in place, and things that are sensed open their shape and shell to thought and become thought. In poetry, one thinks with his heart and senses with his mind. In this case, when sense becomes thought, it opens its borders and becomes free within itself; and when thought is sensed, it "descends" into its own design and is established. In this way, on the site of the imagination, form becomes free, and freedom becomes formable, and poetic thought turns into the "form of imagination" or is imaged and comes into existence in this "body."

From a different perspective, however, in the realm of imagination, thought, like a distorting mirror, reflects the substance of sense (or the subject of the sensory experience), and reprojects it outside in the form that it has nurtured and processed: thought embraces sense, forges it, and projects it; in other words, it places it before us as a topic of thought. Sense, as well, as it "forms" in the mirror, influences its luminousness and bestows upon it a different clarity and luster. Two impactors susceptible to impact are constantly involved in giving birth to themselves through believing in each other. In this process, sense and thought are an inseparable blend: lamp and light. In the realm of "imagination," the separation and distinction between them fades away, like the dark and light of dawn that loses night and day in itself.

Sense and thought reflect themselves in each other. In this oneness, thought can contemplate its incongruous and nonsimultaneous senses congruently and simultaneously. And sense can perceive its varied thoughts as congruous. Like a two-sided mirror, thought simultaneously gives form to its past and future senses, in the same way that sense sees its various scattered thoughts all at once. In this way, "imagination" brings together not only senses and thoughts, but also various times and spaces, takes their distilled essence, and fuses them, such that the imaginer in a single instant possesses life and death, disbelief and faith, union and separation, laughter and weeping, and childhood and old age. It is as though a magical lens gathers together the dispersed and wandering rays of the world in a center, re-emits them in various colors through revolving prisms, playfully adorns the world with colorful tricks, with ugliness and beauty, with happiness and sorrow, and turns them into the shapes of the galloping arena of the enemy and the arena of utter obliteration, or the painting gallery of the friend and the abode of happiness, or both.

In logic and theoretical mathematics, thought responds to the questions that it poses to itself; and in science, it responds to the questions that the world poses. The original source of questions in philosophy, both in thought and in the world, lies in universal thought. In all these arenas, the answer must be based on evidence in the world, or it must interpret it; otherwise, thought spins within itself and does not go beyond illusion and supposition. Poetic thought, however, gives its own evidence or interpretation to the world; it interprets the world, and by doing so, it gives meaning to it, because such thought—similar to myth and religion—is "base building," "design creating,"[23] or foundation creating.

The poet places the world he has created in the workshop of his imagination before the world that exists. Since this creation occurs within the realm of the imagination, it has its very own logic, function, and end; but since it selects its material from existing creation, since it does not remain within the realm of the imagination and necessarily comes into existence in words and joins the actual world, it cannot be totally alien to the laws and order of the world. In any case, the poet is a creation among all the created entities in the world! He places himself in the world, and in agreement or opposition, in any way imaginable, he takes a position vis-à-vis it, and he can in no instance remain detached from it. If so, he would speak in a language that cannot be known about something that cannot be thought: confused speaking in confused thinking. Hence, poetic creation in the unrestricted workshop of the imagination is not willful and whimsical.

On the other hand, however, mathematics and science are logical and "methodical" systems. If the response of thought to them lacks a methodology, it will be in contradiction to itself, and if it is not "orderly," it will be incompatible with the function of the system and will be excluded from that system. Hence, in mathematics and science, thought drives onward toward the boundaries of the system, unless it expands it and moves the boundaries further. Of course, when science cannot answer the questions, it chooses another beginning and approach; in other words, through a "primary hypothesis" and new methodology, it designs another system. In this permanent process, a hypothesis that is not "scientific" frees science from its previous narrow confines, and "unscientific" imagination—which is nurtured by the known facts of science but is not accepted until it leaves them behind—comes to the aid of science. In this state, the scientist, like the poet, is also a creator of designs and a creator of foundations, and his "imaginative" mind functions like that of a poet. But in the new science, since inevitably a system—even though more comprehensive—is established, there is always a boundary like a horizon in front of it. Here, thought is not free and can only move methodically and systematically, and, based on the rules, develop new logical principles and rules from its own logical principles. This thought necessarily has a specific path ahead of it. In philosophy, however, thought can leave its horizon behind. Science is the system of knowing and philosophy, the system of thinking. Philosophical thought can logically (in other words, methodically and systematically) pass beyond the limitations of knowing how to reach "not knowing." It can reason and "prove" that in a different arena, knowing is impossible, or in other words, contemplate "not knowing" and know that it cannot know. Also, it is possible within a philosophical system for thought to develop against the rules—to undo the contradictions—that it has established itself, and contemplate the contradiction in the rule.*

* Note Kant's critique of judgement and his contradiction of principles (antinomies) in *Kritik der reinen Vernunft* [*Critique of Pure Reason*].

The free, fluid, and boundless nature of thought emerges, including in this case.

Poetic thought as well—albeit of a different type—is unruly and cannot be constrained. The "realm of imagination" is the reflecting and re-reflecting of the sensing thought and thinking sense that—like an image in face-to-face mirrors—can be repeated infinitely. In this dawning and growing, sense hunts thought and encloses it in its cage. And thought causes sense to fly out of the cage. Each causes the other to come out of its own domain, a constant departure and return occurring and not remaining in any one place, unless the poet himself chooses that "place" of his own volition and brings this wayfarer down to reside at a certain stage. The beginning of this self-motivated process is within the poet, and its end is also of his own volition. Hence, even though poetic creation is not willful, it is free, unrestricted. This creation occurs in the imagination, which is the place where sense and thought connect.

In knowledge (philosophy, mathematics, science, and so on), where thought operates and expands based on its own laws, thought is only involved in its rational and logical aspects. But now, the emotional and "human" aspect of sense finds its way into the arena of thought and no longer leaves it alone in its cold house. It blows into it like a flame, like a candle, and brings it warmth and light, like spring and autumn that find their way into the unquestionable rotation of the earth and bestow on it another reason and purpose. In knowledge, the thinker—even when he thinks about mankind—tries to think devoid of human dispositions; he tries not to involve emotions and feelings in the workshop of reason. But in poetry, even lifeless things grow in the cultivated field of emotions and feelings and are contemplated with a human dimension. In the imagination, the world possesses the dispositions of the poet, a contemplating man of the heart, a pained, weeping, smiling man, with love and animosity. "Every leaf in the meadow is a book about a different disposition."[24] Man is uprooted from the triviality and futility of the world and falls into the world in some disposition; the house of living and dying, the house of his soul, turns upside down. Even when it deals with our daily commonplace life, not only does poetry not fall into the whirlpool itself, but also it takes our hand, because it both blows its "imagination" like "fresh air" into the breast of our passing life of eating and sleeping and also takes us away to the strange realm of its imagination; and as a result, it opens to us the invisible inner gates.

All that is seen and known—the sleep of fortune and the wakefulness of the sun, the ascension of Christ and the lamp that man gives to the sun, and the nocturnal stars that deceitfully rob the crown of Kavus, and the game of the friend in the arena of beauty who checkmates a moon and a sun with the pawn of the mole of a face*—all grow in the "green field" of the imagination.[25] Things that are known are seen, and things that are seen become known: The thought of fortune shows its face like a sleepy body, knowledge as a lamp, time as a star, and the moving star as a thief.[26] Thoughts become measuring cups,[27] and in exchange, measuring cups find their way into the freedom of thought: thief to star to time; lamp to knowledge; and sleeping body to the contemplation of fortune.[28]

At times the poet—as mentioned before—speaks of his journey in the realm of the imagination, the "story" of that which he has seen in that wonderful realm. In this case, we are mostly dealing with the story in his imagination, not its "images." But at other times—as it so happens—the poet projects the images that form on the canvas of his memory, and he speaks in the language of "images." In this case, we are also dealing with the "image in his imagination,"† which, in remembering the beauty of

* See "I saw the green field of the sky, / and there a sickle moon." [From ghazal 407; Dick Davis, trans. *Faces of Love: Hafez and the Poets of Shiraz* (New York: Penguin, 2013), 36.]

† A ghazal such as "At dawn with a nocturnal hangover / I picked up the wine with the harp and chime" [ghazal 428]. Almost the entire tale is the "imaginary" story of the poet, but in most ghazals, the "story" and the image in the imagination are fused. The following ghazal is an example:

> For years my heart inquired of me
> Where Jamshid's sacred cup might be,
> And what was in its own possession
> It asked from strangers, constantly"
> [ghazal 143; Davis, *Faces of Love*, 42].

the friend, he traces on water.* Thought (memory) with the mediation of the "substance" or the topic of sense (the line of down of the beloved) traces a fleeting "image," an image on water. And the water itself is the "image" of the flood (another substance of sense) that blocks the path to sleep, the path that can only be imagined in thought, and "the image in the imagination" is itself a path that in the external world rests in the breast of the earth.

The beloved's eyebrow (the topic of sense) within sight—in other words, in "insight," in "imagination,"—guides the poet's memory and thought to the prayer niche—which is itself an "image" of the same eyebrow.

The face of the beloved appears before his eyes (beauty in "imagination"), and the lover kisses the face of the moonlight—which is sensed—and such "kissing and embracing" is only possible in the realm of the

* [From ghazal 320:]

Last night the road to sleep
was flooded by my tears
remembering the line of your down
I traced a pattern on the water

with my gown consigned to the flames
and your eyebrow in mind
I raised a wine-cup to that place of prayer

my beloved appeared to me   and from a distance
I placed a kiss upon that moonlike face

gazing at the serving-boy
and listening to the message of the harp
in these two ways
eye and ear told me of my destiny

each bird of thought
that took off from the branches of words
I caught again in the fine net of your curls

[Translation from Geoffrey Squires, trans. *Hafez: Translations and Interpretations of the Ghazals* (Miami: Miami University Press, 2014), 261. Since this translation is based on Khanlari's edition, the order of the couplets is slightly different.]

imagination, and it is in the same "realm" in which moonlight is imagined as an "image" of the beloved's face.

Hence, every bird of thought that flies off from the branches of speech falls into the trap of the beloved's tresses; thought remains "within reach" and is embodied in the senses; and the poet divines his fortune through eyes and ears (through the senses) in the infinity of love.

and till dawn
I drew the image of your face
working in the attic of my sleepless eyes[29]

Blessed by his senses, the poet gives form to his thought in the workshop of the imagination, and he views its image within himself. Images fly in thought, and thoughts reside in images and as a result become "visible."

at every moment the image of your face
blocks the road of my imaginings
to whom shall I tell the things
I see in this shadow play[30]

The realm of the imagination is not the state of understanding, it is the state of unveiling understanding, the state of insight. Our Hafez sees angels at the door of the tavern in nocturnal darkness, and he sees the workshop of his destiny in the green field of the sky. The realm of the imagination of the poet is similar to the allegorical realm of the mystics, and the poetic vision of one is similar to the mystic illumination of the other. Reason's external vision and love's internal vision, the eye of the head and the eye of the heart, appear at the center of the imagination that at every moment has a different hue, shape, disposition, and expression; and new and newer landscapes open wide before the mind's eye. The poet's vision is of magical "lovers' exchange of glances" and a pleasant deception that bewilders those who do not know.

This imaginary vision of poetry is not always revealed in a visible composition and structure. The existence of the image in the imagination (the picture) is not inevitable, and the poem is also possible without it. But it is not possible without "imagination," since without it, poetic vision fades away. In the heroic *Book of Kings*, man's fate is expressed in a language as bare as the sky, with occasional "images" here and there—like the faces of the sky—but not such that it deprives the story of its rapid pace or slows down its movement on a rocky terrain. Despite all this, when, for example, Ferdowsi narrates the story of Rostam and Sohrab or Rostam and Esfandiar, it is perfect poetry throughout. Here, the organs of destiny, or the design of this "lofty palace,"[31] the relationship and connection of the components, and the effect of the denizens of the world on each other, and their encounter with the world, and the creator are all nurtured and created by "imagination." Even though the poet speaks in a language "devoid of images," he is the traveler of the realm of imagination who draws the map, the highs and lows, and the landscapes of this inner realm. Hence, even when it is bereft of "imagined images" and seems devoid of "imagery," its language has some element of imagination.*

The possessor of imagination in a single moment is the possessor of various emotions and thoughts and times and spaces, and he savors the essence of all of them. Contradictory dispositions—which emerge from one another at the dawning of imagination—come together in him, and they acquire the harmony and disharmony of their restless and effusive unity in him: A center from every point of the circumference surrounds the circular rays. The existence of various emotions and thoughts, and the perception of this variety, give the poet a frenzied and mad, "magical-playful" appearance. Even though the foundation of his thinking and worldview is the same, its turning and mechanism are such that they appear to be of various colors. All thoughts and thinking in general are the same, but the dispositions are neither harmonious nor the same. The consistency of sense and thought in "imagination" turns it into a multifaceted mirror that not only shows the top and bottom and the front and back of things but also their interior and exterior. The "imaginative" poet suddenly and

* In the historical part of *Book of Kings*, since the poet is uprooted from the world of imagination and narrates events, and instead of man's destiny, he deals with his story, the "imagined images"—when they are used—cannot compensate for the lack of "imagination" and free the poem.

in a single instant contemplates and experiences a thought and an emotion in various and opposing directions, and he has dispositions of every sort. With a mind that thinks in terms of opposites, he possesses an imagination that processes in terms of opposites, and as a result, often his words appear to be opposite of that which is customary.

> Seek success under conditions that are contrary to custom,
> For I collected my thoughts from disheveled tresses.[32]

The world of plurality and disunity is chaotic and aimless; it is a mass of intertwined, disheveled, and disconnected things, and for this reason, it is demonic. "Renounce the thought of disunion to have union."[33] The message at dawn from the messenger of the invisible will not be received by a distraught mind.[34] The poet gains victory over the thought of disunity and disunity of thought. Of course, consistency of thought in the imagination is of a different sort, and it is different from the system of thought in science or logic. In the imagination of poets, thought at times has a distraught and fleeting face; but at the core, all its components are interconnected by an invisible link. For this reason, the unity of poetry should be sought in the general system of its imagination, not in the trivial order of the couplets.

Consistency of thought in the realm of the imagination, or a collected mind like that of a messenger angel, is acquired at times, *contrary to custom*, precisely from its opposite, from distraction. Since imagination is the place of cultivation and connection and the start of unique single and multiple contradictory states, the sorrow of love is happy, and its happiness is sorrowful, and longing for the sorrow of love, the poet seeks happiness:

> Since the sorrow of love for you
>   can only be found in a happy heart,
> Hoping for the sorrow of love, I will seek a happy heart.[35]

The sorrow of love for the friend nests in happy hearts. The mere existence of such sorrow—which is indicative of love—is itself the original source of happiness and turns its dwelling into the house of happiness.

Sorrow and happiness become one and the same, indistinguishable. Although those unencumbered by love "are pleased and happy with merrymaking and glee," for lovers, "sorrowful longing for the beloved is the source of happiness."[36] Often in this "mirrorlike"[37] imagination, which absorbs in itself sunrise and sunset and light and darkness and reflects them in each other through its transparent surface, they appear to be one and the same; in this seven-times fermentation wine cellar, soberness and drunkenness, solitude and togetherness, pain and comfort, separation and union, and misfortune and fortune not only split open each other's shell and seep through each other, but somewhere and under certain conditions, they become one soul and one body. This association and connectivity of opposites at times bestows contradiction and irony on the words of our Hafez, making his words appear upside down and twisted, which is not merely the magic of expression, but is born of the magical power of a mind that thinks in opposites and the reflection of an imagination that processes contraries.* The poet speaks "from the treasure of sorrow for the friend in the ruins of the heart,"[38] from a sorrow as precious as a treasure and a treasure as ruined as sorrow, from the heart that is a treasure house in ruins and a ruined house with precious treasure. The religious jurist at the seminary issues a religious decree in his drunkenness that "wine is prohibited, but better than religiously endowed property."[39] In drunkenness, he is truthful; until he falls into the misguided path of intoxication, he cannot return to the straight path. Only by passing though the desert of transgression can he reach the right path; and still, he is a sinner in his deed worthy of reward, since he issues a just religious decree in an unjust situation. It is as though he who throws stones at the cup of another thus breaking the jug and subjecting the drunkards to the religious punishment of lashes becomes "wise and learned" once again "with one sip of wine" that causes "lack of reason" and stupor.[40] In his leaning toward expedient and utilitarian reason, the poet contemplates repentance, albeit repentance "at

* For instance, see the following ghazal [194]: "When the jasmine-scented ones sit, they make the dust of sorrow settle / When fairy-faced beauties quarrel, they take away the tranquility of the heart."

the hands of the wine-selling idol" and pledging "not to drink wine again unaccompanied by a face that adorns a festive gathering";[41] but because the wine seller is an idol, she is herself an adorner of feasts, and because she is a wine seller, she is a breaker of repentance. Hence, the poet does not repent except in the presence of "an idol who breaks repentances."[42] In this manner, his repentance is an impossibility. In other words, he repents of repenting. And besides, suppose that he does repent!

> Come, for the flourishing of this workshop
> will not decrease
> From the piety of one like you,
> or the debauchery of one like me.[43]

Not that in the revolving of the world of existence and the destiny of the universe, the piety of one or the debauchery of the other would be ineffectual. If this were all there were, he would say, come, for the flourishing of this workshop will not increase from your piety nor decrease from my debauchery. It does not even cross the poet's mind that the piety of the other would be able to make anything flourish. He considers such piety to be harmful by its very nature, albeit ineffectual, precisely like his own ineffectual debauchery. The distinction between good and bad is erased. But concealed here is the stinging sneer of derision: not merely that all piety and debauchery are the same; rather, the piety of *one like you* and the debauchery of *one like me* are the same. An unvoiced thought can be detected behind the transparent mirror of the words: there is hypocrisy in that piety, but not in this debauchery. Hence, the distinction between good and bad, which had been erased, continues to exist at the core: not in practicing piety and debauchery, not in one's deeds, in appearances and display, but in contemplating hypocrisy and sincerity, in the work of the heart, in the invisible aspects of existence, between "being like you" and "being like me"! And yet, one like me who does not engage in hypocrisy is a debaucher, a doer of bad deeds. Then, how could one tell that I would be better than you, a hypocrite? And yet, suppose I were, in such a case; being better is not a source of happiness nor would it have any effect on the "flourishing of this workshop."

Throughout, the *Divan* of our Hafez is filled with this kind of multifaceted, labyrinthine and colorful language that is not merely due to the unmatched power and mastery of speech and language. The poet certainly is a skillful "player" in the domain of language, because he brings into existence the deception of his creation. But the irony, figurative speech, sarcasm, and ambiguity that rises from it—saying something and meaning something else and giving the words multilayered, exposed, and hidden meanings—is rooted in the "upside-down functioning"[44] of imagination, his colorful imagination. The Tongue of the Invisible comes from the invisible realm, and the magic of expression, from the magic of imagination. For this reason, the poetry of our elder, like nature, is a concealed, perceptible phenomenon, and the deeper one delves into it, the more other-worldly one finds it. Once the thoughts that are sleeping in the "cage" of his words awaken, like migrating birds in a cloudy and windy sky, they fly away in song.

And the "wakefulness" of thought unveils the poem; and until we open the door of the cage of the poem, the birds of thought will not be released. In poetry, words must also be opened, like thought, because words are the arena of poetic creation and the keeper and concealer of its mystery.

> When I bring the reed pen that is the fish to write,
> You ask the N and the pen for interpretation.[45]

"N and the pen and all that it writes."* What has been written by that pen and what has Hafez read on the Preserved Tablet[46] on which we must find the interpretation of his words? The reed pen and *nun*,† both grow in water. Regarding this Koranic verse, interpreters of the Koran have stated that *nun* means the fish on the back of which the creator firmly placed earth,‡ hence, it means the base and foundation of the world. The pen

* Surah 68, verse 1 [of the Koran].

† *Nun* in Arabic means "fish." [Nun is also the name of the letter *n*.]

‡ See the translation and interpretation of the same verse in Tabari's commentary on the Koran, *Kashf al-Asrar* [translated as *The Unveiling of Mysteries* by William C. Chittick (Louisville, KY: Fons Vitae, 2016)] and the interpretation by Abolfotuh Razi.

referred to in the Koran, however, was created before anything else, and all that which occurs up to the Day of Resurrection is written with it: the pen of destiny of the master of eternal beginning! Now there is a relationship and a connection between the turning of the pen in the ocean of poetry and the turning of the pen of the creator in the world of creation. It is as though the pen of the poet says "that which the master of eternal beginning said,"[47] and emulating him, he "designs" the foundation of the earth and the ceiling of the sky, or rewrites the destiny of the world.

In the face of Hafez's talented nature, which is as clear as water, the "water of life"[48] has crept behind the veil of darkness from embarrassment. This poetry itself is the water that remedies life.* This water is hidden behind the veils of darkness, and only prophets and the chosen can gain access to this light in the heart of darkness.

Moreover, while the poet possesses the reed pen that is the fish, Jonah has also been called the possessor of the fish.† This prophet, as well, like the poet, found the water of life of deliverance in darkness, in the belly of the fish that was swimming in the darkness at the bottom of the sea, and he returned to the shore from there. Hence, behind the hidden heart of thought there is a veiled similarity between the two composers of words, the poet and the prophet. His poetry, which flows out from the depths of roots like a pleasant stream, is like the words of a prophet in whose soul the thoughts of God descend and on whose tongue they resonate to reveal the mysteries. Thus, the meaning of the poetry of one is found in the verses of the other. The reed pen that is the fish, as well, like the pen of eternity, creates; and the interpretation of the poetry must be sought in the prophet's divine revelation and the tongue of the invisible, which is

* "The veil of darkness concealed the water of life, since / It was embarrassed before the poetry of Hafez and his clear-as-water talented nature." [From ghazal 305.] And also, "Hafez, your poetry gave me a drink from the water of life / Leave the physician, come and read the prescription of my drink." [From ghazal 382.]

† *Zo al-nun* [of the fish] and *saheb al-hut* [the possessor of the fish] in surah 21, verse 86 [in some versions, verse 87] and surah 68, verse 48. Also see *Qor'an-e Majid,* vol. 2 (Tehran: Sazman-e Owqaf, 1975), translated, compiled, and interpreted by Zeynol'abedin Rahnema, 130.

the "dawn" of speakers. Language rises from this dawn; and it is a divine matter that has been entrusted to the poet and prophet alike, like the eye that sees in the dark placed in the star, the patient pregnancy in soil, the growth in plants, and flight in the wing. These words are neither the form nor the clothing, but are the formable substance of thought. Such words unveil the veil in the veil, and in every unveiling, they remove a veil from the face of thought; and in removing every veil, they push aside a veil from speech, because these words, like thought, are mysterious themselves, since they are his water of life that flows in my stream. "The delightfulness and beauty of words is God-given."[49] In the view of our Hafez, the words of the poet come from the words of the friend, and both are of the same essence. Hence, they are both ancient:

> in the time of Adam   in the garden of Eden
> Hafez' lines
> illustrated the pages of the book of flowers.[50]

Hence, they are both sacred:

> At dawn a cry came from the heavens —
> And Reason said, "I see
> The very angels know by heart
> Hafez's poetry!"[51]

And they both, in "voyaging in time and space, traverse a hundred-year-long path overnight,"[52] are victorious over the revolving universe. The "poems of Hafez, whose words are sweet," can make the heavens dance,[53] and

> Venus's odes will not flourish
> Once Hafez begins to sing.[54]

But because the words of the poet are of man and not of the divine, they are of the senses and emotions, and they have an existential nature and quality. The burning of the fire of the heart can be recognized "from burning words."[55] The deer of the poetry that comes from strange plains and whose musk is scattered by the breeze in the meadow of the soul is a weeping laughter. "How can a despondent heart compose a novel poem?"[56] But a "fresh sweet poem"[57] from a happy heart also drips with blood.

> I don't know who fired the arrow
> into the poet's heart
> I know only that his blood   drips from every fresh line[58]

God with his word opened the world to us; the poet, as well, with his words opens his world to us. Among our poets, rarely does anyone know this world of poetry as perfectly as he does, and is aware of himself as a poet:

> When I bring the reed pen that is the fish to write,
> You ask the N and the pen for interpretation.
> I fused the soul with wisdom,
> From the mix, I planted the resulting seed.
> Delightfulness is apparent in this composition,
> Thus is the marvel of poetry, the core of its components' soul.
> Come, and from the scent of this delightful hope,
> Make the olfactory of the soul fragrant forever.
> For this musk comes from the bosom of angels,
> Not from the deer that flees the people.[59]

"Being a poet" is the delightful combining and successful harmonizing of the truth of words and the essence of the soul, the planting of the seeds of the soul and of wisdom, the sprinkling of seeds by the hand of the wind, and the nurturing of the fresh scent of hope, a fragrant eternal soul and an ambergris musk from the covered neck and timid body of the fairy of paradise; it is from ideal beauty, not the scent of the deer that flees from the people.

And the wild, startled gazelle of poetry is only tame to lovers. If what the poet says stems from the words of the friend, and if the words of the friend stem from his thought and creation, the purpose of creation is love, and the poet who emulates the game of the friend in a different state and rewrites what he has provided as a sample is the lover. To be a poet is to be in love. In the same way that the nightingale learns words through the blessing of the rose, the nightingale that "Hafez favors" also sings because of "the scent of the rosebush of union" with the beloved.[60] He is himself the anemone who has come, branded by love;[61] he has lived in love and has departed longing for love. Love is his seed, his tree, and his season of spring. He sleeps in the soil of love, he burgeons under the rain of love, and he walks on the ground of love. The water of love runs in the stream of his soul and "opens his chest, makes the affairs easy for him, removes the knot from his tongue," and opens the doors of the universe to him, so that he can traverse the world like a bird in flight or a running deer to find and create his own world.

God's creation occurs in the arena of all that exists, in the reality of life and death; and for this reason, it is evolving and diminishing, it is imperfect and incomplete. It is what we see. But he is absolute. Hence, he does not yearn for more beauty and for something better, since the desire for perfection is a part of him, not beyond him. His work and purpose are "one and the same," precisely the same. God does not have any desire or ideal.

But the poet is an incomplete creator with incomplete creation in the twilight of mystery, in the "deceptive magic" of words; and since they are magic, they never rejoin reality and do not become one with it; they do not reach perfection, and since they are deceptive, at every moment, they force the creator into another magical game; they do not end. In this state, aware of his incompleteness, the creator yearns for completeness and perfection, yearns to "be God," and for that matter, not with a creation like this world, but a perfect and ideal world. The poet seeks the impossible, and for this reason, necessarily and undoubtedly, he does not succeed. Because of his awareness of the incompleteness of himself and of his poetry, he lives in the landscape of longing and the ideal. But longing moves horizontally and always flees ahead of those who yearn. He himself is here, and his unstable abode is there; hence, he is "in the wrong time and the wrong place," because although he is now standing here, the bird of his heart takes flight in the air of a different time and space. It flies off a branch from this forest, but before it returns, it journeys in the air of longing. Poetry is the "story of longing."[62] Our Hafez consoles the "lost heart,"[63] telling it that it will in the end reach its Mecca and Canaan.[64] But "protect me from this desert, this road without end!"[65] In this "story of longing," my elder is a wayfarer who will never arrive, a permanent traveler who on his way to his destination constantly passes beyond himself and his path, leaving both behind. He succeeds in *going* and is an unsuccessful wayfarer, *not arriving.* In such case, that "reed pen that is the fish," which was as powerful as fate, often remains helpless in the hand.

> The pen does not have the tongue to utter the secret of love
> The story of longing is beyond all utterance.[66]

Appendix ❁ *Notes*

Appendix

This appendix provides the original Persian of the set-off couplets in this translation, identified and alphabetized by the first line of the English translation of the couplet. Bracketed numbers in the appendix refer to ghazal numbers.

A nightingale was holding in its beak [77]

بلبلی برگ گلی خوش رنگ در منقار داشت
و اندر آن برگ و نوا خوش ناله‌های زار داشت
گفتمش در عین وصل این ناله و فریاد چیست
گفت ما را جلوه معشوق در این کار داشت

A pair of clever companions, and of old wine, a couple of stones [477]

دو یار زیرک و از باده کهن دومنی
فراغتی و کتابی و گوشه چمنی
من این مقام به دنیا و آخرت ندهم
اگر چه در پی ام افتند هر دم انجمنی

Along the path of love, indeed [125]

در ره عشق نشد کس به یقین محرم راز
هر کسی بر حسب فکر گمانی دارد

although as a *hafez* I am well-known [457]

من ار چه حافظ شهرم جوی نمی‌ارزم
مگر تو از کرم خویش یار من باشی

and till dawn [320]

نقش خیال روی تو تا وقت صبحدم
بر کارگاه دیده بی‌خواب می‌زدم

Appreciate the preciousness of time as much as you can [473]

وقت را غنیمت دان آن قدر که بتوانی
حاصل از حیات ای جان این دم است تا دانی

arise and let us dedicate our lives [77]

خیز تا بر کلک آن نقاش جان افشان کنیم

کاین همه نقش عجب در گردش پرگار داشت

Although I have been immersed a hundred ways [313]

هر چند غرق بحر گناهم ز صد جهت

تا آشنای عشق شدم ز اهل رحمتم

At dawn a cry came from the heavens [199]

صبحدم از عرش می‌آمد خروشی عقل گفت

قدسیان گویی که شعر حافظ از بر می‌کنند

At dawn, I was telling the wind the story of my longing [440]

سحر با باد می‌گفتم حدیث آرزومندی

خطاب آمد که واثق شو به الطاف خداوندی

At dawn, my good fortune came to my bedside [176]

سحرم دولت بیدار به بالین آمد

گفت برخیز که آن خسرو شیرین آمد

At dawn, the nightingale told the zephyr the story [130]

سحر بلبل حکایت با صبا کرد

که عشق روی گل با ما چه‌ها کرد

at every moment the image of your face [357]

هر دم از روی تو نقشی زندم راه خیال

با که گویم که در این پرده چه‌ها می‌بینم

Be my beloved [52]

یار من باش که زیب فلک و زینت دهر

از مه روی تو و اشک چو پروین من است

Bring wine! Qur'an reciters, clerics [200]

می خور که شیخ و حافظ و مفتی و محتسب

چون نیک بنگری همه تزویر می‌کنند

but if you are not prepared [144]

تو کز سرای طبیعت نمی‌روی بیرون

کجا به کوی طریقت گذر توانی کرد

Come, for the flourishing of this workshop [477]

بیا که رونق این کارخانه کم نشود

به زهد همچو تویی یا به فسق همچو منی

Come, let us scatter flowers [374]

بیا تا گل برافشانیم و می در ساغر اندازیم

فلک را سقف بشکافیم و طرحی نو دراندازیم

اگر غم لشکر انگیزد که خون عاشقان ریزد

من و ساقی به هم تازیم و بنیادش براندازیم

Dark night and the desert, where can one reach [117]

شب ظلمت و بیابان به کجا توان رسیدن
مگر آن که شمع رویت به رهم چراغ دارد

Do what you want, but do not pursue hurting others [76]

مباش در پی آزار و هر چه خواهی کن
که در شریعت ما غیر از این گناهی نیست

Drunkenly, let us remove the veil [375]

سر خدا که در تتق غیب منزویست
مستانه‌اش نقاب ز رخسار برکشیم

each night all night [324]

پاسبان حرم دل شده‌ام شب همه شب
تا در این پرده جز اندیشه او نگذارم

Even though covered in the dust of poverty [346]

گر چه گردآلود فقرم شرم باد از همتم
گر به آب چشمه خورشید دامن تر کنم

Even though the affairs of the world are clenched like a bud [274]

چو غنچه گر چه فروبستگیست کار جهان
تو همچو باد بهاری گره گشا می‌باش

Excited by the intoxicated narcissus eyes [379]

ز شوق نرگس مست بلندبالایی
چو لاله با قدح افتاده بر لب جویم

Fall in love, for if not, some day [435]

عاشق شو ار نه روزی کار جهان سر آید
ناخوانده نقش مقصود از کارگاه هستی

From the alley of the friend [454]

ز کوی یار می‌آید نسیم باد نوروزی
از این باد ار مدد خواهی چراغ دل برافروزی

from the dawn of time until eternity's evening [206]

از دم صبح ازل تا آخر شام ابد
دوستی و مهر بر یک عهد و یک میثاق بود

Give me wine, oh cupbearer [286]

ساقیا می ده که رندی‌های حافظ فهم کرد
آصف صاحب قران جرم بخش عیب پوش

give my futile heart the elixir it craves [248]

ای صبا نکهتی از کوی فلانی به من آر
زار و بیمار غمم راحت جانی به من آر

Hafez although we have no choice [53]

گناه اگر چه نبود اختیار ما حافظ

تو در طریق ادب باش گو گناه من است

Hafez, talk of your delightfully deceptive magic [429]

حافظ حدیث سحرفریب خوشت رسید

تا حد مصر و چین و به اطراف روم و ری

Hark! Do not despair [255]

هان مشو نومید چون واقف نه‌ای از سر غیب

باشد اندر پرده بازیهای پنهان غم مخور

how can eyes see you as you truly are [300]

تو را چنان که تویی هر نظر کجا بیند

به قدر دانش خود هر کسی کند ادراک

How can one benefit from union with the beauty of a king [428]

که بندد طرف وصل از حسن شاهی

که با خود عشق بازد جاودانه

ندیم و مطرب و ساقی همه اوست

خیال آب و گل در ره بهانه

How could we claim to be without sin in a place [489]

جایی که برق عصیان بر آدم صفی زد

ما را چگونه زیبد دعوی بی‌گناهی

How joyfully and tenderly you strut, oh young spring branch [429]

خوش نازکانه می‌چمی ای شاخ نوبهار

کشفتگی مبادت از آشوب باد دی

بر مهر چرخ و شیوه او اعتماد نیست

ای وای بر کسی که شد ایمن ز مکر وی

How long shall our hearts grieve [391]

غم دل چند توان خورد که ایام نماند

گو نه دل باش و نه ایام چه خواهد بودن

However old, incapable [321]

هر چند پیر و خسته دل و ناتوان شدم

هر گه که یاد روی تو کردم جوان شدم

Humans and spirits are dependent on the existence of love [452]

طفیل هستی عشقند آدمی و پری

ارادتی بنما تا سعادتی ببری

Humans cannot be found in the terrestrial world [470]

آدمی در عالم خاکی نمی‌آید به دست

عالمی دیگر بباید ساخت و از نو آدمی

I am a bird [317]

طایر گلشن قدسم چه دهم شرح فراق

که در این دامگه حادثه چون افتادم
من ملک بودم و فردوس برین جایم بود
آدم آورد در این دیر خراب آبادم

I am a lover, a libertine, an admirer of beauty [311]

عاشق و رند و نظربازم و می‌گویم فاش
تا بدانی که به چندین هنر آراسته‌ام

I am ashamed of my soiled robe [311]

شرمم از خرقه آلوده خود می‌آید
که بر او وصله به صد شعبده پیراسته‌ام

I am slave to he [37]

غلام همت آنم که زیر چرخ کبود
ز هر چه رنگ تعلق پذیرد آزادست

I am that magical poet [324]

منم آن شاعر ساحر که به افسون سخن
از نی کلک همه قند و شکر می‌بارم

I am the falcon on the wrist of the king [343]

شهباز دست پادشهم این چه حالت است
کز یاد برده‌اند هوای نشیمنم

I did not fall from the mosque into the tavern on my own [111]

من ز مسجد به خرابات نه خود افتادم
اینم از عهد ازل حاصل فرجام افتاد

I don't know who fired the arrow [240]

تیر عاشق کش ندانم بر دل حافظ که زد
این قدر دانم که از شعر ترش خون می‌چکید

I drink from the decanter secretly [149]

صراحی می‌کشم پنهان و مردم دفتر انگارند
عجب گر آتش این زرق در دفتر نمی‌گیرد

I have been struck by an arrow of the firmament [348]

خورده‌ام تیر فلک باده بده تا سرمست
عقده دربند کمر ترکش جوزا فکنم
جرعه جام بر این تخت روان افشانم
غلغل چنگ در این گنبد مینا فکنم

I never paid attention to the workings of the world [22]

مرا به کار جهان هرگز التفات نبود
رخ تو در نظر من چنین خوشش آراست

I offered both worlds to my experienced heart [48]

عرضه کردم دو جهان بر دل کارافتاده

بجز از عشق تو باقی همه فانی دانست

I shall not lament your absence [254]

از دست غیبت تو شکایت نمی‌کنم

تا نیست غیبتی نبود لذت حضور

I uprooted the silhouette of that spruce fir [146]

من آن شکل صنوبر را ز باغ دیده برکندم

که هر گل کز غمش بشکفت محنت بار می‌آورد

if ever the breeze of union with you [234]

نسیم زلف تو چون بگذرد به تربت حافظ

ز خاک کالبدش صد هزار لاله برآید

If my wounded heart has any aspirations [492]

دل خسته من گرش همتی هست

نخواهد ز سنگین دلان مومیایی

If one night [334]

گر خلوت ما را شبی از رخ بفروزی

چون صبح بر آفاق جهان سر بفرازم

If the wind of calamity casts chaos into both worlds [60]

گر باد فتنه هر دو جهان را به هم زند

ما و چراغ چشم و ره انتظار دوست

If you go to the heavens [407]

گر روی پاک و مجرد چو مسیحا به فلک

از چراغ تو به خورشید رسد صد پرتو

If you must have sunlight at midnight, cast off the veil [263]

به نیمشب اگرت آفتاب می‌باید

ز روی دختر گلچهر رز نقاب انداز

If your heart is about to burst [263]

ز جور چرخ چو حافظ به جان رسید دلت

به سوی دیو محن ناوک شهاب انداز

In that time without beginning [371]

سلطان ازل گنج غم عشق به ما داد

تا روی در این منزل ویرانه نهادیم

in the beauty of your face [90]

در روی خود تفرج صنع خدای کن

کآیینهٔ خدای نما می‌فرستمت

In the time before time began [152]

در ازل پرتو حسنت ز تجلی دم زد

عشق پیدا شد و آتش به همه عالم زد

in the time of Adam in the garden of Eden [206]

شعر حافظ در زمان آدم اندر باغ خلد

دفتر نسرین و گل را زینت اوراق بود

it has grown dark within [483]

درون‌ها تیره شد باشد که از غیب

چراغی برکند خلوت نشینی

Last night in my sleep I dreamed that a moon had risen [439]

دیدم به خواب دوش که ماهی برآمدی

کز عکس روی او شب هجران سر آمدی

Last night the wine-seller [286]

دوش با من گفت پنهان کاردانی تیزهوش

وز شما پنهان نشاید کرد سر می فروش

Like a bird, I flew out of the terrestrial cage [335]

مرغ سان از قفس خاک هوایی گشتم

به هوایی که مگر صید کند شهبازم

Like a cypress, gleefully [355]

سر به آزادگی از خلق برآرم چون سرو

گر دهد دست که دامن ز جهان درچینم

like Jamshid drink from that visionary cup [488]

همچو جم جرعه ما کش که ز سر دو جهان

پرتو جام جهان بین دهدت آگاهی

Look at these conditions, I said [470]

زیرکی را گفتم این احوال بین خندید و گفت

صعب روزی بوالعجب کاری پریشان عالمی

Love arises from a hidden subtlety [66]

لطیفه‌ایست نهانی که عشق از او خیزد

که نام آن نه لب لعل و خط زنگاریست

Might I go mad in this passion, since from night to day [356]

مگر دیوانه خواهم شد در این سودا که شب تا روز

سخن با ماه می‌گویم پری در خواب می‌بینم

My body's dust is as a veil [342]

حجاب چهره جان می‌شود غبار تنم

خوشا دمی که از آن چهره پرده برفکنم

My whole heart and being became so filled with the friend [332]

چنان پر شد فضای سینه از دوست

که فکر خویش گم شد از ضمیرم

No friendship is seen in anyone [169]

یاری اندر کس نمی‌بینیم یاران را چه شد
دوستی کی آخر آمد دوستداران را چه شد
آب حیوان تیره گون شد خضر فرخ پی کجاست
خون چکید از شاخ گل باد بهاران را چه شد
کس نمی‌گوید که یاری داشت حق دوستی
حق شناسان را چه حال افتاد یاران را چه شد
لعلی از کان مروت برنیامد سال‌هاست
تابش خورشید و سعی باد و باران را چه شد
شهر یاران بود و خاک مهربانان این دیار
مهربانی کی سر آمد شهریاران را چه شد
گوی توفیق و کرامت در میان افکنده‌اند
کس به میدان در نمی‌آید سواران را چه شد
صد هزاران گل شکفت و بانگ مرغی برنخاست
عندلیبان را چه پیش آمد هزاران را چه شد
زهره سازی خوش نمی‌سازد مگر عودش بسوخت
کس ندارد ذوق مستی میگساران را چه شد
حافظ اسرار الهی کس نمی‌داند خموش
از که می‌پرسی که دور روزگاران را چه شد

No matter which way I went, my fear only increased [94]

از هر طرف که رفتم جز وحشتم نیفزود
زنهار از این بیابان وین راه بی‌نهایت

no one profits from the market of life [440]

در این بازار اگر سودیست با درویش خرسند است
خدایا منعمم گردان به درویشی و خرسندی

Not only today do we drink wine [243]

ما می به بانگ چنگ نه امروز می‌کشیم
بس دور شد که گنبد چرخ این صدا شنید

Nurturing the thought of having the capacity of the sea [290]

خیال حوصله بحر می‌پزد هیهات
چه‌هاست در سر این قطره محال اندیش

O Hafez, on the last day, if you bear [80]

حافظا روز اجل گر به کف آری جامی
یک سر از کوی خرابات برندت به بهشت

O knowing heart how long will you have to know [436]

تا کی غم دنیای دنی ای دل دانا
حیف است ز خوبی که شود عاشق زشتی

O morning breeze, abet me now, tonight, because [42]

ای صبا امشبم مدد فرمای
که سحرگه شکفتنم هوس است

O selfishness! Leave me, you greedy thing [492]

مرا گر تو بگذاری ای نفس طامع
بسی پادشایی کنم در گدایی

O tie a cup to my shroud [266]

پیاله بر کفنم بند تا سحرگه حشر
به می ز دل ببرم هول روز رستاخیز

Oh Hafez, drink wine, be a clever libertine, and rejoice [9]

حافظا می خور و رندی کن و خوش باش ولی
دام تزویر مکن چون دگران قرآن را

one cannot find the precious pearl alone [234]

به سعی خود نتوان برد پی به گوهر مقصود
خیال باشد کاین کار بی حواله برآید

Our elder said that the creator's pen made no error [105]

پیر ما گفت خطا بر قلم صنع نرفت
آفرین بر نظر پاک خطاپوشش باد

Paradise, the shade of its Tuba tree [353]

باغ بهشت و سایه طوبی و قصر و حور
با خاک کوی دوست برابر نمی‌کنم

Purely because of his love for you, Hafez became [24]

حافظ از دولت عشق تو سلیمانی شد
یعنی از وصل تواش نیست به جز باد به دست

Rise and display your stature, oh graceful idol [336]

خیز و بالا بنما ای بت شیرین حرکات
کز سر جان و جهان دست فشان برخیزم

Seek success under conditions that are contrary to custom [319]

در خلاف آمد عادت بطلب کام که من
کسب جمعیت از آن زلف پریشان کردم

since poets first used their pens [184]

کس چو حافظ نگشاد از رخ اندیشه نقاب
تا سر زلف سخن را به قلم شانه زدند

Since the sorrow of love for you [368]

چون غمت را نتوان یافت مگر در دل شاد
ما به امید غمت خاطر شادی طلبیم

So what if the Magian elder became my spiritual leader? [69]

گر پیر مغان مرشد من شد چه تفاوت

در هیچ سری نیست که سری ز خدا نیست

Speak to me of minstrels and wine [3]

حدیث از مطرب و می گو و راز دهر کمتر جو
که کس نگشود و نگشاید به حکمت این معما را

Strive to be truthful [28]

به صدق کوش که خورشید زاید از نفست
که از دروغ سیه روی گشت صبح نخست

the angel kneeling before Adam [474]

ملک در سجده آدم زمین بوس تو نیت کرد
که در حسن تو لطفی دید بیش از حد انسانی

The army of tyranny rules from shore to shore [49]

از کران تا به کران لشکر ظلم است ولی
از ازل تا به ابد فرصت درویشان است

The bird of my soul that sang from the Lote tree [310]

مرغ روحم که همی‌زد ز سر سدره صفیر
عاقبت دانهٔ خال تو فکندش در دام

The city is devoid of lovers [189]

شهر خالیست ز عشاق بود کز طرفی
مردی از خویش برون آید و کاری بکند

The flaming torch of the sun [87]

زین آتش نهفته که در سینه من است
خورشید شعله‌ایست که در آسمان گرفت

The pen does not have the tongue to utter the secret of love [440]

قلم را آن زبان نبود که سر عشق گوید باز
ورای حد تقریر است شرح آرزومندی

The story of longing as recorded in this book [354]

حدیث آرزومندی که در این نامه ثبت افتاد
همانا بی‌غلط باشد که حافظ داد تلقینم

There is a vast difference between the lover and the beloved [244]

میان عاشق و معشوق فرق بسیار است
چو یار ناز نماید شما نیاز کنید

There is no end to the story of me and the beloved [310]

ماجرای من و معشوق مرا پایان نیست
هر چه آغاز ندارد نپذیرد انجام

They call you from the empyrean pinnacle [37]

تو را ز کنگره عرش می‌زنند صفیر
ندانمت که در این دامگه چه افتادست

to me the air of my beloved's house [333]

هوای منزل یار آب زندگانی ماست
صبا بیار نسیمی ز خاک شیرازم

to spend time in the company [232]

هوای منزل یار آب زندگانی ماست
صبا بیار نسیمی ز خاک شیرازم

To use the lashes of my eyes, for honor's sake [42]

از برای شرف به نوک مژه
خاک راه تو رفتنم هوس است

Veils are removed from the earth and the heavens [187]

ز ملک تا ملکوتش حجاب بردارند
هر آن که خدمت جام جهان نما بکند

Venus's odes will not flourish [258]

زل سرایی ناهید صرفه‌ای نبرد
در آن مقام که حافظ برآورد آواز

We saw the fresh beauty of your face and came [366]

سبزه خط تو دیدیم و ز بستان بهشت
به طلبکاری این مهرگیاه آمده‌ایم

What is the heart's purpose [393]

مراد دل ز تماشای باغ عالم چیست
به دست مردم چشم از رخ تو گل چیدن

What kind of sugar is there in this city [455]

چه شکرهاست در این شهر که قانع شده‌اند
شاهبازان طریقت به مقام مگسی

When I am with you, a year seems a day [464]

آن دم که با تو باشم یک سال هست روزی
وان دم که بی تو باشم یک لحظه هست سالی

When I bring the reed pen that is the fish to write ["The Wild Deer"]

چو من ماهی کلک آرم به تحریر
تو از نون والقلم می‌پرس تفسیر

When the spring cloud saw [454]

رسم بدعهدی ایام چو دید ابر بهار
گریه‌اش بر سمن و سنبل و نسرین آمد

Whenever I desire to see my soul [347]

آن زمان کآرزوی دیدن جانم باشد
در نظر نقش رخ خوب تو تصویر کنم

Whosoever is not alive through love in this circle [244]

هر آن کسی که در این حلقه نیست زنده به عشق
بر او نمرده به فتوای من نماز کنید

Why let the world upset you? Why, and for how long? [159]

غم دنیای دنی چند خوری باده بخور
حیف باشد دل دانا که مشوش باشد

Why would one who has chosen seclusion need sights to see? [33]

خلوت گزیده را به تماشا چه حاجت است
چون کوی دوست هست به صحرا چه حاجت است

Wish for the spring of life, oh heart [115]

بهار عمر خواه ای دل وگرنه این چمن هر سال
چو نسرین صد گل آرد بار و چون بلبل هزار آرد

With your scent, like the rose, at every moment [389]

چو گل هر دم به بویت جامه در تن
کنم چاک از گریبان تا به دامن
تنت را دید گل گویی که در باغ
چو مستان جامه را بدرید بر تن
من از دست غمت مشکل برم جان
ولی دل را تو آسان بردی از من

You are not less than an atom [387]

کمتر از ذره نه‌ای پست مشو مهر بورز
تا به خلوتگه خورشید رسی چرخ زنان

You said that our Hafez reeks of hypocrisy [485]

گفتی از حافظ ما بوی ریا می‌آید
آفرین بر نفست باد که خوش بردی بوی

Your love will come to the rescue, if you, like Hafez [94]

عشقت رسد به فریاد ار خود به سان حافظ
قرآن ز بر بخوانی در چارده روایت

Notes

Translator's Introduction

1. Readers familiar with the books of the late renowned scholar Ali Dashti, who wrote about several major Persian classical poets based mainly on his personal and intellectual experience with their poetry, might find Meskoob's book to be similar to Dashti's 1957 *Naqshi az Hafez* (Tehran: Amir Kabir Publishers, 1978). The resemblance, however, is superficial, since while Dashti writes "about" Hafez and his poetry, Meskoob submerges himself in the ghazals intellectually, spiritually, and emotionally to experience that which the poet has experienced.

2. In the ghazals, Hafez's first-person speaker is sometimes the singular *I* and often the plural *we*. This usage also adds to the inherent ambiguity of the poems. Translators often render the plural persona as singular.

3. From personal correspondence in March 2016. I had just begun translating this book and was not happy with my rendition of the first chapter, when I found that Geoffrey Squires had won the Lois Roth Translation Prize for his translations of Hafez's ghazals. When I contacted him after more than fifty years and shared my concerns about the work I was doing, he was traveling but kind enough to send this enlightening response.

4. For example, see Dick Davis, "On Not Translating Hafez," *The New England Review* 25, no. 1, 2: 310–18.

5. Dick Davis, trans. *Faces of Love: Hafez and the Poets of Shiraz* (New York: Penguin, 2013).

6. Geoffrey Squires, trans. *Hafez: Translations and Interpretations of the Ghazals* (Miami: Miami University Press, 2014).

7. In my original translation, I had quoted extensively from Davis's translations. Unfortunately, however, due to disallowance by the private business establishment that holds the copyright to his translations, I had to substantially curtail my use of quotations from Davis's work.

8. Robert Bly and Leonard Lewisohn, trans. *The Angels Knocking at the Door: Thirty Poems of Hafez* (New York: HarperCollins Publishers, 2008).

9. Mohammad Qazvini and Qasem Ghani, eds. *Divan-e Hafez* (Tehran: Amir Kabir Publishers, 1969). The only English translation based on this edition that includes all the ghazals with the numbers that correspond to the original as well as Meskoob's text is by Reza Saberi, *The Poems of Hafez* (Lanham MD: University Press of America, 1984). Saberi's translations are extremely literal and even then, they are not error free.

10. Parviz Natel-Khanlari, *Divan-e Ghazaliyyat-e Hafez*, 2nd printing (Tehran: Nil Publishers, 1983).

11. For these and many other terms in Hafez's poetry see the entry, *Encyclopaedia Iranica*, s.v. "Hafez viii. Hafez and Rendi," by Franklin Lewis, http://www.iranicaonline.org/articles/hafez-viii.

12. Khanlari's edition of Hafez's poems is also available online.

13. Shahrokh Meskoob, *Goftogu dar Bagh* (Tehran: Bagh-e Ayeneh Publishers, 1992).

14. M. R. Ghanoonparvar, *Translating the Garden* (Austin: The University of Texas Press, 2001).

15. Ali Banuazizi, *Karnameh-ye Natamam: Darbareh-ye Siyasat va Farhang* (Paris: Khavaran Publications, 1994).

Foreword

1. A ghazal is usually a love poem consisting of between seven and twelve couplets. The entire poem has the same meter, and the second hemistich of every couplet has the same rhyme as the first couplet, both hemistiches of which are rhymed. A ghazal is somewhat similar to the English sonnet.

2. From ghazal 20 by Sa'di.

3. Modified line from ghazal 39. The phrase comes from the following couplet: "The sorrow of love is no more than one tale, astonishing that / No matter from whose tongue I hear, it is not repeated."

4. The quoted phrase is a variation of a segment of the following couplet by Sheykh Mahmud Shabestari: "The world is like tresses, down, a mole, and eyebrows / Each of which is fine where it is." The couplet is found in his *Golshan-e Raz* (*The Mystic Rose Garden*). For more information on *The Mystic Rose Garden*, see endnote 6 in the chapter, "My Rose-Colored Elder." Meskoob's reference is also possibly to ghazal 287. The couplet from this ghazal is translated by Squires, as follows:

> sweet your airs and graces
> comely your mole and down
> beautiful your eyes and your brow
> your stature and bearing fine.
> (Squires, *Hafez*, 234)

From This Hidden Fire . . .

From ghazal 87. The title comes from the couplet that is translated as follows:

The flaming torch of the sun
that rises in the eastern sky
is lit from the hidden fire inside my breast.
(Geoffrey Squires, trans. *Hafez: Translations and Interpretations of the Ghazals* [Miami: Miami University Press, 2014], 419)

1. From ghazal 144. The couplet that contains the phrase is translated by Squires as:

but if you are not prepared
to abandon the house of nature
how can you embark on the spiritual way.
(Squires, 336)

2. From ghazal 342. The phrase "shackled frame of the body" comes from the following couplet: "How can I soar in the celestial air / When trapped in the shackled frame of the body?" Squires translates the couplet as follows:

how can I range like a bird
in the air of paradise
when my body is trapped in contingency
like a prisoner nailed to a board.
(Squires, 333)

For another translation, see Dick Davis, trans. *Faces of Love: Hafez and the Poets of Shiraz* (New York: Penguin, 2013), 124.

3. From ghazal 184. Squires translates the couplets that Meskoob paraphrases in the paragraph as follows:

Last night I dreamed that the angels
were beating at the tavern gate
kneading Adam's clay
they made measures out of it

the hidden seraphims
the purest of the pure
sat down and drank with me
who beg from door to door

and as "God be thanked that now / there is peace between Him and me." Squires, 356. See also Davis, 40, for the translation the same couplets.

4. From ghazal 184. The couplet paraphrased by Meskoob also appears in Robert Bly and Leonard Lewisohn, trans. *The Angels Knocking at the Door: Thirty Poems of Hafez* (New York: HarperCollins Publishers, 2008), 39.

5. Paraphrase of a couplet from ghazal 290. The quoted segment is from the following couplet in this ghazal: "Nurturing the thought of having the capacity of the sea, alas / What is in the mind of this droplet that dreams the impossible?"

6. From ghazal 184. For a different translation, see Bly and Lewisohn, *The Angels Knocking*, 39.

7. From ghazal 184. Translated in Davis, *Faces of Love*, 41. Squires translates the couplet as follows:

Since poets first used their pens
to comb the tresses of speech
no one like Hafez has unveiled
the complexion of our minds.
(Squires, *Hafez*, 356)

See also Bly and Lewisohn, 40.

8. From ghazal 206. The quoted segment comes from a couplet that Squires translates as follows:

if the shadow of the loved one fell upon us lovers
what does it matter
for we wanted him and he was filled with desire.
(Squires, 253)

9. "Ostad-e Azal" or "master of eternal beginning," meaning God. From ghazal 380. Squires translates the phrase as "eternal Master" in the following couplet from this ghazal:

I am like a parrot placed behind a mirror
what the eternal Master tells me to say   I say.
(Squires, 292)

10. "Angel of good tidings" is my translation of Sorush, who is a special guardian angel in Zoroastrianism.

11. Khezr is a mythical figure dressed in green, a prophet or saint character in Iranian and Islamic mystic tradition, who is associated with Elijah, is believed to have drunk the water of life, the fountain of youth, and is believed to remain alive until the end of time. For a brief historical account of Khezr, see Oliver Leaman, ed., *The Qur'an: An Encyclopedia* (New York: Routledge, 2006), 343–45.

12. From ghazal 483. Squires, *Hafez*, 295.

13. From ghazal 37. The phrase is from Squires's translation, found in the following couplet:

I am slave to he
whose spiritual vocation
is untainted by any lingering attachments
under these wheeling heavens
the velvet blue of the night-sky.
(Squires, 323)

14. From ghazal 37. The phrase translated here as "invisible realm" is contained in the couplet translated as "invisible world." Bly and Lewisohn, *The Angels Knocking*, 29.

15. From ghazals 19, 188, 345, and 373. Reference to Moses in the Sinai desert. The couplet from ghazal 19 is: "The night is dark and the path to the Sinai desert, ahead / Where is the fire on Mount Sinai and when the appointed time for meeting?" The couplet in ghazal 188 from which it is taken is as follows: "The shepherd of the Sinai desert sometimes attains his purpose / When he serves Jethro wholeheartedly for several years." The couplet from ghazal 345 is: "If the fire of Mount Sinai does not help me with the light / What am I to do with the dark night of the Sinai desert?" The couplet from ghazal 373 is:

O You with whom we sealed that covenant
in the valley of faith
let us bring it like Moses to the appointed place
saying   show your face.
(Squires, *Hafez*, 302)

In this couplet, Squires translates *vadi-ye iman*, which I have translated in the previous couplets as "Sinai desert," as "valley of faith."

16. From ghazal 187. The phrase "the cup that reveals the universe" here is a translation of *jam-e jahan nema*, which is the same as *jam-e jam* or *jam-e Jamshid*. The couplet from ghazal 187 in which it appears is: "Veils are removed from the earth and the heavens / For anyone who serves the cup that reveals the universe." See also the couplet from ghazal 143, which is translated by Davis, *Faces of Love*, 42.

17. Meaning "water of life." For Khezr and "water of life," see endnote 11 above.

18. From ghazal 232. Squires translates the couplet that contains the quoted line as follows:

to spend time in the company
of those in authority
is like the longest of long nights

pray for the light of the sun
that it may rise again
(Squires, *Hafez*, 207)

19. From ghazal 467. The quoted phrase is from the following couplet: "I will not complain about the ill-tempered ascetic, it is inevitable that / Every morning that dawns is followed by evening."

20. From ghazal 178. The quoted phrase comes from the following couplet: "The morals police chief became a high priest and forgot his own debauchery / It is only my story that is told at every marketplace." *Mohtaseb*, translated here as "morals police chief," is a possible reference to Amir Mobarezeddin, who up to the age of forty drank wine, but then became religious and imposed restrictions on the people.

21. From ghazal 313. The quoted phrase is translated as "the shadows of confusion" in the following couplet: "and with your bright cup that overflows with joy / lead me out of the shadows of confusion." Squires, *Hafez*, 96.

22. Persian literature, especially mystic literature, contains stories about Alexander of Macedonia, who accompanied by Khezr (see endnote 11) went to the Land of Darkness in search of the water of life (fountain of youth). Among other sources, this legend is told in Ferdowsi's *Book of Kings* and Nezami's twelfth-century *Eskandarnameh*. For an English translation of Nezami's work, see Minoo S. Southgate, trans. *Iskandarnamah: A Persian Medieval Alexander-Romance* (New York: Columbia University Press, 1978).

23. From ghazal 1. Reference to a couplet from this ghazal is available in Davis, *Faces of Love*, 10.

24. From ghazal 439. Squires, *Hafez*, 82.

25. From ghazal 183. The couplet containing the phrase I have translated as "blissful dawn" is translated by Davis as "O dawn of Fortune." Davis, *Faces of Love*, 44. Squires translates the couplet as:

how blessed that morning   and how happy
that night of destiny   when I was set free.
(Squires, 349)

26. From ghazal 488. The couplet paraphrased by Meskoob is translated as:

Dawn   in the tavern   and the mysterious voice
that acts as my guide   said

come back again   you that for so long
have frequented this place
and like Jamshid drink from the visionary cup
whose rays disclose the secrets of heaven and earth.
(Squires, 325)

27. From ghazal 182. For an English translation of the quoted couplets containing part of what Meskoob has paraphrased, see Davis, *Faces of Love*, 67.

28. From ghazal 183. The phrase "from the shackles of life's sorrows" is from the following couplet: "It was Hafez's aspiration and the breath of the risers at dawn / That saved me from the shackles of life's sorrows." The couplet is also translated by Davis, 44. Squires translates the same couplet as follows:

through faith
and the breath of those who rise to pray at dawn
I have been freed from the grievous bonds of time.
(Squires, *Hafez*, 349)

The quoted hemistich is from Davis, 44. Squires translates the couplet as:

Last night   before dawn   I knew deliverance
in the darkness I was given the Water of Life.
(Squires, 349)

29. Hafez is often referred to as Lesan ol-Gheyb (the Tongue of the Invisible).

30. From ghazal 381. The quoted phrase is from the couplet translated as follows:

> Although I am a servant of the king
> when I say my morning prayers
> I am monarch of the kingdom of dawn.
> (Squires, *Hafez*, 190)

31. From ghazal 176. The phrase I have translated as "the beloved king" in Persian is "khosrow-e shirin," which could also be an allusion to Nezami's romance narrative poem, *Khosrow and Shirin*.

32. Phrases from ghazals 33 and 6. Squires translates the couplet from ghazal 33, which includes the phrase I have translated as "chosen seclusion," as:

> What need have I of society
> when I have you
>
> why should I want company
> when I can be alone with you
>
> why should I criss-cross the desert
> when I know where you dwell
>
> why should I beg when I am in
> the very presence of munificence.
> (Squires, *Hafez*, 368)

See also Bly and Lewisohn, *The Angels Knocking*, 37–38.

33. Paraphrase of the first couplet of ghazal 183. See endnote 28 above.

34. From ghazal 381. Squires, *Hafez*, 190.

35. From ghazal 111. For another translation of the couplet containing the quoted segment, see Bly and Lewisohn, *The Angels Knocking*, 57.

36. From ghazal 183. The couplet that contains the quoted line is translated as:

> for turning my face towards the mirror of beauty
> I saw what it was there   that was true.
> (Squires, *Hafez*, 349)

See also Davis, *Faces of Love*, 44.

37. From ghazal 90. Squires, 13.

38. Jamshid was the legendary Persian king who is credited with the invention of wine and many other things that made life more comfortable and secure for his people. See Rudi Mathee, "Wine and Wine Drinking in Iran (Persia)" in M. R. Ghanoonparvar, *Traditional, Regional, and Modern Foods* (Costa Mesa, CA: Mazda Publishers, 2006), 260–65.

39. From ghazal 187.

40. Keykhosrow was a legendary king of Persia who appears in Ferdowsi's *Book of Kings*.

41. Paraphrase from ghazal 143. The couplet paraphrased by Meskoob is translated by Davis, *Faces of Love*, 42, and by Bly and Lewisohn, *The Angels Knocking*, 27.

42. This line is from a poem in praise of wine (qasideh no. 49) by the eleventh-century Persian poet, Manuchehri-Damghani.

43. From ghazal 116. A rather literal translation of the couplet that Meskoob paraphrases is: "If wine has no other benefit for you, it is enough / that, for a moment, it makes one unaware of the temptations of reason."

44. Paraphrase of the first couplet from ghazal 129. My translation of this couplet is: "If not for wine that makes our heart forget its sorrow, / the dread of events would uproot our foundation."

45. From ghazal 278. Squires, *Hafez*, 83.

46. Perhaps a reference to ghazal 423. Squires translates the couplet that contains the quoted phrase as:

> in your lust for the lips of young boys
> how long will you go on
> staining the pure jewel of the spirit
> with liquid ruby
> (Squires, 93)

See also Bly and Lewisohn, *The Angels Knocking*, 5.

47. Reference to the following couplet from ghazal 90:

> in the beauty of your face   admire God's handiwork
> in the mirror of my heart   behold the divine.
> (Squires, 13)

48. This segment is a paraphrase of ghazal 111, including the following couplets:

> When the image of your face
> was reflected in the wine
> the laughing cup sent the seer wild with desire
>
> since the very first day
> when you appeared veiled before mankind
> people have perceived only the mirror of illusion.
> (Squires, 103)

For another translation of the same couplets, see Bly and Lewisohn, *The Angels Knocking*, 57.

49. From ghazal 119. The couplet that contains the quoted line is as follows: "The heart that reveals the unseen and holds the cup of Jamshid / What care does it have if a precious stone is lost for a moment?"

50. From ghazal 263.

51. From ghazal 263.

52. From ghazal 348.

53. From ghazal 263. This is a reference to the above-quoted couplet: "If you must have sunlight at midnight, cast off the veil / From the rosy face of the daughter of the vine."

54. From Hafez's poem, "Saqinameh." *Saqinameh* is a term that refers to poems addressed to a *saqi*, or a cupbearer, involving themes such as death and the transiency of the world. This is a paraphrase from the following couplet in this poem: "Cupbearer, give me the wine from which the cup of Jamshid / Boasts of sight in nonexistence."

55. From ghazal 266. Squires, *Hafez*, 153. See also Davis, *Faces of Love*, 111.

56. From ghazal 111. The couplet that contains the quoted line is also translated in Bly and Lewisohn, *The Angels Knocking*, 57.

57. From ghazal 232. Squires translates the couplet that contains the quoted line as follows:

> the theater of the heart
> has no room for adversaries
> when the devil leaves the angel makes its entry.
> (Squires, *Hafez*, 207)

58. From ghazal 37. See also Bly and Lewisohn, *The Angels Knocking*, 29.

59. From ghazal 263. A translation of the couplet to which Meskoob refers is as follows: "When your heart aches from the cruelty of the wheel of time, Hafez / Shoot an arrow of a meteor at the demon of suffering."

60. From ghazal 218. The couplet to which Meskoob refers is as follows: "Without the lamp of the cup, I cannot rest in seclusion / Because the people of the heart's corner must be illuminated."

61. From ghazal 234. Squires's translation of the couplet that is paraphrased by Meskoob is as follows:

> As the sun of wine rises in the east of the cup
> the cheeks of the serving-boy
> bloom like a garden of tulips.
> (Squires, *Hafez*, 100)

62. From ghazal 413. Paraphrase of the following couplets: "The down of the beloved's face that eclipsed the moon / is a beautiful ring, of which there is no way out" and "Oh cup-bearer, bring the lamp of wine on the path of the sun / And let it light the torch of morning."

63. From ghazal 488. Squires, *Hafez*, 325.

64. From ghazal 488. Squires's translation of the verse paraphrased by Meskoob is as follows: "do not venture this far without Khezr your guide / for fear of losing your way in the dark." Squires, 325.

65. From ghazal 149. The couplet from which the quoted phrase is taken is: "The lovers have such joy with his ruby wine since / it holds no engraved image other than truthfulness."

66. From ghazal 28. The entire couplet from which this line is quoted is: "Strive to be truthful and the sun will be born from your breath / For the false dawn's face was blackened from falsehood."

67. This is a reference to a ghazal that is not included in the Qazvini and Ghani edition of the *Divan*. In Davis's translation it begins with the following couplet: "Good news, my heart! The breath of Christ is wafting here / Its sweetness brings the scent of One who'll soon appear." Davis, *Faces of Love*, 69.

68. From ghazal 488. In Iranian ancient popular mythology, it was believed that the earth is held by the horns of a bull that stands on the top of a fish. See Sadeq Hedayat, *Neyrangestan*, 3rd ed. (Tehran: Amir Kabir Publishers, 1963), 171. The couplet summarized by Meskoob appears in Squires's translation as follows:

> O heart if you are granted
> the suzerainty of poverty
> the smallest of your provinces will extend
> from the moon to the earth's foundations.
> (Squires, *Hafez*, 325)

69. Simorgh is a benevolent, Iranian, mythical bird of enormous size that appears in many works of art and literature. For more detail, see the entry in *Encyclopaedia Iranica*, s.v. "simorg," http://www.iranicaonline.org/articles/simorg.

70. Paraphrase of two couplets from ghazal 488, which are translated as follows:

> but my Lord
> what do you know of poverty
> do not give up the privileges you enjoy
> at the court of Turanshah
> Hafez
> have you no shame at this display of greed
> what have you done
> to ask for this and the next world as reward
> (Squires, *Hafez*, 325)

71. From ghazal 199. The Persian verb, *mokhammar mikonand*, translated here as "leaven," also means "ferment." See also Davis, *Faces of Love*, 79 for a translation of the couplet that is paraphrased here by Meskoob.

72. From ghazal 428. The couplet from which the quoted phrase is taken is as follows: "Bring the ship of wine, so that we may ride happily / Away from this sea whose shores are invisible."

73. From ghazal 313. The quoted phrase is translated as "bright cup" in the following rendition of the couplet: "and with your bright cup that overflows with joy / lead me out of the shadows of confusion." Squires, *Hafez*, 96.

74. From ghazal 405. The couplet from which this phrase is taken is: "Should you find a head on the threshold of the tavern / Do not kick it, for his intentions are not clear."

75. From ghazal 196. The phrase comes from the following couplet: "Those who turn dust into gold with a glance / For them to look our way, is there a chance?"

76. From ghazal 357. Squires, *Hafez*, 101.

77. From ghazals 27 and 490. The couplet that contains the phrase "monastery of the Magi" from ghazal 27 is as follows: "Into the monastery of the Magi came my beloved with goblet in hand / Drunk from wine, and the wine drinkers drunk from her drunken narcissus eyes." Squires translates the same phrase as "the temple of wine" in his rendition:

> I drink in your drunken eyes
> as drunk you make your entrance
> to the temple of wine.
> (Squires, 404)

The phrase also appears in the following couplet from ghazal 490: "In all the monastery of the Magi, no one is as frenzied as I am / With my robe pawned somewhere and my wine and notebook, somewhere else." Squires translates the same couplet as:

> In all these ruined Temples
> there is no one as foolish as me
> who has pawned his gown one place
> and his notebook somewhere else.
> (Squires, 297)

78. From ghazal 144. The couplet that contains the phrase is translated as:

> but if you are not prepared
> to abandon the house of nature
> how can you embark on the spiritual way.
> (Squires, 336)

79. From Hafez's poem, "Ahu-ye Vahshi" (The Wild Deer). The quoted phrase is found in the following couplet from this poem: "Beside a spring, by a stream / With moist eyes in a conversation with the self."

80. From ghazal 357. The couplet that contains the quoted paraphrased phrase is translated as follows:

> In this ruined Magian den
> I see the light of the divine
> strange   this light   and that I perceive it
> here of all places.
> (Squires, *Hafez*, 101)

81. *Hafez* means "memorizer" (of the Koran).

82. From ghazal 199. Davis, *Faces of Love*, 78.

83. The Persian is *foruharha*, meaning Essences in Zoroastrianism.

84. In ancient Peripatetic philosophy, that which is issued from God's essence for the first time.

85. From ghazal 69.

86. From ghazal 177. The quoted phrase is from the following couplet: "I am a slave to the aspirations of that clever libertine who disregards consequences / And who, even though a beggar, knows how to make gold."

87. From ghazal 184. For a translation of the paraphrased couplet, see Davis, *Faces of Love*, 40. Squires translates the same couplet as:

> there is some excuse for
> the unending wars of religion
> for unable to see reality
> people cling to illusion.
> (Squires, *Hafez*, 356)

88. From ghazal 173. The quoted phrase is from the following couplet: "The plant temptresses all adorned themselves / It is only our beloved who came with God-given beauty."

My Rose-Colored Elder . . .

From ghazal 203. The title of this chapter is taken from the following couplet: "My rose-colored elder, regarding the blue attired / Gave me no chance; else there were stories to be told."

1. From ghazal 39. The phrase comes from the following couplet: "The sorrow of love is no more than one tale, astonishing that / No matter from whose tongue I hear, it is not repeated."

2. From ghazal 310.

3. From ghazal 193. The quoted line is from the following couplet: "The worldly wise are the pivot of the compass of existence, but / Love knows that they are bewildered within this circle." Squires translates this couplet as:

> reason would suggest
> that we are the pivot of the compass
> but love knows we are spinning round.
> (Geoffrey Squires, trans. *Hafez: Translations and Interpretations of the Ghazals* [Miami: Miami University Press, 2014], 305)

4. From ghazal 452. The quoted phrase is from the following couplet: "Humans and spirits are dependent on the existence of love / Devote yourself to love to enjoy its bliss."

5. From ghazal 127. Squires translates this line as: "have you ever seen a mirror not clouded with sighs." Squires, *Hafez*, 262.

6. In Persian, *Golshan-e Raz* is a collection of poems written by the fourteenth-century Persian mystic Mahmud Shabestari. For an English translation and commentary online see E. H. Whinfield, trans. *Gulshan I Raz: The Mystic Rose Garden*, Internet Archive, http://www.archive.org/stream/gulshanirazmysti00shabuoft/gulshanirazmysti00shabuoft_djvu.txt.

7. From ghazal 286. Dick Davis, trans. *Faces of Love: Hafez and the Poets of Shiraz* (New York: Penguin, 2013), 100.

8. From ghazal 317. The quoted phrase is rendered as "bird from paradise." Davis, 114.

9. "Old wolf" is a reference to the world. From the following consecutive couplets in Hafez's poem, "Saqinameh":

Come, cupbearer, bring me that juice that burns the mind
That would make the lion burn the forest, should he drink it
Give it to me, that I may go to the firmament as a lion-catcher
To turn the trap of this old wolf upside down.

10. From ghazal 126. The phrase "beauty of the beloved" comes from the following couplet in this ghazal: "Without the beauty of the beloved, the soul does not desire the world / Anyone who does not have this truly does not have that."

11. From ghazal 286. The phrase "to your health" is from the following couplet: "Then he handed me a cup from the brightness of which in the heavens / Venus began to dance and play the harp, cheering 'to your health.'" See also Davis, *Faces of Love*, 100.

12. For the most part, this segment is a paraphrase of ghazal 286.

13. The quoted line is from the following couplet: "Heed my advice, son, be not sad about the world / I gave you a pearl of wisdom, if you are able to grasp it." See also Davis, *Faces of Love*, 100.

14. From the following couplet from ghazal 18 by Sa'di: "Eating, sleeping, anger, and carnal desire mean chaos, ignorance, and darkness / Animals have no knowledge of the world of humankind."

15. From ghazal 286. See also Davis, *Faces of Love*, 101. "Imperial monarch" (*sahabqeran* in Persian) is rendered as "the Lord of Time" in Davis's translation.

16. From ghazal 159. The quoted line is from the following couplet: "One raised in affluence will not find his way to the friend / Being in love is the manner of clever libertines who can withstand calamity." See also Davis, *Faces of Love*, 68.

17. Reference to the couplet from ghazal 286 cited above.

18. From ghazal 94. The phrase "guiding star" comes from the following couplet: "In this dark night of mine, I have lost my way / Come into view from where you are, oh guiding star." Squires translates the couplet as follows:

in this dark night I cannot see
where I am going
let the Pole Star come out of hiding
and point me the way.
(Squires, *Hafez*, 269)

19. The quoted segment is a paraphrase of the second line of the following couplet from Rumi's *Masnavi*: "The green garden of love which is endless / Has many fruits but sorrow and happiness"; from Mowlavi (Jalalu'ddin Rumi), *The Mathnawi*, ed. Reynold A. Nicholson, 3rd ed. (Tehran: Hermes Publishers, 2007), 81.

20. From ghazal 22. The couplet that contains the phrase is: "I know not who is inside my wounded heart / That I am silent while he cries and roars." Squires, translates the couplet as follows:

> I do not know
> who this person is within me
> I who am heartsore
>
> for when I am quiet he is in uproar.
> (Squires, *Hafez*, 281)

21. From ghazal 428. Squires translates this line, as follows: "our existence is an enigma / our answers only fables and spells." Squires, 102.

22. From ghazal 440. The quoted phrase is from the following couplet: "At dawn I was reciting to the wind the story of longing / When a voice said, 'Be aware of God's favor.'" Squires translates the couplet as follows:

> I confided in the wind all my fond hopes
> trust in God's grace the wind replied.
> (Squires, 294)

23. From ghazal 317. See also Davis, *Faces of Love*, 114.

24. In this and the previous two paragraphs, the author's persona speaks in the same voice as Hafez.

25. In Persian, the phrase that I have translated as "flourishing ruins" is *kharababad*. Meskoob points out later that Hafez distinguishes between this concept and other concepts that he uses to describe the world as ruins.

26. From ghazal 343. Squires, *Hafez*, 205.

27. From ghazal 266. Davis, *Faces of Love*, 111.

28. From ghazal 492. The quoted phrase is from the following couplet: "Greetings, like the fragrant scent of friendship / To that pupil of the eye of brightness."

29. From ghazal 383. The quoted phrase is from the following couplet: "You would not have become enchanted by the world / Had you listened to the advice of the literati."

30. From ghazal 154. Here, Meskoob quotes the first line of the eighth couplet and the last line of the final couplet of this ghazal. The eighth couplet is as follows: "Love, youth, and being a clever libertine are all we desire / Once all these come together, one can strike the ball of speech." The final couplet is as follows: "For the sake of the Koran, turn away from deception and hypocrisy / Perhaps in the meantime, one could strike the polo ball of some pleasure."

31. From ghazal 230. The quoted phrase is from the following couplet: "The bride of the world is a beauty, but be warned / This lady will not wed anyone."

32. From ghazal 310. The lote tree (*sedrat al-montaha*) is a tree in paradise beyond which angels are not allowed and do not have the ability to go.

33. From ghazal 353. My translation. For other translations, see also Davis, *Faces of Love*, 48; Robert Bly and Leonard Lewisohn, trans. *The Angels Knocking at the Door: Thirty Poems of Hafez* (New York: HarperCollins Publishers, 2008), 51; Abbas Aryanpur Kashani, trans. *Odes of Hafiz: Poetical Horiscope* (Lexington, KY: Mazda Publishers, 1984), 226; and Squires, *Hafez*, 347.

34. From ghazal 248. The quoted phrase is from the following couplet:

> O boy
> do not put back today's pleasures till tomorrow
> or else bring me a written guarantee from fate.
> (Squires, 142)

35. This is a paraphrase of the following couplet in ghazal 340: "My father [Adam] sold the garden of paradise for two grains of wheat / Why shouldn't I sell the kingdom of the world for one grain of barley?"

36. From ghazal 429. The couplet from which the quoted phrase is taken is as follows: "Hey, sober up, for the bird in the meadow is inebriated / Hey, wake up, for the sleep of nonexistence is imminent."

37. From ghazal 429.

38. From ghazal 359. The quoted line comes from the following couplet:

> Happy the day I move on from this desolate staging-post
> in search of my love and comfort for my soul.
> (Squires, *Hafez*, 391)

39. From ghazal 37. Squires's translation of this couplet is as follows:

> do you not hear the falconer's command
> from the high turrets of heaven
> calling you home.
> (Squires, 322)

Bly and Lewisohn translate the couplet as:

> People on the battlements of heaven are
> Blowing a whistle to bring you back.
> How does it happen that you tripped the noose?
> (Bly and Lewisohn, *The Angels Knocking*, 29)

40. Paraphrase of a couplet from ghazal 111:

> if I have gone downhill from mosque to tavern
> it was not me but the working out of fate
> how can we stop revolving like a compass
> we who have fallen into the cycle of days.
> (Squires, 103)

See also Bly and Lewisohn, 57.

41. From ghazal 335.

42. From ghazal 387.

43. From ghazal 150. The couplet containing the quoted phrase from ghazal 150 is as follows: "And if she places under the curl of her locks the seed that is the mole / Most likely she would ensnare the bird of wisdom." The term *daneh-ye khal*, which I have translated as "the seed that is the mole," is translated by Squires as "the grain of his mole" in his translation of the same couplet:

and if he carefully arranges his hair
to cover the grain of his mole
how many wise birds will then fall into his snare.
(Squires, *Hafez*, 92)

44. From ghazal 342. Davis, *Faces of Love*, 124. Squires's translation of this couplet is as follows:

The dust of my body
veils the face of my soul
blessed be the moment
I remove that veil.
(Squires, 333)

45. From ghazal 342. The sentence including the quoted phrase is a paraphrase of the following couplet: "How can I soar in the celestial air / When trapped in the shackled frame of the body?" See also Davis, 124. Squires translates the couplet as follows:

how can I range like a bird
in the air of paradise
when my body is trapped in contingency
like a prisoner nailed to a board.
(Squires, 333)

46. From ghazal 428. The couplet from which the quoted phrases are taken is as follows: "The companion, the minstrel, and the cupbearer are all him / The illusion of water and clay is an excuse on the way."

47. From Hafez's, "The Wild Deer." The quoted line from this poem is found in the following couplet: "Two lonely beings, two wanderers, two who have no one / Wild beasts and traps in ambush behind and ahead."

48. From ghazal 485.

49. From ghazal 199. This is a reference to the couplet that is translated in Davis, *Faces of Love*, 78. Squires translates the couplet:

These preachers who make great show
in the *mehrab* and the pulpit
when they are in private
get up to other things.
(Squires, *Hafez*, 287)

50. From ghazal 200. Davis, 57.

51. From ghazal 352. Squires translates the couplet that contains the quoted phrase as follows:

O you who in your mercy veils our faults
hide from the gaze of those who wish me ill
these audacious thoughts I have when I am alone
(Squires, *Hafez*, 373)

52. From ghazal 290. The quoted phrase comes from the following couplet: "I tremble like the willow tree over my faith / For my heart is in the hands of an infidel with bowed eyebrows."

53. From ghazal 144. The couplet that contains the phrase is translated by Squires as:

but if you are not prepared
to abandon the house of nature
how can you embark on the spiritual way.
(Squires, *Hafez*, 336)

54. From ghazal 400. A paraphrase of the following couplet: "I fear my faith will be ruined since / The prayer niche of your eyebrow removes my presence of mind for prayers."

55. From ghazal 400. The quoted phrase comes from the following couplet: "My tall, coquettish, cunning beloved / Cut short my tall tale of piety."

56. From ghazal 9. The couplet paraphrased by Meskoob is translated as follows:

I suspect that those who mock us revelers
may at the end of the day
ruin their faith in this place of ruination.
(Squires, *Hafez*, 55)

57. From ghazal 343. Squires, 205.

58. From ghazal 194. The quoted line is taken from the following couplet: "Like Mansur, those who have reached their goal are on the gallows / As they call Hafez to this threshold, they drive him away."

59. From ghazal 286. The quoted phrase is from the following couplet: "Heed my advice, son, be not sad about the world / I gave you a pearl of wisdom, if you are able to grasp it." See also Davis, *Faces of Love*, 100.

60. From ghazal 159. Davis, 68.

61. From ghazal 346. The couplet is Hafez's typical manner of giving his patron, possibly Shah Shoja', a backhanded compliment by calling him generous (the undiminishing spring of the sun) and at the same time refusing to beg. I am indebted to M. M. Khorrami for providing the relevant explanations for this couplet.

62. From ghazal 492. Aryanpur, *Odes of Hafiz*, 262.

63. From ghazal 492.

64. From ghazal 346. See endnote 61 above.

65. From ghazal 354.

66. From ghazal 290.

67. From ghazal 303. The quoted line is from the following couplet: "But for the thought of your lips, nothing exists in my yearning heart / May no one be in search of an impossible dream."

68. From ghazal 143. See also Davis, *Faces of Love*, 43, and Bly and Lewisohn, *The Angels Knocking*, 27.

69. From ghazal 348. The quoted line is contained in the following couplet from this ghazal: "The source of happiness lies where the beloved is / I will endeavor to perhaps hurl myself there."

Another World . . .

From ghazal 470. The chapter title comes from the following couplet: "Humans cannot be found in the terrestrial world / Another world must be built, and an Adam anew."

1. From ghazal 348. See endnote 69 in the chapter "My Rose-Colored Elder."

2. From ghazal 232. Squires translates the couplet that contains the quoted line, as follows:

> the theater of the heart
> has no room for adversaries
> when the devil leaves the angel makes its entry.
> (Geoffrey Squires, trans. *Hafez: Translations and Interpretations of the Ghazals* [Miami: Miami University Press, 2014], 207)

3. From ghazal 276. The quoted phrase is from the following couplet: "Oh heart entrapped by her tresses, lament not your distress / When a clever bird falls into a trap, it must persevere."

4. From ghazal 470.

5. In ancient Zoroastrian beliefs, air, water, earth, and fire were considered the sacred elements of which the entire world is made.

6. From ghazal 341. The quoted phrase comes from the following couplet: "Whether or not I drink wine, why bother with others / I am the keeper of my own secret and the knower of my time." Squires translates the couplet as follows:

> what business is it of any of you
> whether I indulge or not
>
> Hafez ever mysterious
> spirit of the age.
> (Squires, *Hafez*, 359)

7. From ghazal 379. The quoted phrase is from the following couplet: "Scold me not for growing on my own in this meadow / I grow as they nurture me."

8. From ghazal 374. The quoted line is a paraphrase of the following couplet: "They do not know of eloquent words and pleasant singing in Shiraz / Come, Hafez, let us hurl ourselves to another kingdom." See also Dick Davis, trans. *Faces of Love: Hafez and the Poets of Shiraz* (New York: Penguin, 2013), 23. Squires translates the couplet as:

in Shiraz it seems
no one values eloquence or verse
come Hafez
take yourself and us to some other place.
(Squires, *Hafez*, 110)

9. From ghazal 374. See also Davis, 22.

10. From ghazal 11. The quoted phrase is from a couplet that Squires translates as follows: "O you who know nothing of the pleasures of drinking / know that we have seen our beloved's face in the cup." Squires, *Hafez*, 72.

11. Yamakan or Yamagan is a village in which the eleventh-century Persian poet, philosopher, and Isma'ili scholar and religious leader, Naser Khosrow, spent the final years of his life. "The angry spokesman of Yamakan" is a reference to Naser Khosrow and his often indignant anger toward Sunni religious leaders, among others. For an enlightening account of Naser Khosrow, see Alice C. Hunsberger, *Nasir Khusraw, the Ruby of Badakhshan: A Portrait of the Persian Poet, Traveller and Philosopher* (London: I. B. Tauris, 2000).

12. The reference is to Hasan Sabbah, the tenth- and eleventh-century Isma'ili leader and propagator and his fortress, Alamut, located in northern Iran.

13. From ghazal 189.

14. From ghazal 281. The quoted phrase comes from the following couplet: "Even though she has moved a hundred stages away from the alley of loyalty / May the blight of the revolving of the firmament in the soul and body not affect her."

15. From ghazal 470. The paraphrase and the quoted phrase refer to the following couplets that follow each other in this ghazal:

The happy and the pampered have no path to the alley of clever
    libertines
A wayfarer who burns down the world is allowed, not an
    inexperienced man without sorrow
Humans cannot be found in the terrestrial world
Another world must be built, and an Adam anew.

16. From ghazal 407. The quoted phrase is from the following couplet: "If like Christ you go to the heavens, pure and incorporeal / A hundred rays will reach the sun from your lamp."

17. From ghazal 407.

18. From ghazal 374. The quoted phrase is from the couplet that Squires translates, p. 110, as follows:

Come let us scatter petals   fill the cup
shatter heaven's vault   and then rebuild anew.

19. From ghazal 374. The quoted phrase is from the couplet that Squires translates as follows:

O minstrel since you have a melodious lute to hand
play us a fine tune
so that waving our hands and stamping our feet
we may sing out a heady ghazal.
(Squires, *Hafez*, 110)

For a different translation of this couplet, see Davis, *Faces of Love*, 22.

20. Meskoob here uses *sarvar-e dana*, which is the modern Persian translation for Ahura Mazda.

21. By using the adjective *old* for Zoroaster, Meskoob is perhaps alluding to ghazal 3, in which Hafez uses *pir-e dana* (wise elder).

22. This is Meskoob's paraphrase of the fifth couplet of ghazal 374. For a translation of the couplet, see Davis, *Faces of Love*, 22.

23. From ghazal 69. The quoted phrase is a paraphrase of a line from the following couplet: "So what if the Magian elder became my spiritual leader? / No head exists devoid of some mystery of God."

24. From the following couplet in ghazal 66: "Love arises from a hidden subtlety / Called neither ruby lips nor rust-colored down."

25. From ghazal 428. The quoted phrase is a paraphrase of a line from the following couplet: "Our existence is a puzzle, Hafez / The solving of which is the stuff of sorcery and fable." Squires translates the same couplet as:

Hafez our existence is an enigma
our answers only fables and spells.
(Squires, *Hafez*, 102)

26. From ghazal 193. Squires translates this couplet as follows:

reason would suggest
that we are the pivot of the compass
but love knows we are spinning round.
(Squires, 305)

27. From ghazal 203. The quoted phrase is a paraphrase of the following couplet: "Like the compass, the heart turned in every direction / And within that circle, it was a static wanderer." Squires translates the same couplet as: "Like a compass the heart spun in every direction / even at its center it turned upon itself." Squires, 324.

28. From ghazal 71. The quoted line is from the following couplet: "What is this simple high ceiling full of images / No sage in the world knows the answer to this puzzle."

29. From ghazal 71.

30. From ghazal 87 by the eleventh- and twelfth-century Persian poet, Sana'i. The quoted phrase refers to the following couplet: "Like a flower, you were all body; thus it was as long as it was / Like wine, she became life; let it be thus as long as it will be."

31. From ghazal 3. See also Davis, *Faces of Love*, 128. Squires translates the same couplet as follows:

> come speak of minstrels and wine and less of fate
> for no wise man has ever unpicked that knot
>
> or will.
> (Squires, *Hafez*, 401)

32. From ghazal 184. The phrase "seventy-two factions," sometimes translated as "sects," is from the following couplet: "The war of the seventy-two factions, leave all that aside / They followed the path of myth, since they did not see the truth." See also Davis, 40.

33. From ghazal 206. The quoted segment is from the following couplet in Squires's translation:

> if the shadow of the loved one fell upon us lovers
> what does it matter
> for we wanted him and he was filled with desire.
> (Squires, *Hafez*, 253)

34. From ghazal 428. My translation of these couplets. Squires translates only a few couplets from this ghazal; his translation of the second line of the second couplet is as follows: "the earthly image of water and clay / simply a means a way." Squires, 102.

35. From ghazal 193. The couplet that is summarized by Meskoob is translated by Squires as follows:

> my eyes are not the only place
> where your face appears
> sun and moon act as its mirror also.
> (Squires, 305)

36. Mansur Hallaj was a ninth- and tenth-century Persian Sufi who is famous for having proclaimed, "I am the Truth" or "I am God," because of which, it is commonly believed, he was executed by hanging.

37. Bayazid Bastami was a ninth-century Persian Sufi who is known as the King of the Mystics, and who is believed to have attained unity with God.

38. From ghazal 428. The quoted line is from the following couplet: "How can one benefit from union with the beauty of a king / Who is in love with himself for all eternity?"

39. From a poem in the prologue of Sa'di's *Golestan* (Flower Garden). The following lines from which Meskoob uses the phrase are found in some versions of *Golestan*:

> The four opposing unruly humors
> Are happy together for a few days
> When one of these four becomes dominant
> Sweet life leaves its frame.

40. From ghazal 48.

41. From Hafez's "Saqinameh." *Old wolf* here means "the world." From the following consecutive couplets in Hafez's poem, "Saqinameh":

Come, cupbearer, bring me that juice that burns the mind
That would make the lion burn the forest, should he drink it
Give it to me, that I may go to the firmament as a lion-catcher
To turn the trap of this old wolf upside down.

42. From ghazal 48.

43. From qasideh 30 by the fourteenth-century Persian poet, Obeyd Zakani, a contemporary of Hafez, in praise of Amidolmolk, the vizier. The quoted line is from the following couplet: "The enemy dreams delusively about his position / Such false delusions, such an impossible dream."

44. From ghazal 184. Meskoob paraphrases the following couplet: "The heavens could not endure the burden of trust / They drew lots and the name of crazy me was drawn." See also Davis, *Faces of Love*, 40. Squires translates the same couplet as:

the angels could not bear
the weight of heaven's trust
so the lot fell to man
and this one who is insane.
(Squires, *Hafez*, 356)

45. From ghazal 178. The couplet paraphrased by Meskoob appears in Squires's translation as follows:

I have heard nothing sweeter than the song of love
which is the only reminder
we have of our lives
beneath this circling cupola of the sky.
(Squires, 344)

46. From ghazal 380. The phrase rendered as "the master of eternal beginning" is translated as "eternal Master" in the following couplet:

I am like a parrot placed behind a mirror
what the eternal Master tells me to say   I say.
(Squires, 292)

47. From ghazal 117. Squires translates this couplet as follows:

how could I find my way in the darkness
through the twists and turns of your curls
did not your face illumine them like a lamp.
(Squires, 60)

48. From ghazal 26. The phrase translated here as "disheveled hair" comes from the couplet that Squires translates as follows:

Halfway through the night you came to the side of my bed
wine in hand blouse torn and your hair all over the place.
(Squires, 23)

Davis translates the phrase as "Her hair hung loose." Davis, *Faces of Love*, 4. Bly and Lewisohn, translate it as "Her hair was still tangled." Robert Bly and Leonard Lewisohn, trans. *The Angels Knocking at the Door: Thirty Poems of Hafez* (New York: HarperCollins Publishers, 2008), 7–8.

49. From ghazal 244. Islamic law requires the performance of special prayers by the side of a deceased person before burial.

50. From ghazal 117. See the set-off couplet marked by endnote 47 above.

51. From ghazal 152. Squires, *Hafez*, 340.

52. From ghazal 387.

53. From ghazal 435. The quotation comes from the couplet that Squires translates as follows:

Let those who are full of themselves
die in themselves

let them not know the *ekstasis* of love.
(Squires, *Hafez*, 91)

54. From ghazal 435. My translation. See also Bly and Lewisohn, *The Angels Knocking*, 49.

55. From ghazal 366. The translation of the phrase is mine. See a translation of the couplet in Davis, *Faces of Love*, 86. Squires translates this couplet as follows:

from the edge of nothingness we have found our way
to the house of love
we have made the long journey to the province of being.
(Squires, *Hafez*, 330)

56. From ghazal 11. The quoted line is from Squires's translation of the following couplet: "he who finds life through love will never die / for in time's register we shall live for ever." Squires, 72.

57. From ghazal 206. Squires, 253. Reuben Levy translates the couplet, as: "From the dawn of past eternity to the end of everlasting night / our fond love rested on one firm pact and one covenant." *An Introduction to Persian Literature* (New York: Columbia University Press, 1969), 133.

58. From ghazal 206. Squires translates the couplet from which the quoted passage is taken as follows:

before that green roof and enamelled vault
were raised to the sky my eyes
were fixed on the vault of my beloved's eyebrow.
(Squires, 253)

Levy translates the same couplet as follows: "Long ago, when this green roof and azure sky were being raised above / my beloved's eyebrow formed an archway to the vision of my eye." Levy, 133.

59. Paraphrase of a couplet in ghazal 178. The couplet is translated by Squires as follows: "my heart alone has loved from Beginning to End / I know of no one else who has been so faithful." Squires, 344.

60. Paraphrase of a line from ghazal 22. The paraphrase comes from the following couplet: "They endear me in the monastery of the Magi / Since the fire that never dies is in my heart." Squires translates the couplet, as follows:

it is for this that the Magi
hold me in such high esteem
that in my heart there is
an inextinguishable flame.
(Squires, 341)

61. From ghazal 60.

62. From ghazal 407. Paraphrase of the following couplet: "Say to the skies, do not sell me your grandeur, since in love / the harvest of the moon is bartered for one grain of barley, and the cluster of the Pleiades, for two." See also Davis, *Faces of Love*, 37.

63. From Book One of Rumi's *Masnavi*. Line from the following couplet: "Wine became intoxicated from us, not we from it / The world was created because of us, not we because of it." In most versions of this line, *qaleb* (frame, form) is used instead of *alam* (world).

64. From ghazal 317. For another translation of this line, see Davis, *Faces of Love*, 114.

65. From ghazal 90. Squires, *Hafez*, 13.

66. Modified paraphrase of a line from ghazal 193. The couplet from which Meskoob paraphrases is translated by Squires as follows:

my eyes are not the only place
where your face appears
sun and moon act as its mirror also.
(Squires, *Hafez*, 305)

67. From ghazal 317. The phrase is from the following couplet: "I was an angel and supreme paradise was my place / Adam brought me to this flourishing monastery in ruins." See also Davis, *Faces of Love*, 114.

68. From ghazal 366. Also see Davis, 86. Squires translates the couplet as follows:

we glimpsed the fresh growth on the chin of the beloved
so from the gardens of paradise
we came looking for the tender shoots
of his loving-kindness.
(Squires, *Hafez*, 330)

69. From ghazal 1. Reference to the following couplet: “How can I have a refuge of pleasure in the caravanserai of the beloved, since at every moment / The camel’s bell cries, ‘Pack up your belongings’?” See also Davis, *Faces of Love*, 10. Squires, translates the couplet as follows:

what respite do we have
here in this stopping place   this halt
what tenure of pleasure
    nothing lasts   the caravan moves on
    nothing remains.
(Squires, 414)

70. From ghazal 152. Paraphrase of the following couplet: “My celestial soul, desiring the well of your chin / Reached with its hand the locks of your curled tresses.”

71. From ghazal 239.

72. From ghazal 393. My translation of this couplet. Bly and Lewisohn translate the couplet as follows:

What is our purpose in admiring the garden
Of this world? The answer is: Let the man inside
Your eye reach out and take roses from Your face.
(Bly and Lewisohn, *The Angels Knocking*, 21)

73. From ghazal 423. My translation of the couplet that contains the phrase *ruined monastery* is: “Cleanse yourself and then wander into the tavern / so that you would not contaminate this ruined monastery.” Squires translates the couplet as:

clean yourself up before you enter
the sacred precincts of these Magian ruins
so that they are not sullied by the likes of you.
(Squires, *Hafez*, 93)

See also Bly and Lewisohn, 5.

74. From ghazal 317. The phrase is from the following couplet: “I was an angel and supreme paradise was my place / Adam brought me to this flourishing monastery in ruins.” See also Davis, *Faces of Love*, 114.

75. From ghazal 266. The quoted adjectives are from the opening couplet of this ghazal: “My heart is unruly for a crazed, seditious one / Who breaks promises, is murderous and inconstant.” Squires translates the couplet as follows:

My heart has been stolen
by this wandering street-dancer with a painted face
who stirs things up

untrustworthy   fickle   murderous   dangerous.
(Squires, *Hafez*, 152)

76. From ghazal 29. The quoted phrase comes from the following couplet: "The plains and valleys are lush and pleasant; let us not neglect / Wine, since all the world is but a mirage."

77. From ghazal 335. The quoted line comes from the following couplet: "Like a bird, I flew out of the terrestrial cage / Hoping to be hunted by the royal falcon."

78. Regarding Mansur, see endnote 36.

79. From ghazal 336. My translation of the couplet. Squires translates this couplet as follows:

> rise up before us   you who move sweetly
> so that moving and circling   we may abandon ourselves.
> (Squires, *Hafez*, 420)

80. This is the paraphrase of the first line of the first couplet from ghazal 336. For a translation of the entire ghazal, see Davis, *Faces of Love*, 120–21. Squires translates this line as follows:

> When shall I be one with you   so that finally I may arise
> souring clear of the world's snares   like a bird of paradise
> (Squires, 420)

81. From ghazal 471. The quoted line is from the following couplet: "Debating the how and why results in headache, oh heart / Pick up the cup and take respite from your life for a moment."

82. From ghazal 125.

83. From ghazal 143. The quoted phrase is from the following couplet: "Though God was with him in all conditions / The lover could not see Him and called Him from afar."

84. From ghazal 300. Squires, *Hafez*, 200.

85. From ghazal 125. The quoted phrase is a reference to the following couplet: "The beloved is not the one with beautiful tresses and slender waist / Be the slave to the face of the one who has that certain something."

86. Paraphrase of a line from ghazal 3. The couplet that contains the line that is paraphrased is: "The beautiful face of the beloved has no need for my imperfect love / What need would a beautiful face have for powder and paint?" See also Davis, *Faces of Love*, 128. Squires translates the couplet as:

> what need has my perfect companion
> of my imperfect love
> what need has such a face of beautification.
> (Squires, 401)

87. From ghazal 385. The quoted line comes from the following couplet: "Without you, I say, I do not want life / Listen, oh messenger, and take my message to her."

88. Paraphrase of the following couplet from ghazal 4: "The wise can be ensnared with good temper and kindness / A wise bird cannot be caught with ropes and traps." See also Davis, *Faces of Love*, 118. Squires's translation of the couplet is:

courtesy and kindness
are the only ways to win over men of vision
the bird of wisdom is not trapped or snared.
(Squires, *Hafez*, 12)

89. From ghazal 125. The quoted phrase is contained in the following couplet: "The beloved is not the one with beautiful tresses and slender waist / Be the slave to the face of the one who has that certain something."

90. From ghazal 66.

91. From ghazal 348. The quoted line is contained in the following couplet from this ghazal: "The source of happiness is there, where the beloved is / I will endeavor to perhaps hurl myself there."

92. From ghazal 357. Squires, *Hafez*, 101.

93. From ghazal 357. Squires, 101.

94. From ghazal 81. The quoted line is from the following couplet: "Talk of love is not that which is uttered by the tongue / Oh cupbearer, give me wine and stop this debate."

95. From ghazal 22. In his argument, Meskoob paraphrases the following two couplets from ghazal 22: "They endear me in the monastery of the Magi / Since the fire that never dies is in my heart." Squires translates this couplet as:

it is for this that the Magi
hold me in such high esteem
that in my heart there is
an inextinguishable flame.
(Squires, *Hafez*, 341)

The second couplet referenced is: "I know not who is inside my wounded heart / That I am silent while he cries and roars." Squires translates this couplet as:

I do not know
who this person is within me
I who am heartsore

for when I am quiet   he is in uproar.
(Squires, 281)

96. Reference to ghazals 1 and 428. The couplet from ghazal 1 is translated by Squires as:

how can those who stand carefree on the shore
comprehend
the dark   the waves   the terrors of the sea.
(Squires, 414)

See also Davis, *Faces of Love*, 10. The couplet from ghazal 428 is as follows: "Bring the ship of wine, so that we may ride happily / Away from this sea whose shores are invisible."

97. From Hafez's poem, "The Wild Deer." The quoted line is found in the following couplet from this poem: "Beside a spring, by a stream / With moist eyes in a conversation with the self."

98. From ghazal 348. See endnote 91.

99. From ghazal 158. The quoted line is Squires's translation from the following couplet:

> if the ascetic does not take the road of excess
> he has some excuse
> for love is a journey that requires a guide.
> (Squires, *Hafez*, 74)

100. From ghazal 234. Squires, 100.

101. From ghazal 227. The quoted phrase is found in the following couplet: "Pure essence is needed to become worthy of grace / Not all stone and mud can turn into pearl and coral."

102. From ghazal 371. Squires, *Hafez*, 352. Bly and Lewisohn translate the couplet as:

> The Sultan of Pre-Eternity gave us the casket of love's grief
> As a gift; therefore we have turned our face
> Toward this wrecked caravanserai that we call "the world."
> (Bly and Lewisohn, *The Angels Knocking*, 15)

103. From ghazal 143. The couplet paraphrased by Meskoob is: "A pearl outside the shell of time and place / Made requests to those lost along the seashore." See also Davis, *Faces of Love*, 42; and Bly and Lewisohn, 27.

104. From ghazal 336. The quoted phrase is from Squires's translation of the following couplet:

> if you give me leave I will give you my oath
> that if you were to take me as your slave
> I would give up lordship over the earth.
> (Squires, *Hafez*, 420)

105. From ghazal 255. Paraphrase of the following couplets:

> Lost Joseph will return to Canaan, do not lament
> The hovel of sorrow will once again flower, do not lament
> Oh sorrowful heart, your mood will mend, do not despair
> Your distraught mind will be calm again, do not lament.

See also Davis, *Faces of Love*, 29.

106. From ghazal 254. Squires, *Hafez*, 53.

107. From Hafez's poem, "The Wild Deer." The quoted line is from the following couplet: "The advisor's counsel is merely this / That the stone thrower of separation is waiting in ambush."

108. Paraphrase of the following couplet from a poem by the fifteenth-century Persian poet, Jami: "I was from the clan of dreg drainers at the time / When there was no sign left of the vine and vine planter."

109. Paraphrase of the following couplet from a poem entitled "Bahar-e Ghamangiz" by contemporary Iranian poet, Hushang Ebtehaj: "We will find our way out from among its blood and water / We will come out of this wave and storm." *Bukhara*, vol. 80 (March–April 2011): 270.

110. From ghazal 77. Squires, *Hafez*, 379.

111. Paraphrase of the first couplet of ghazal 493. Squires's translation of the couplet, is as follows:

> O sovereign beauty   redress my loneliness
> without you my heart begins to fail   come back.
> (Squires, 376)

112. From ghazal 77. See Squires's translation in the set-off quote above.

113. Shirin and Farhad are lovers, as told by the twelfth- and thirteenth-century Persian poet Nezami-Ganjavi in verse in his *Khosrow and Shirin*. Leyli and Majnun are legendary Arab lovers; the most famous version of their love story in verse is also by the poet Nezami-Ganjavi.

114. From ghazal 353. The quoted segment is from Squires's translation of the following couplet:

> I shall not compare
> the dust of my dear one's street
> to the gardens of paradise
> the shade of the Tuba tree
> or the abode of the heavenly maidens.
> (Squires, *Hafez*, 347)

115. From ghazal 461. Reference to a couplet from this ghazal, which Squires translates as follows:

> What language can Hafez use
> to describe your beauty
>
> since like the divine attributes
> you are beyond comprehension.
> (Squires, 28)

116. From ghazal 362. The quoted line is from the following couplet: "Gone is the enemy, and so are tears / Since all existence is alive from your scent."

117. From ghazal 332.

118. From ghazals 123 and 363. The couplet from ghazal 123 that is paraphrased in the text is translated by Bly and Lewisohn as follows:

> I brought my bloody tears to my doctor.
> He said: 'These symptoms all associate with love problems. Burning and bitter medicines are indicated.'
> (Bly and Lewisohn, *The Angels Knocking*, 47)

Dard-e eshq, which I have translated as "ailment of love" in the text, is rendered as "love problems" in the above translation. It is also rendered as "my pain" in Squires's translation of the following couplet from ghazal 363: "My pain comes from my beloved / and the remedy too." Squires, *Hafez*, 10.

119. From ghazal 101. Davis, *Faces of Love*, 32.

120. From ghazal 471. The quoted phrase is from the following couplet: "By analogy, I discerned that on the path of love, reason's prudence / Is like a dewdrop that draws a figure on an ocean."

121. From ghazal 357. Squires, *Hafez*, 101.

122. From a famous qasideh (ode) by the ninth- and tenth-century Persian poet, Rudaki: "The air is wafting the scent of the Oxus stream / the mind is reviving the memory of dear friends left behind." From Hadi Hasan, *A Golden Treasury of Persian Poetry* (Delhi: Ministry of Information and Broadcasting, 1965), 6.

123. From ghazal 356.

124. "The seven cities of love" is a reference to the seven stages that a mystic wayfarer must go through as described in the twelfth- and thirteenth-century Persian mystic poet Attar's allegorical poem, *The Conference of the Birds*, as well as Rumi's *Masnavi*. For a translation, see Farid ud-Din Attar, *The Conference of the Birds*, trans. Afkham Darbandi and Dick Davis (London: Penguin, 1984).

125. From ghazal 348. The quoted segment has been modified by Meskoob to fit his narrative, from the following couplet: "The source of happiness lies where the beloved is / I will endeavor to perhaps hurl myself there."

126. From the following couplet in Rumi's *Masnavi*, Book One, Part 105: "The legs of men of reason are wooden / Wooden legs are most noncompliant."

127. From ghazal 94. My translation. Squires translates the couplet as:

> but love will answer your call
> if like Hafez you are one of those
> who knows the Koran by heart
> in each of its fourteen recensions.
> (Squires, *Hafez*, 270)

128. From ghazal 38. The quoted phrase is from the couplet that Squires translates as follows:

> being with you
> postponed my doom
> but now with your fateful absence
> I sense my time has come.
> (Squires, 278)

129. From ghazal 234. Squires, 100.

130. From ghazal 303. Meskoob's paraphrase and the quoted phrase come from the following couplets that follow one another in the ghazal:

But for the thought of your lips, nothing exists in my yearning heart
May no one be in search of an impossible dream.
The one who was killed for your love is a forlorn Hafez, but
Pass by my grave and I will forgive you my blood.

131. From ghazal 24. Bly and Lewisohn, *The Angels Knocking*, 43.

132. From ghazal 49. Paraphrase of the following couplet: "The riches for which there is no threat of being diminished, / I say, truly is the wealth of dervishes." Squires translates this couplet as:

the only wealth that does not in the end decline
to put it simply
is the wealth of the dervishes' piety.
(Squires, 338)

133. Paraphrase of a couplet in ghazal 488. The couplet is translated by Squires as:

O heart if you are granted
the suzerainty of poverty
the smallest of your provinces will extend
from the moon to the earth's foundations.
(Squires, *Hafez*, 325)

134. From ghazal 49. The quoted phrase comes from the following couplet: "I am a slave to the view of the Asef of our time, who / In appearance is a nobleman and in manners, like a dervish." Asef was the chief vizier to King Solomon. In Hafez's poetry, Asef is generally identified as Jalaleddin Dowlatshah, who was the minister to Shah Shoja', Hafez's favorite ruler, who was in power during his time. Squires translates the same couplet as:

I am the slave of the Asaf of our times
for his outward nobility   his inner grace.
(Squires, 338)

135. From ghazal 358. The couplet from which the quoted phrase comes is translated by Squires as follows:

the mark of the people of God is to be a lover
keep that to yourself
for I see no sign of it in the sheikhs of this city.
(Squires, 406)

136. The reference is to "emblem of love" in the following couplet from ghazal 400: "I thought I could conceal the emblem of love with my flashy robe / My tears, the tattletales, revealed my secret."

137. Mansur Hallaj. See endnote 36.

138. From ghazal 461. The quoted line is from the couplet that Squires translates as follows:

What language can Hafez use
to describe your beauty

since like the divine attributes
you are beyond comprehension.
(Squires, *Hafez*, 28)

139. From ghazal 474. Squires, 257.

140. From ghazal 444. The quoted phrase is from Squires's translation of the following couplet:

who ever saw such a body
created of the spirit
God forbid that we earthly creatures
should sully the hem of his coat.
(Squires, 172)

141. From ghazal 444. Squires, 172.

142. From ghazal 206. The couplets that are paraphrased by Meskoob in this paragraph are translated by Squires, as follows:

from the dawn of time until eternity's evening
love and friendship are bound by one covenant

before that green roof and enamelled vault
were raised to the sky   my eyes
were fixed on the vault of my beloved's eyebrow

if the shadow of the loved one fell upon us lovers
what does it matter
for we wanted him and he was filled with desire

if the thread of my prayer-beads has snapped   forgive me
for my hand was laid on the arm of the silver-limbed boy

and if on the Night of Power
I consumed my morning draught
do not complain
for my beloved turned up drunk
and there on the ledge of the prayer-niche
was a jug of wine

in the time of Adam   in the garden of Eden
Hafez' lines
illustrated the pages of the book of flowers.

(Squires, 253–54)

143. From ghazal 379.

144. From ghazal 88. The quoted phrase is from the following couplet: "The story of the fear of Resurrection Day, as told by the city preacher / Is an allusion he made to the time of separation."

145. From ghazal 26. The phrase translated here as "with her torn dress, singing a love song" comes from the couplet that Squires translates as follows:

> Halfway through the night you came to the side of my bed
> wine in hand   blouse torn   and your hair all over the place.
> (Squires, *Hafez*, 23)

See also Davis, *Faces of Love*, 4; and Bly and Lewisohn, *The Angels Knocking*, 7–8.

146. Paraphrase of lines from two consecutive couplets in ghazal 42. Squires translates the couplets as:

> to sleep one night with you
> one transcendent night
> tender yet exalted
> and in the darkness to pierce that pearl.
> (Squires, *Hafez*, 130)

See also Davis, 14.

147. From ghazal 42. The quoted phrase is from the following couplet: "Like Hafez, in spite of the pretenders / I wish to compose cleverly libertine poetry." See also Davis, 14.

148. From ghazal 474. Squires, *Hafez*, 257.

149. From ghazal 177. The quoted line is from the following couplet: "Your mole is the pivotal point of my vision / The jeweler appreciates a unique gem."

150. From ghazal 472. The quoted line is from the following couplet, as translated by Squires:

> the splendor of your good fortune
> captures the hearts of king and beggar alike
> may the evil eye spare you
> who are both lover and beloved.
> (Squires, *Hafez*, 167)

151. *Jan* connotes life, life force, and soul; both the derivatives *janan* and *jananeh* connote the beloved and, in mysticism, God.

152. From ghazal 457. Squires, *Hafez*, 268. The word *hafez* here is interpreted as "memorizer of the Koran."

153. From ghazal 354. The quoted line is from the following couplet: "If the friend should choose someone other than me, he is the judge / May it be forbidden for me to choose my soul over the beloved."

154. Regarding *jan*, see endnote 151; *omr* means "life," and usually "length or span of life."

155. From ghazal 27. From the following couplet translated by Squires as:

> come back   so that my life may come back
> even though the spent arrow   does not return.
> (Squires, *Hafez*, 404)

156. From ghazal 253. The quoted phrase is from the following couplet: "I live without life, do not be surprised at this / Who counts the day of separation as a part of life?" Squires translates the couplet as follows:

I exist rather than live
but why should you be surprised
for being without you cannot be counted as life.
(Squires, 122)

157. From ghazal 464. Squires translates this couplet as follows:

with you one year would go by like a day
without you one moment seems like a whole year.
(Squires, 274)

158. From ghazals 206 and 184. Squires's translation of the couplet that contains the quoted phrase from ghazal 206, is as follows:

before that green roof and enamelled vault
were raised to the sky my eyes
were fixed on the vault of my beloved's eyebrow.
(Squires, 253)

For a translation of the couplet from ghazal 184, also see Davis, *Faces of Love*, 40.

159. From ghazal 321. Davis, 2.

160. From ghazal 348.

161. From ghazal 95. The couplet paraphrased by Meskoob here is translated by Squires as follows:

if you want to embellish the world
for all eternity
ask the wind for just one moment
to lift your veil.
(Squires, *Hafez*, 156)

162. Paraphrase of parts of ghazal 95. For a translation of the entire ghazal, see Squires, 385–86.

163. From ghazal 470. The paraphrase and the quoted phrase refer to the following couplet: "Humans cannot be found in the terrestrial world / Another world must be built, and an Adam anew."

164. From ghazal 33. My translation. See also Bly and Lewisohn, *The Angels Knocking*, 37. For a loose translation of this ghazal, see Squires, *Hafez*, 368.

165. Paraphrase of a line from the following couplet from ghazal 3: "If that Turk from Shiraz would appease my heart / For the sake of her Hindu beauty mark, I would give away Samarkand and Bokhara." Squires translates the couplet as follows:

What would I give what would I not give
whole cities

Samarkand   Bokhara

for that one dark Indian mole.
(Squires, 8)

See also Davis, *Faces of Love*, 28.

166. From ghazal 359. The quoted phrase is from a couplet that Squires translates as follows: "if my heart is seized with terror at Alexander's prison / I shall gather my things and go to Solomon's kingdom." Squires, 391.

167. Paraphrase of parts of several couplets from ghazal 359, including the following couplets translated by Squires:

Happy the day I move on   from this desolate staging-post
in search of my love   and comfort for my soul

and

in my longing for you   like a mote dancing
I shall make my way to the edge of the shining sun.
(Squires, 391)

See also the previous endnote.

168. From ghazal 337. The quoted line is from the couplet that Squires translates as follows:

since I cannot endure
exile and estrangement here
I shall return to my own city
and be a person of importance there.
(Squires, 221)

169. From ghazal 333. Squires, 192.

170. From ghazal 375. Squires translates the couplet paraphrased by Meskoob as follows:

where can I find those graceful eyebrows
curved like the new moon
so that I may catch in the hook
of my golden polo-stick
that celestial sphere.
(Squires, 286)

171. From ghazal 334. Paraphrase of the following couplet: "If ever once again I reach the tip of your tresses / I shall lose many heads, like balls to your polo stick."

172. From ghazal 375. See endnote 170.

173. From ghazal 52. The quoted phrase "eyes that see the world" comes from the following couplet: "To see you, one must have eyes that see the soul / How could my eyes that see the world be capable of that?"

174. From ghazal 348. The quoted segment is contained in the following couplet from this ghazal: "The source of happiness lies where the beloved is / I will endeavor to perhaps hurl myself there."

175. Reference to Mansur Hallaj; see endnote 36.

176. From the following couplet in ghazal 143: "A pearl outside the shell of time and place / Made requests to those lost along the seashore." Also see translations of this couplet in Bly and Lewisohn, *The Angels Knocking*, 27; and Davis, *Faces of Love*, 42.

177. From ghazal 255. The couplet that contains the quoted phrase is translated by Squires as:

> if the tide of nothingness sweeps away the ground of your being
> since Noah is your Master do not despair at this.
> (Squires, *Hafez*, 315)

178. Leyli and Majnun are legendary Arab lovers; the most famous version of their love story in verse is by the twelfth- and thirteenth-century Persian poet, Nezami-Ganjavi.

179. From ghazal 255. The phrase "the Canaan of the lost Joseph" refers to the following couplet from this ghazal: "Lost Joseph will return to Canaan, do not lament / The hovel of sorrow will once again flower, do not lament." See also Davis, *Faces of Love*, 29.

180. From ghazal 437. The quoted line is from the following couplet: "Oh you from whose alley the story of paradise is but a tale / The beauty described of heavenly maidens is but one depiction of your face."

181. From ghazal 372. The quoted line is from the following couplet: "Preacher, refrain from giving frenzied lovers advice / With the dust of the alley of the friend, we would not even look at paradise."

182. Paraphrase from ghazal 415. The quoted paraphrase is from the following couplet: "Anyone who says that the dust at the door of the friend is collyrium / Tell him to look straight into my eyes and say this."

183. Paraphrase from ghazal 472. The paraphrase comes from the following couplet: "Oh morning breeze, bring the dust from the door of the friend / For Hafez to illuminate the eye of his heart." Squires translates the same couplet as follows:

> O wind bring me some dust from the door
> of he whom I revere
> so that I may illumine my heart with it.
> (Squires, *Hafez*, 168)

184. From ghazal 416. Paraphrase of the following couplet, which is translated by Squires as:

> O hoopoe happy bird be my guide on the road
> for my eyes are filled with tears
> of longing for the dust at the door.
> (Squires, 24)

185. From ghazal 392. The quoted line is from the following couplet: "Do you know what wealth is? It is to see the friend / To choose begging in his alley over being a king."

186. From ghazal 470. Paraphrase of the following couplet: "Humans cannot be found in the terrestrial world / Another world must be built, and an Adam anew."

From the House of Nature . . .

From ghazal 144. The chapter title comes from the couplet that Squires translates as:

but if you are not prepared
to abandon the house of nature
how can you embark on the spiritual way.
(Geoffrey Squires, trans. *Hafez: Translations and Interpretations of the Ghazals* [Miami: Miami University Press, 2014], 336)

1. "The Sage of Tus" is a reference to the tenth- and eleventh-century Persian poet, Ferdowsi, and the "battle chronicle of the champions" is a reference to his *Shahnameh*, or *Book of Kings*.

2. Refers to the proverbial *haft khan-e Rostam*, or the seven perilous feats of Rostam, the greatest champion in *Book of Kings*.

3. From ghazal 359. The quoted phrases are from a couplet that is translated by Squires as follows: "if my heart is seized with terror at Alexander's prison / I shall gather my things and go to Solomon's kingdom." Squires, *Hafez*, 391.

4. From ghazal 359. Squires, 391.

5. From ghazal 333. The quoted phrase is from the couplet from this ghazal that Squires translates as follows:

I belong to the country of my loved one
not the province of strangers
O You who protect me   return me to my friends.
(Squires, 192)

6. From ghazal 178. Squires translates the phrase *gonbad-e davvar*, which I have rendered as "the revolving dome," as "this circling copula" in the following couplet from which it is taken:

I have heard nothing sweeter than the song of love
which is the only reminder
we have of our lives
beneath this circling copula of the sky.
(Squires, 344)

7. From ghazal 45. The couplet that contains the quoted phrase is translated by Squires as follows:

I see nothing
that could be regarded as stability

in this turbulent world
nothing of real value.
(Squires, 210)

See also Robert Bly and Leonard Lewisohn, trans. *The Angels Knocking at the Door: Thirty Poems of Hafez* (New York: HarperCollins Publishers, 2008), 63.

8. Paraphrase of a couplet in ghazal 74. The couplet that contains the quoted phrase is translated by Squires as follows:

boy seize your chance
as we wait on the shores of the sea of oblivion
for the space between shore and sea
is nothing.
(Squires, 412)

The two couplets that contain the quoted phrases are also translated by Bly and Lewisohn, 9.

9. Modified line from ghazal 37. The couplet paraphrased by Meskoob is translated by Squires as follows:

accept what is given to you
and do not knit your brow
for the portal of free will
does not open to us.
(Squires, 323)

See also Bly and Lewisohn, 30.

10. From ghazal 41. Paraphrase from two couplets in this ghazal. The first couplet, as translated by Squires, is as follows:

if you have got hold of some wine
and someone to share it with
don't take risks my friend
for these are dangerous times.
(Squires, 89)

The second couplet, as translated by Squires, is as follows:

are not the upturned heavens
like some bloody colander
that scatters the remains of kings
Khosrow's head and Parviz' crown.
(Squires, 89)

In Meskoob's text, the phrase that has been correctly translated here as "bloody colander" by Squires is in Persian *khunafshan*, which is possibly a typo in Meskoob's text, as it appears as *khunasham* (bloodthirsty).

11. From ghazal 41. The quoted phrase is from the following couplet: "Do not seek joy and pleasure from the vicious circle of the firmaments / For the pure wine of this vat is all dregs." Squires translates this couplet as follows:

friends
do not expect the wheeling firmament
to bring you happiness
for the pure wine is mixed with the lees.
(Squires, 89–90)

12. From ghazal 88. Paraphrase of the following couplet: "Do not veer from the path, with the opportunity that the spheres have given you / Who told you that this old hag has given up her deceitfulness?"

13. From ghazal 37. The phrase translated here as "the bride of a thousand grooms" is from the following couplet: "Do not expect loyalty from this inconstant world / For this hag is the bride of a thousand grooms." Squires translates the couplet as follows:

and do not expect this treacherous world
to honor its word
for it is like an old crone
who has taken a thousand men to her marriage bed.
(Squires, *Hafez*, 323)

See also Bly and Lewisohn, *The Angels Knocking*, 30.

14. From ghazal 29. Paraphrase of the following two couplets: "Oh eyes, awaken; there is no refuge / From the relentless deluge in this slumber house" and "The plains and valleys are lush and pleasant; let us not neglect / Wine, since all the world is but a mirage."

15. Paraphrase of a couplet from ghazal 111. Squires translates the couplet as follows:

these reflections   and the different images that we see
are nothing but the light of the wine-boy's cheek
falling onto the wine.
(Squires, *Hafez*, 103)

See also Bly and Lewisohn, *The Angels Knocking*, 57.

16. From ghazal 207. The quoted line is from the following couplet: "Oh the injustice and plunder in this trap / Oh the passion and compassion in that gathering."

17. From ghazal 269. Paraphrase of the following couplet: "The firmament puts the reigns of aspired goals in the hands of the ignorant / You are a man of virtue and knowledge, which is enough to warrant blame."

18. From ghazal 7. The phrase is from the following couplet: "Ask of the mystery behind the veil from drunken libertines / These high-ranking ascetics lack this disposition."

19. From Hafez's poem, "Saqinameh." From the following couplet: "The same is true of this faraway desert / In which the army of Salm and Tur was lost." The reference to Salm and Tur is from Ferdowsi's *Book of Kings*.

20. From ghazal 29. See endnote 14.

21. From ghazal 94. My translation. Squires translates this couplet as follows:

lost in the wilderness
at every turn my apprehension grows

beware the desert and its winding trails.
(Squires, *Hafez*, 270)

22. From ghazal 383. The quoted phrase is from the following couplet: "You would not have become enchanted by the world / Had you listened to the advice of the literati."

23. From ghazal 317. The quoted phrase is from the couplet translated in Dick Davis, trans. *Faces of Love: Hafez and the Poets of Shiraz* (New York: Penguin, 2013), 114.

24. From ghazal 259. The quoted phrase is from the following couplet: "In this illusory state, do not hold anything but a cup / In this small playground of a house, do not play any game but love."

25. From ghazal 121. The quoted phrase is my translation of the following couplet: "While you are on earth, relish your abilities / For your time of disabilities will be long, under the earth." See also Bly and Lewisohn, *The Angels Knocking*, 55.

26. From ghazal 77. Squires, *Hafez*, 379.

27. The quoted phrase is from ghazal 178. Squires translates the phrase as "the song of love" in the following:

I have heard nothing sweeter than the song of love
which is the only reminder
we have of our lives
beneath this circling cupola of the sky.
(Squires, 344)

28. From ghazal 477. Paraphrase of a couplet that is translated by Squires as follows:

Two engaging companions
two jugs of mellow wine
time a book the corner of some meadow
away from everyone.
(Squires, 63)

29. From ghazal 1. Davis, *Faces of Love*, 10.

30. From ghazal 391. Squires, *Hafez*, 157.

31. From ghazal 436. Squires, 266.

32. From ghazal 274. Paraphrase of a line from the following couplet: "Even though the affairs of the world are clenched like a bud / Like the wind in spring, be an opener of knotted buds."

33. From ghazal 341. The quoted segment is a paraphrase of the following couplet: "Whether or not I drink wine, why bother with others / I am the keeper of my own secret and the knower of my time."

34. From ghazal 473.

35. From ghazal 288. The phrase comes from the following couplet: "Appreciate this night of companionship and demand your right to joyfulness / For there is moonlight that brightens the heart and a pleasant tulip field."

36. From ghazal 473.

37. From ghazal 473.

38. From ghazal 456. The quoted line is from the following couplet: "Every leaf in the meadow is a book about a different disposition / What a pity should you neglect the nature of all things."

39. From ghazal 22.

40. From ghazal 393.

41. From ghazal 347.

42. From ghazal 177. The quoted line is from the following couplet: "Your mole is the pivotal point of my vision / The jeweler appreciates a unique gem."

43. From ghazal 56. The quoted line is from the following couplet: "Every new flower that adorns the meadow / Is the gift of the color and scent of her companionship."

44. From ghazal 345. The quoted line comes from the following couplet: "What can I do with the rose and the rose garden without you, oh cypress in motion / Why should I pull on the tresses of the hyacinth and what should I do with the lily's face?"

45. From ghazal 94. The quoted phrase is a reference to the following couplet: "Your love will come to the rescue, if you, like Hafez, / Recite the Koran from memory in fourteen versions." Squires translates the couplet as:

> but love will answer your call
> if like Hafez you are one of those
> who knows the Koran by heart
> in each of its fourteen recensions.
> (Squires, *Hafez*, 270)

46. From ghazal 74. Squires's translation from the following couplet:

> boy   seize your chance
> as we wait on the shores of the sea of oblivion
> for the space between shore and sea
> is nothing.
> (Squires, 412)

47. From ghazal 126. The quoted line comes from the following couplet in this ghazal: "Without the beauty of the beloved, the soul does not desire the world / Anyone who does not have this truly does not have that."

48. From ghazal 334.

49. From ghazal 52.

50. From ghazal 362. The quoted phrases come from the following couplet: "Since the loveliness of the faces of the tulip and the rose is blessed by your beauty / Oh cloud of kindness, rain on me, the earthly one, as well."

51. From ghazal 101. Paraphrase of the following couplets:

> Take the goblet graciously, since it is made
> From the skull of Jamshid, Bahman, and Qobad

Who knows where King Kavus has gone?
Who comprehends how the throne of Jamshid was cast to the wind?

See also Davis, *Faces of Love*, 32.

52. From ghazal 101. Paraphrase of the following couplet: "Yearning for the lips of Shirin, I still see / that from Farhad's tears of blood, tulips grow." See also Davis, *Faces of Love*, 32.

53. From ghazal 101. Paraphrase of the following couplet: "Does the tulip know of time's disloyalty / That from birth to death it would not set down the cup of wine?" See also Davis, *Faces of Love*, 32.

54. From ghazal 367. Paraphrase of a line from the following couplet: "Tell the bud, be not sad about the entangled affairs / For you shall receive help from the breath of the morning breeze."

55. From ghazal 465. The quoted line comes from two couplets from this ghazal. Squires translates them as follows:

One morning I went to the garden to pick a rose
when suddenly to my ear
came the sound of the nightingale

wretched like me
it was afflicted with love for a flower
and across those lawns gave voice to its plangent cry.
(Squires, *Hafez*, 49)

56. From ghazal 145. The phrase is a reference to the following couplet: "May the arrival of the rose and the daffodil be a safe and happy one / The violet came happy and joyful, and the jasmine brought mirth."

57. From ghazal 176. The quoted line is from the following couplet: "When the zephyr heard from the nightingale what Hafez said / It came sprinkling amber to gaze at the scented florae."

58. From ghazal 146. My translation. See also Davis, *Faces of Love*, 54.

59. From ghazal 320. Paraphrase of the following couplet, which Squires translates as:

Last night the road to sleep
was flooded by my tears
remembering the line of your down
I traced a pattern on the water.
(Squires, *Hafez*, 261)

60. Paraphrase of the first couplet of ghazal 253. Squires translates the couplet as follows:

O you whose bright cheeks
gladden the garden of our lives
come back
for without the rose-bloom of your face

we shall come to the end
of the spring-time of being.
(Squires, 122)

61. From ghazal 115.

62. The phrase appears in ghazals 115, 253, and 255. In addition to the quoted couplet from ghazal 115 above, the "spring of life" appears in ghazal 215 (see endnote 60) and in the following couplet from ghazal 255, which Squires translates as: "if the springtime of life comes back to the beds of flowers / the songbird will be shaded by the parasol of the rose." Squires, *Hafez*, 315. See also Davis, *Faces of Love*, 29.

63. From ghazal 454.

64. From ghazal 486. The quoted line is from the following couplet: "The birds of the garden are rhyme critics and humorists / That the master poet can drink wine listening to old Persian love songs." Squires translates this couplet as follows: "the birds of the garden deploy their verbal skills / so the master can drink to the sound of old ghazals." Squires, *Hafez*, 62.

65. From ghazal 51. The quoted phrase comes from the following couplet: "The one who taught Hafez the fine points of the modes of composing love songs / Is my sweet-tongued beloved with incomparable words."

66. From ghazal 277. Paraphrase of the following couplet: "The nightingale learned eloquence through the bounty of the rose, if not / All the words and songs would not have been placed on its beak."

67. From ghazal 392. Paraphrase of the following couplet: "Sometimes, like the breeze, tell the rose hidden secrets / Sometimes, learn from the nightingales the secret of making love."

68. From ghazal 392.

69. From ghazal 167. Paraphrase of the following couplet: "By her scent, the ailing heart of lovers, like the zephyr / Was sacrificed for the face of the daffodil and the eyes of the narcissus."

70. From ghazal 164. Squires, *Hafez*, 417. For other translations of this couplet, see also Davis, *Faces of Love*, 126; and Bly and Lewisohn, *The Angels Knocking*, 19.

71. From ghazal 174. Paraphrase of the following couplet: "The tulip sensed the aroma of sweet wine in the morning air / With a wounded heart, it returned hoping for a remedy." Squires translates the same couplet as follows:

in the morning air
the tulip scents the bouquet of wine
its heart scarred it too has come back
hoping to salve its wound.
(Squires, 179)

72. From ghazal 164. Paraphrase of the following couplet: "Having long suffered the sorrow of separation, the nightingale / Goes to the pavilion of the rose in loud lament." Squires's translation of the couplet is: "after the long tyranny of absence / the

nightingale / will fly clamoring to the court of the rose." Squires, 417. For other translations of this couplet, see Davis, *Faces of Love*, 126; and Bly and Lewisohn, *The Angels Knocking*, 19.

73. From ghazal 277. Paraphrase of the following couplet: "It is fitting for the heart of the ruby to bleed / From the sorrow of its value lost to pottery."

74. From ghazal 269. The quoted line is from the following couplet: "The firmament puts the reigns of aspired goals in the hands of the ignorant / You are a man of virtue and knowledge, which is enough to warrant blame."

75. From ghazal 346. The quoted line is from the following couplet: "The tulip is the cupbearer and the narcissus is drunk, yet I am blamed for debauchery / I have much to complain about, oh lord, but whom should I choose as a judge?"

76. From ghazal 176. Paraphrase of the following couplet: "When the spring cloud saw the world's habit of breaking promises / It wept over the jasmine, the hyacinth, and the daffodil."

77. From ghazal 176.

78. From ghazal 238. Paraphrase of the following couplets: "With woad, the world drew a crescent on the eyebrow of the feast / The crescent of the feast should be seen on the eyebrow of the beloved"; "Did the breeze of your down pass in the morning over the meadow / That the rose, sensing your scent, ripped open its gown, like morning"; and "Seeing the moon of your face in the night of your tresses / My night turned bright as day with your face."

79. From ghazal 388. Paraphrase of the following consecutive couplets: "Spring and the rose became joyful and repentance-breaking / With the happiness of the rose's face, uproot sorrow from your heart" and "The zephyr arrived, and in enthusiasm, the rosebud / Opened up and ripped its dress apart."

80. From ghazal 388. Paraphrase of the following consecutive couplets: "Learn the path of truthfulness from water that is pure of heart / Seek truthfulness from the free-spirited cypress and the meadow"; "From the zephyr's thievery, see the curl that has fallen on the rose's face / And the hyacinth's tresses on the jasmine's face"; "The bud bride arrived from the harem with good omens / Her beauty steals one's heart and religious faith"; and "The frenzied nightingale, crying out in song / Emerged from the house of sorrow to be united with the rose."

81. From ghazal 389.

82. From ghazal 440. My translation. Squires translates the couplet as follows:

> I confided in the wind   all my fond hopes
> trust in God's grace   the wind replied.
> (Squires, *Hafez*, 294)

83. From ghazal 454.

84. From ghazal 176. The quoted phrase is a reference to the following couplet: "At dawn, my good fortune came to my bedside / And told me, arise, the beloved king has come."

85. From ghazal 144. Paraphrase of a couplet, which Squires translates as follows:

but if you are not prepared
to abandon the house of nature
how can you embark on the spiritual way.
(Squires, *Hafez*, 336)

86. The quoted line is from the following couplet, which opens Ferdowsi's *Book of Kings*: "In the name of the Lord of the soul and the intellect / Nothing in the mind transcends this thought." This couplet is translated by Arthur George Warner and Edmond Warner, in *The Sháhnáma of Firdausi* (London: K. Paul Trench, Trubner Co., 1905–25), as follows: "In the name of the Lord of both wisdom and mind, / To nothing sublimer can thought be applied."

87. A qasideh, some of the characteristics of which are described by the author later in following pages, is a poem consisting of more than twenty couplets, which shares some of the characteristics of an English ode. Similar to a ghazal, the entire poem has the same meter, and the second hemistich of every couplet has the same rhyme as the first couplet, both hemistiches of which are rhymed.

88. Manuchehri-Damghani, a famed eleventh-century Persian court poet of the Ziyarid and Ghaznavid dynasties.

89. Bizhan is a champion in Ferdowsi's *Book of Kings* who is captured and imprisoned in a well by the enemy, Afrasiyab, and eventually rescued by Rostam.

90. Reference to Mani's illustrated book, *Arzhang* or *Artang*, usually referred to in English as the *Book of Pictures*. For more detail, see, Zsuzsanna Gulácsi, *Mani's Pictures: The Didactic Images of the Manichaeans from Sasanian Mesopotamia to Uygur Central Asia and Tang-Ming China* (Leiden, Netherlands: Brill, 2015). See also *Encyclopaedia Iranica*, s.v. "Aržang" by J. P. Asmussen, http://www.iranicaonline.org/articles/arzang-mid.

91. The first day of spring.

92. From the *Divan* of Manuchehri, a qasideh in praise of Ali ebn Omran.

93. From ghazal 247. The quoted phrase is from the following couplet: "The world and all that is in it is but a trifle, insignificant / Do not spare the enlightened such a trifle."

94. The couplet that follows is from Manuchehri's qasideh 26 in praise of Sultan Mas'ud Ghaznavi.

95. From Manuchehri's qasideh 22 in praise of Sultan Mas'ud Ghaznavi.

96. From Manuchehri's qasideh 34 in praise of Sultan Mas'ud Ghaznavi.

97. From Manuchehri's qasideh 77 in praise of Sultan Mas'ud Ghaznavi.

98. From ghazal 244.

99. From ghazal 42. Davis, *Faces of Love*, 14. Squires translates the couplet as follows:

to sweep the road in front of you
with the tips of my eyelashes
to honor you.
(Squires, *Hafez*, 130)

100. This may be a reference to *Akhlaq al-Ashraf* [*Ethics of the Aristocracy*], a satirical work by the fourteenth-century Persian poet Obeyd Zakani.

101. Shah Shoja' was a Mozaffarid king and Hafez's longest and most favored patron.

102. From ghazal 144. Squires, *Hafez*, 336.

103. From a poem in the prologue of Sa'di's *Golestan*. The following lines from which Meskoob uses the phrase are found in some versions of *Golestan*:

The four opposing unruly humors
Are happy together for a few days
When one of these four becomes dominant
Sweet life leaves its frame.

104. From ghazal 274.

105. From ghazal 476. The quoted phrase is from the following couplets:

Breeze of the morning of happiness, go to the address you know
To the alley of that person, at the time that you know
You are the messenger of the sanctuary of secrets, my eyes await you
Blow as you know out of human kindness, not because I order you to.

Squires translates the couplets as follows:

O happy morning breeze
carrying the message you know
go to the appointed street
at the appointed time you know

my eyes will follow you
as you carry my secret there
out of simple human kindness
not because I tell you
hasten in the way you know.
(Squires, *Hafez*, 125)

106. From ghazal 130.

107. From ghazal 492. The quoted phrase is from the following couplet: "Greetings, like the fragrant scent of friendship / To that pupil of the eye of brightness."

108. From ghazal 43. Squires translates the line from the ghazal as follows:

breeze teasing the nostrils
at every breath

pleasing not just the senses
but the very soul.
(Squires, *Hafez*, 40)

109. From ghazal 115. Squires translates the couplet containing the phrase as follows:

Plant the tree of friendship
so that it may bear the fruit
of your heart's desire

uproot the sapling of enmity
for it will produce
nothing but suffering.
(Squires, 215)

110. From ghazal 145. From the following couplet: "In bringing good news, the Zephyr is Solomon's hoopoe / Which brought good tidings of joy from the flower garden of Sheba."

111. With different spellings, *saba* means both "zephyr" and "Sheba."

112. From ghazal 476. See endnote 105.

113. From ghazal 42. Davis, 14.

114. From ghazals 234 and 93. The quoted phrase "a hundred thousand tulips" is from the following couplet from ghazal 234: "When the breeze from your tresses passes over the tomb of Hafez / From the dust of his corpse, a hundred thousand tulips bloom." Squires translates this couplet as follows:

If ever the breeze of union with you
blows over Hafez' grave
from the earth of his corpse   tulips in profusion will grow.
(Squires, *Hafez*, 100)

The phrase *zephyr Christ* is from the following couplet from ghazal 93: "Oh zephyr Christ, may you always be happy / For the soul of the heartbroken Hafez was revived by your breath."

115. From ghazal 95. Paraphrase taken from the following couplet: "I and the zephyr, destitute, two inept wanderers / I, intoxicated by your mesmerizing eyes and it, by the scent of your locks." Squires translates the couplet as follows:

I and the morning breeze
are like a pair of vagabonds
I   drunk on the charms of your gaze
It   on the scent of your hair.
(Squires, 156)

116. From ghazal 237. The quoted line is from the following couplet: "I have many tales of the heart to tell the morning breeze / But because of my ill fortune, tonight, dawn will not arrive."

117. From ghazal 249. Paraphrase of three consecutive couplets, which Squires translates as follows:

O that a breath of wind
would bring me the scented dust
from the road of my friend

would blow away the sorrows from my heart
and bring me news of the one who possesses it
relay those uplifting words

that come from the mouth of my beloved
and bring me tidings from the secret world

and so that I might perfume my senses
with the gentleness of your breeze
bring me a waft of my beloved's breath.
(Squires, *Hafez*, 241)

118. From ghazal 248. Squires, 142.

119. From ghazal 354. The quoted phrase is from the following couplet: "The story of longing as recorded in this book / Is the same error-free story that Hafez taught me."

120. From ghazal 342. The quoted phrase is a paraphrase of the following couplet: "How can I soar in the celestial air / When trapped in the shackled frame of the body?" Squires translates the couplet as follows:

how can I range like a bird
    in the air of paradise
when my body is trapped in contingency
    like a prisoner nailed to a board.
(Squires, *Hafez*, 333)

See also Davis, *Faces of Love*, 124.

Strive to Be Truthful . . .

From ghazal 28. The title of this chapter is taken from the following couplet: "Strive to be truthful and the sun will be born from your breath / For the false dawn's face was blackened from falsehood."

1. From ghazal 407. My translation. See also Dick Davis, trans. *Faces of Love: Hafez and the Poets of Shiraz* (New York: Penguin, 2013), 36.

2. From ghazal 87. The phrase quoted comes from a couplet translated by Squires as follows:

The flaming torch of the sun
that rises in the eastern sky
is lit from the hidden fire inside my breast.
(Geoffrey Squires, trans. *Hafez: Translations and Interpretations of the Ghazals* [Miami: Miami University Press, 2014], 419)

3. The twelfth- and thirteenth-century Iranian mystic, Shams Tabrizi, was Rumi's spiritual guide.

4. From ghazal 28.

5. The original term in Persian, which is translated as "false dawn," is *sobh-e nokhost* (first morning).

6. From ghazal 436. The quoted line is from the following couplet: "The contamination of the robe means the corruption of the world / Where is a wayfarer, a man of the heart, one with a pure nature?" Squires's translation of this couplet is as follows:

the Sufi's stained robe
brings ruin upon the world
where shall I find a true wayfarer
by nature pure   a citizen of the heart.
(Squires, *Hafez*, 266)

7. From ghazal 65. The translation of the line is from Davis, *Faces of Love*, 39.

8. The quoted phrase is a saying attributed to the prophet Mohammad.

9. From ghazal 177. Paraphrase of the following couplet: "Do not serve for wages like a beggar / For the friend himself knows how to take care of servants."

10. From a couplet in story 4, chapter 7 of Sa'di's *Golestan*, as translated by Thackston. The couplet is: "When master and teacher are lenient, children play leapfrog in the marketplace." Wheeler M. Thackston, *The Gulistan (Rose Garden) of Sa'di* (Bethesda, MD: Ibex Publishers, 2008), 132.

11. From ghazal 71. The quoted phrase is from the following couplet: "The ascetic who is a slave to appearances knows not of our disposition / There is no place for taking offense at what he says of us."

12. From ghazal 436. Paraphrase of the following couplet: "The contamination of the robe means the corruption of the world / Where is a wayfarer, a man of the heart, one with a pure nature?" Squires's translation of this couplet is as follows:

the Sufi's stained robe
brings ruin upon the world
where shall I find a true wayfarer
by nature pure   a citizen of the heart.
(Squires, *Hafez*, 266)

13. From ghazal 199. I have here paraphrased Davis's translation from Davis, *Faces of Love*, 78.

14. From ghazal 283. The quoted phrase refers to the following couplet: "Oh heart, let me give you good guidance on the path of salvation / Do not pride yourself on debauchery, and neither sell piety." Squires translates this couplet as follows:

O heart let me direct you
on the right road to salvation
do not flaunt your license   or your abstinence.
(Squires, *Hafez*, 180)

15. From ghazal 203. The quoted phrase comes from the following couplet: "My rose-colored elder, regarding the blue attired / Gave me no chance; else there were stories to be told." Sufis dressed in blue.

16. From ghazal 94. The phrase "guiding star" comes from the following couplet: "In this dark night of mine, I have lost my way / Come into view from where you are, oh guiding star." Squires translates the couplet as follows:

in this dark night I cannot see
where I am going
let the Pole and Star come out of hiding
and point me the way.
(Squires, *Hafez*, 269)

17. Sohrab, Siavosh, Esfandiar, and Rostam are among the heroes from Ferdowsi's *Book of Kings*.

18. Mazdak was a reformist Zoroastrian prophet of the Sasanian era. Opposed by the orthodox Zoroastrian priests, he and his followers were massacred by King Anushirvan, Khosrow I.

19. Regarding Mansur Hallaj, see endnote 36 in the chapter "Another World."

20. Babak Khorramdin was a ninth-century Persian revolutionary who rebelled against the Abbasids and was eventually betrayed by a friend and executed savagely on the order of the Abbasid Caliph.

21. Although Anushirvan is known throughout Iranian history as Anushirvan the Just, in recent centuries, his status as a just king has been questioned, especially considering his having massacred the Mazdakites and all his own brothers and offspring. Meskoob seems to favor this revisionist view.

22. Paraphrase of an aphorism from Sa'di's *Golestan*, story 1, chapter 1. Thackston translates the line referenced as follows: "The wise have said, 'A prudent lie is better than a seditious truth.'" Thackston, *The Gulistan*, 12.

23. From ghazal 28.

24. Paraphrase of a couplet from ghazal 87. The couplet that contains the phrase is from a couplet translated by Squires as follows:

The flaming torch of the sun
that rises in the eastern sky
is lit from the hidden fire inside my breast.
(Squires, *Hafez*, 419)

25. From ghazal 16. The quoted phrase is from the following couplet: "Now I wash my robe with the water of ruby-red wine / One cannot cast off one's destiny from the dawn of creation."

26. From ghazal 69. The quoted lines are from the following couplet: "So what if the Magian elder became my spiritual leader? / No head exists devoid of some mystery of God."

27. From ghazal 256. The quoted phrase comes from the following couplet: "Since our destiny was decided without our presence / If it disagrees with you slightly, do not fault it."

28. The quoted line is from the following couplet of Rumi's *Masnavi*, section 29: "We did not exist, thus our request did not exist / Your grace would hear without our speaking."

29. From ghazal 407. Davis, *Faces of Love*, 37. See also Robert Bly and Leonard Lewisohn, trans. *The Angels Knocking at the Door: Thirty Poems of Hafez* (New York: HarperCollins Publishers, 2008), 36.

30. Ahriman, akin to Satan, is the force or spirit of evil, and Yazdan, akin to God, is the force of good.

31. From ghazal 111. Squires translates this couplet as follows: "if I have gone downhill from mosque to tavern / it was not me but the working out of fate." Squires, *Hafez*, 103. See also Bly and Lewisohn, *The Angels Knocking*, 57.

32. From ghazal 256. The quoted phrase comes from the following couplet: "I resolve not to drink wine and not to sin / If fate should agree with my resolve."

33. From ghazal 105.

34. From ghazal 71. The quoted line is from the following couplet: "What kind of magnanimity is this, oh Lord, and what kind of almighty wisdom / That there are all these hidden wounds and no chance for a sigh?"

35. From ghazal 123. The quoted phrase is a reference to the following couplet: "Even though our dreg-draining elder has neither gold nor power / With his divine generosity, he conceals errors." See also Bly and Lewisohn, *The Angels Knocking*, 47.

36. From the following couplet in the prologue of Sa'di's *Golestan*: "See the lord's generosity and kindness: his servants have sinned and he is ashamed." Thackston, *The Gulistan*, 2.

37. From ghazal 80. Davis, *Faces of Love*, 35. Squires translates the couplet as follows:

> Hafez if you raise a cup on Judgment Day
> you will walk straight from the tavern into heaven.
> (Squires, *Hafez*, 289)

See also Bly and Lewisohn, *The Angels Knocking*, 34.

38. From ghazal 20. The couplet that contains the quoted phrase is translated by Squires as follows:

> we who are free and without pretence
> who are not concerned with trying to save face
> are better than these po-faced hypocrites
> as those in the know know.
> (Squires, *Hafez*, 69)

39. From ghazal 284. The quoted line is from the following couplet: "God's kindness exceeds our transgressions / How would you know of this hidden secret? Be silent!"

40. From ghazal 199. The couplet that contains the quoted phrase is: "As though they do not believe in judgment day / They carry out so much fraud and deception with regard to the Judge's affairs." Squires translates the couplet as:

> one might almost conclude
> that they did not really believe in the day of judgment
> the way they come before the great judge of all

with their false claims their bending of the rules.
(Squires, *Hafez*, 287)

See also Davis, *Faces of Love*, 78.

41. From ghazal 76. Squires translates this couplet as follows:

do what you will but do no harm to others
there is no other sin according to our *sharia*.
(Squires, 224)

42. From ghazal 232. The quoted line is from the following couplet: "The pious and the mischievous show their goods / Who knows what will be accepted and what will catch the eye." Squires translates the couplet as:

good and bad
each one sets out his stall
we shall see who catches the eye
whose wares are acceptable in the end.
(Squires, 207)

43. From ghazal 435. The quoted phrases are from the following couplet: "Do not tell the pretender the secrets of love and drunkenness / That he may die from the ailment of egotism." Squires translates the couplet as:

Let those who are full of themselves
die in themselves

let them not know the *ekstasis* of love.
(Squires, 91)

See also Bly and Lewisohn, *The Angels Knocking*, 49.

44. From ghazals 221, 266, and 342. The couplet paraphrased by Meskoob from ghazal 221 is translated by Squires as:

Hafez you cloud your own vision like a veil
remove your self
happy the person who sees to part the curtain.
(Squires, 160)

The couplet from ghazal 266 is as follows: "Between the lover and the beloved is no barrier / You, Hafez, are yourself the veil that must be removed from in between." Squires translates this couplet as follows:

nothing can come between lover and beloved
Hafez remove the veil from yourself yourself.
(Squires, 153)

See also Davis, *Faces of Love*, 111. The couplet paraphrased by Meskoob from ghazal 342 is translated by Squires as follows:

The dust of my body
veils the face of my soul

blessed be the moment
I remove that veil.
(Squires, 333)

See also Davis, 124.

45. From ghazal 49. The quoted phrase is a reference to the following couplet: "The army of tyranny rules from shore to shore, but / From the dawn of eternity to the end of time is the chance for mendicants." Squires translates the couplet as: "though the armies of oppression straddle the world / their time is now for all eternity." Squires, 338.

46. From ghazal 37. Paraphrase of a couplet from ghazal 37, which Squires translates as:

I am slave to he
whose spiritual vocation
is untainted by any lingering attachments
under these wheeling heavens
the velvet blue of the night-sky.
(Squires, 323)

See also Bly and Lewisohn, *The Angels Knocking*, 29.

47. From ghazal 470. Paraphrase of the following couplet: "Humans cannot be found in the terrestrial world / Another world must be built, and an Adam anew."

48. Paraphrase of the following couplet by the tenth-century Persian poet, Daqiqi: "One is gold, engraved with the king's name / The other, Yemeni-tempered metal."

49. From ghazal 66. The quoted line is from the following couplet: "Stop hurting his heart with your lamentation, Hafez / For eternal salvation means not hurting others."

50. From ghazal 440. Squires, *Hafez*, 294.

51. Paraphrase from Sa'di's *Golestan*, chapter three, story 22. See the translation in Thackston, *The Gulistan*, 85.

52. From ghazal 477. The quoted phrase is a line from the following couplet: "A couple of astute companions, and of old wine, a couple of stones, / Some time for leisure, a book, and the corner of a meadow." Squires, translates the couplet as follows:

Two engaging companions
two jugs of mellow wine
time   a book   the corner of some meadow
away from everyone.
(Squires, *Hafez*, 63)

53. From Hafez's, "The Wild Deer." The reference is to the following couplet from this poem: "Beside a spring, by a stream / With moist eyes in a conversation with the self."

54. Also from Hafez's, "The Wild Deer." The quoted phrase comes from the following couplet: "Do not renounce wine and sitting alongside flowers / But do not close your eyes to the drunken world."

55. From ghazal 199. This is a reference to a couplet from this ghazal Squires translates as:

These preachers who make great show
in the *mehrab* and the pulpit
when they are in private
get up to other things.
(Squires, *Hafez*, 287)

See also Davis, *Faces of Love*, 78.

56. From ghazal 200. The line is from the following couplet: "They rob love of its honor and lovers of their chance to flourish / They find fault with the youth and scold the old." See also Davis, 56.

57. From ghazal 41. The translation of the line is from the following couplet: "Even though wine is delightful and the wind scatters flowers / Do not drink wine to the sound of the lyre, for the ears of the morals police are sharp." See also Davis, 60.

58. From the following couplet from the prologue of Sa'di's *Golestan*, Thackston translates as: "People who claim to be seeking Him know nothing, for those who do know are never heard from again." Thackston, *The Gulistan*, 3.

59. Regarding Mansur Hallaj, see endnote 36 in the chapter "Another World."

60. From ghazal 243.

61. From ghazal 149.

62. From ghazal 311.

63. From ghazal 12. The quoted phrase comes from the following couplet: "When could this goal be achieved, oh lord / For my collected mind and her tousled tresses to be companions?"

64. The eleventh-century Persian poet, philosopher, and Isma'ili scholar. For more detailed information on Naser Khosrow, see endnote 11 in the chapter "Another World."

65. Reference to the tenth- and eleventh-century Persian poet Onsori-Balkhi.

66. From ghazal 37. Squires, *Hafez*, 323. See also Bly and Lewisohn, *The Angels Knocking*, 29.

67. From ghazal 388. The quoted phrase comes from the following couplet: "Learn the path of truthfulness from water that is pure of heart / Seek truthfulness from the free-spirited cypress and the meadow."

68. From ghazal 388. Paraphrase of the same couplet quoted above, in the previous endnote.

69. From ghazal 355.

70. From ghazals 5, 278, and 356. The couplet from ghazal 5 that contains the quoted phrase is as follows: "That bitter wine the Sufi called the mother of all evil / Is to us more delightful and sweet than kisses from virgins." Squires translates the couplet from ghazal 278 that contains this phrase, rendering it "potent wine," as follows:

I want a potent wine
that will knock a strong man out
so that for a while I may forget

the iniquity of these times.
(Squires, *Hafez*, 83)

The couplet from ghazal 356 that contains this phrase is as follows: "The Sufi-burning bitter wine will uproot my foundations / Place your lips upon my lips, oh cup-bearer, and take my sweet soul."

71. From ghazal 338. The quoted phrase is from the following couplet: "I am a lover of a beautiful face and magnificent tresses / I am enchanted by drunken eyes and pure, fine wine." See also Davis, *Faces of Love*, 122.

72. From ghazal 350. From the following couplet: "Resolved to repent, I thought to seek a divination by holy writ / As spring that breaks repentances arrives, what am I to do?" Squires translates the couplet as follows:

Resolving to repent first thing today
I said to myself   I shall consult the omens
but spring which shatters all good resolutions
has now arrived   so what is to be done.
(Squires, *Hafez*, 44)

73. From ghazal 489.

74. From ghazal 311.

75. From ghazal 3. Paraphrase of a couplet from this ghazal, which Squires translates as follows:

O you who are dearer to me
than my own soul
pay heed
for gilded youth values the counsel of elders
more than its own life.
(Squires, *Hafez*, 402)

See also Davis, *Faces of* Love, 129.

76. From ghazal 3. Squires's translation of this couplet is as follows:

come speak of minstrels and wine   and less of fate
for no wise man has ever unpicked that knot
or will.
(Squires, 401)

See also Davis, 128.

77. From ghazal 9. Squires translates this couplet as follows:

Hafez   drink your fill   indulge   feel free
without as others do turning the Koran
into a snare of hypocrisy.
(Squires, 56)

78. Paraphrase of a well-known saying attributed to Loqman-e Hakim, a legendary sage whose name has also been mentioned in the Koran.

79. Regarding Naser Khosrow, see endnote 11 in the chapter "Another World."

80. The reference is to Sa'di.

81. From ghazal 91. From the following couplet: "Wine, beautiful beloveds, and being a clever libertine are not yours, Hafez / Take them all, and I will allow you."

82. The concepts of *sargardan* (wanderer, bewildered) and *sargardani* (bewilderment, wandering) are found in several ghazals and "The Wild Deer" (see endnote 47 in the chapter "My Rose-Colored Elder"), including the following couplet from ghazal 472: "When the head of the lover is not the dust at the door of the beloved / How could he be free of the suffering of bewilderment." Squires translates the couplet as follows:

how can the head of he
who is not dirt at his beloved's gate
still the turmoil of his mind.
(Squires, *Hafez*, 168)

83. From ghazals 232 and 288. The word I have translated as "negligence" is translated as "disdain" by Squires in the following couplet from ghazal 232:

Hafez' disdain for this worldly pavilion
comes as no great surprise
for everyone knows that those who frequent the tavern
become oblivious to everything.
(Squires, *Hafez*, 208)

The word also appears in the following couplet from ghazal 288: "Life passed in negligence, Hafez, come with us to the tavern / So that your jovial drunken friends teach you something pleasant."

84. From ghazals 312 and 327. The phrase from ghazal 312 is a reference to the following couplet: "The pledge breaker will be broken, indeed / The wise keep their promises." Squires translates this couplet as follows: "those who break treaties will themselves be broken / for wise men hold such pledges to be inviolable." Squires, 171. The phrase from ghazal 327 is from the following couplet: "Oh wise elder, do not fault me because of the tavern / For in setting aside the cup, I have a pledge-breaking heart."

85. From ghazals 218 and 490. The phrase appears in ghazal 218 in the following couplet: "Suppose like a lily I throw a prayer rug over my shoulder / Like a rose, the color of wine on the robe is being a Muslim." It also appears in a couplet from ghazal 490, which is translated by Squires as follows:

if what Hafez has is truly Muslim
alas if after today Tomorrow comes.
(Squires, 298)

86. From ghazal 347. The concept of the "fear of being deceitful" appears in several ghazals, including this couplet from ghazal 347: "Away from me, oh preacher, and speak no further nonsense / I am no longer the one who listens to words of deception."

87. From ghazal 347. The quoted line is from the following couplet: "There is no hope for Hafez's deliverance from vice / Since this is his fate, what can I do?"

88. Possible paraphrase of a combination of couplets in numerous ghazals including ghazals 53 and 313. Squires translates the couplet from ghazal 53 as follows:

> Hafez   although we have no choice but err
> be courteous and say   the fault was mine.
> (Squires, *Hafez*, 99)

Squires translates the couplet from ghazal 313 as follows:

> although I have been immersed a hundred ways
> in the ocean of sin
> since this was set down long ago
> in the book of fate.
> (Squires, 96)

89. From ghazal 355. The quoted phrase and paraphrase come from the following couplet: "Like a cypress, I will free-spiritedly raise my head above the people, / If it becomes possible for me to leave this world."

90. A contemporary of Hafez, Obeyd Ẕakani was a poet and satirist from the city of Qazvin who also spent a part of his life in his favorite city, Shiraz.

91. Salman Savaji was a fourteenth-century Persian poet and eulogist and a contemporary of Hafez.

92. From ghazal 477, selected couplets. My translation. Squires translates these same couplets as follows:

> Two engaging companions
> two jugs of mellow wine
> time   a book   the corner of some meadow
> away from everyone
>
> I would not give up such things
> for this world and the next
> even if a pack of zealots were on my heels

and

> in the whirlwind of events we can no longer see
> if the rose or jasmine survive
>
> let us see what the mysterious hand depicts
> in Jamshid's visionary cup
> for no one can recall such times

and

> and with this sandstorm sweeping through the garden
> it is a miracle

> that any colors or scents remain.
> (Squires, 63)

93. From ghazal 470.

94. From ghazal 455.

95. *Safarnameh*, translated by Wheeler M. Thackston as *Book of Travels* (New York: Bibliotheca Persica, 1986), is an account of Naser Khosrow's seven-year journey in the Islamic world and his pilgrimage to Mecca. *Zad al-Mosaferin* [Pilgrim's Provisions] is considered the most important source for understanding Naser Khosrow's beliefs, in which he expounds on Isma'ili philosophy and theology. For more information on Naser Khosrow, see endnote 11 in the chapter "Another World."

96. Anvari was a famed twelfth-century Persian poet at the court of Sultan Sanjar.

97. From ghazals 470 and 487. The phrase "seven seas" is contained in the following couplet from ghazal 470: "How could Hafez's weeping measure up to the richness of love / Since in this sea, the seven seas are but a dewdrop." It also appears in the following couplet from ghazal 487: "Plunge into God's sea for a moment and do not think / That one hair of yours will get wet from the water of the seven seas."

98. From ghazal 39. The phrase comes from the following couplet: "Shiraz, with Rokni stream and this pleasant breeze, / Do not fault it, as this is the beauty mark on the face of the seven climes."

99. Possibly a reference to the following couplet from ghazal 428: "Go and set this trap for another bird / For Anqa nests in high places." The mythical bird Anqa is sometimes identified as Simorgh. For more explanation of Simorgh, see endnote 69 in the chapter "From This Hidden Fire."

100. From ghazal 23. Reference to the following couplet: "See what the apple of your chin says / A thousand Egyptian Josephs have fallen into our well." Squires translates the couplet as follows: "listen to what your apple-dimple says / a thousand Josephs have fallen into my pit." Squires, *Hafez*, 162.

101. From ghazal 41. The quoted phrase is a paraphrase of the following couplet: "Hide the wine cup in your patched sleeve / As from the mouth of the jug, the times are spilling blood." Squires translates the same couplet as follows:

> better to hide the cup
> up your ragged sleeve
> for nowadays blood flows freely
> as from the neck of a flask.
> (Squires, 89)

See also Davis, *Faces of Love*, 60.

102. From ghazal 374. A paraphrase of the following couplet: "They do not know of eloquent words and pleasant singing in Shiraz / Come, Hafez, let us hurl ourselves to another kingdom." Squires translates the couplet as:

in Shiraz it seems
no one values eloquence or verse
come Hafez
take yourself and us to some other place.
(Squires, 110)

See also Davis, 23.

103. From ghazal 283. The quoted phrase is from the following couplet: "Homemade wine, afraid of the morals police / We drink to the face of the beloved with cheers of 'to your health.'" Squires translates this couplet as:

let us toast each other openly and drink
what previously we consumed behind closed doors
for fear of the regime.
(Squires, 180)

104. From ghazal 283. The quoted phrase is from the following couplet: "To the tune of the harp, let us tell those stories / The hiding of which made the pot of the chest boil." Squires translates the couplet as follows: "let us tell those tales that we have been bursting to tell / and to the sound of the harp." Squires, 180.

105. From ghazal 234. The phrase is from the following couplet, which is translated by Squires as:

As the sun of wine rises in the east of the cup
the cheeks of the serving-boy
bloom like a garden of tulips.
(Squires, 100)

106. From ghazal 283. See endnote 104.

107. From ghazal 283. Reference to the following couplet: "In the alley of the tavern last night, they were carrying him on their shoulders / The prayer leader of the city, who carried his prayer rug on his shoulder." Squires translates the couplet as follows:

last night I saw them coming from the tavern
carrying on their shoulders
the Imam who leads Friday prayers
with his prayer rug slung over his shoulders.
(Squires, *Hafez*, 180)

108. From ghazal 285. Both phrases in quotations are from the following consecutive couplets:

In the era of the king who forgives errors and conceals offenses
Hafez became a drinker from the jug, while the mufti drinks from the cup
The Sufi left the corner of the monastery to sit by the vat of wine
As soon as he saw that the morals police chief was carrying a large flagon
 on his shoulder.

109. From ghazal 283. The quoted phrase refers to the following couplet: "Oh heart, let me give you good guidance on the path to salvation / Do not pride yourself on debauchery, and neither sell piety." Squires translates this couplet as follows:

O heart let me direct you
on the right road to salvation
do not flaunt your license   or your abstinence.
(Squires, *Hafez*, 180)

110. From ghazal 283. Reference to the following couplet: "Other than praising his glory, do not chant anything in your mind / For the ear of his heart is intimate with the message of the messenger angel." Squires translates the couplet as follows:

and may your heart's orisons
be only to his glory
for his heart is the confidant of the angel Soroush.
(Squires, 180)

111. From ghazal 283. The quoted line is from the following couplet: "The king's luminous decision is where light is manifested / Should you seek to be close to him, strive to be pure of intent." Squires translates this couplet as follows:

we see signs of divine illumination
in the king's clear-sighted judgments
if you want to be part of his inner circle
ensure that your reasons are pure.
(Squires, 180)

112. From ghazal 283. The quoted line is from the following couplet: "Kings know the secrets to the wellbeing of the kingdom / You are but a reclusive beggar, oh Hafez, do not roar." Squires translates the couplet as follows:

kings know the secret
of what is best for their kingdom
Hafez

a beggar in the corner should not raise his voice.
(Squires, 181)

113. From ghazal 207. The quoted line is from the following couplet: "It was in my heart that I would never be without my friend / What is to be done that my efforts and my heart were wrong?" See also Davis, *Faces of Love*, 58.

114. From ghazal 207. The phrase "blood in its heart and feet in the mud" is from the following couplet: "Last night, remembering the rivals, I went to the tavern / I saw the vat with blood in its heart and feet in the mud." The phrase "the claws of the hawk of fate" is from the following couplet: "Did you hear the roaring laughter of that strutting partridge, Hafez / That was neglectful of the claws of the hawk of fate." See also Davis, 59.

115. From ghazal 207. My translation. Also see Davis, 59.

116. Regarding Khezr, see endnote 11 in the chapter "From This Hidden Fire."

117. From ghazal 169. My translation. Also see Davis, *Faces of Love*, 6–7; and Squires, *Hafez*, 202–3. This is the only instance in which Meskoob quotes the entire poem.

118. From ghazal 169.

119. From ghazal 255. Paraphrase of the following couplet: "Oh heart, should the flood of annihilation uproot the foundations of existence / Since, in the storm, Noah is your ship's captain, do not lament." See also Davis, 30; and Bly and Lewisohn, *The Angels Knocking*, 13.

120. From ghazal 255. My translation. See also Davis, 29.

121. From ghazal 232. Squires, *Hafez*, 207.

122. From ghazal 49. Squires translates this couplet as: "though the armies of oppression straddle the world / their time is now for all eternity." Squires, 338.

No One Like Hafez . . .

From ghazal 184. The title of the chapter is taken from the couplet that is translated by Squires as:

> since poets first used their pens
> to comb the tresses of speech
> no one like Hafez has unveiled
> the complexion of our minds.
> (Geoffrey Squires, trans. *Hafez: Translations and Interpretations of the Ghazals* [Miami: Miami University Press, 2014], 356)

1. Verse 35 of the Koranic chapter, "Light."

2. From ghazal 184. Squires, *Hafez*, 356. See also Dick Davis, trans. *Faces of Love: Hafez and the Poets of Shiraz* (New York: Penguin, 2013), 41; and Robert Bly and Leonard Lewisohn, trans. *The Angels Knocking at the Door: Thirty Poems of Hafez* (New York: HarperCollins Publishers, 2008), 40.

3. From ghazal 407. The phrase "the green field" is from the following couplet: "When I saw the green field of the firmament and the sickle of the new moon / I recalled what I planted, and that it was time to harvest." See also Davis, 36.

4. From ghazal 320. The quoted segment is from the couplet that Squires translates as follows:

> each bird of thought
> that took off from the branches of words
> I caught again in the fine net of your curls.
> (Squires, *Hafez*, 261)

5. From ghazal 428. The couplet that contains the quoted phrase is translated by Squires as:

Hafez our existence is an enigma
our answers only fables and spells.
(Squires, 102)

6. From ghazal 380. The couplet that contains the quoted phrase is translated by Squires as:

I am like a parrot placed behind a mirror
what the eternal Master tells me to say I say.
(Squires, 292)

7. From Sa'di's ghazal 309. Paraphrase of a line from the following couplet: "If I say that I am not distraught / The color of the face reveals the inner secret."

8. From ghazal 290. The quoted segment is from the following couplet in this ghazal: "Nurturing the thought of having the capacity of the sea, alas / What is in the mind of this droplet that dreams the impossible?"

9. From ghazal 375. Squires translates this same couplet as follows: "drunk we shall rip the veil / from the face of the mystery." Squires, *Hafez*, 286.

10. From ghazal 429.

11. The discrepancy regarding the function of the chess pieces as used by Meskoob is due to the fact that the Persian terms for most of the chess figures are different from those in English. For instance, the equivalent of the pawn in Persian is *infantryman*, the queen is *vizier*, the knight is *horse*, and the bishop is *elephant*.

12. From ghazal 470. Paraphrase of a line from the following couplet: "Humans cannot be found in the terrestrial world / Another world must be built, and an Adam anew."

13. From ghazal 35. Paraphrase of a line from the following couplet: "Even though the intoxication of love has ruined me / The foundation of my existence is those flourishing ruins."

14. From ghazal 128. The quoted phrase is from the following couplet: "What can the mooing of a calf echo? Do not be enamored / Who is the Samarian to win a hand from the white hand?"

15. From ghazal 128. The Arabic phrase *yad-e beyza* translated as "white hand" is a reference to the following verse (XXVII:12) from the Koran: "And put thy hand into the bosom of thy robe, it will come forth white but unhurt. This will be one among nine tokens unto Pharaoh and his people."

16. *Sehr-e halal*, or "legitimate or permissible magic," in Persian connotes elegant art and literature.

17. From ghazal 178. The quoted phrase is from the following couplet: "Never have I heard a more pleasant sound than the sound of the words of love / A memento left in this revolving dome." Squires translates the couplet as follows:

I have heard nothing sweeter than the song of love
which is the only reminder
we have of our lives

beneath this circling copula of the sky.
(Squires, *Hafez*, 344)

18. From ghazal 324. Squires, 393.

19. From ghazal 429. The quoted phrase is from the following couplet: "Hafez, the talk of your delightfully deceptive magic has reached / As far as Egypt and China and near to Rome and Rey."

20. From ghazal 184. The quoted phrase is a paraphrase of the following couplet, from Squires's translation:

since poets first used their pens
to comb the tresses of speech
no one like Hafez has unveiled
the complexion of our minds.
(Squires, *Hafez*, 356)

Also see Davis, *Faces of Love*, 41.

21. From ghazal 324. Squires, 393.

22. From ghazal 342. Paraphrase of the first line of the couplet translated by Squires as follows:

The dust of my body
  veils the face of my soul
blessed be the moment
  I remove that veil.
(Squires, 333)

See also Davis, *Faces of Love*, 124.

23. From ghazal 374. The quoted phrase refers to the couplet: "Come, let us scatter flowers and pour wine into goblets / Split the vault of the heavens and make a new design." Squires translates the couplet as follows:

Come let us scatter petals   fill the cup
shatter heaven's vault   and then rebuild anew.
(Squires, 110)

See also Davis, 22.

24. From ghazal 456. The quoted line is from the following couplet: "Every leaf in the meadow is a book about a different disposition / What a pity should you neglect the nature of all things."

25. From ghazal 407. The passage is a paraphrase of several couplets from this ghazal:

I said, Oh fortune, you have been asleep and the sun has risen
She said, Despite all this, do not give up your past hope.
If you go to the heavens, like Christ, pure and incorporeal
Your lamp will bestow a hundred rays upon the sun.
Do not rely on the star that robs the night, because this robber
Took away the crown of Kavus and the royal belt of Keykhosrow.

Another of the referenced couplets is as follows: "May the evil eye stay removed from your beautiful mole, as in the chess game of beauty / Even your pawn would win over the sun and the moon." For a translation of the entire ghazal, see Davis, *Faces of Love*, 36–37.

26. From ghazal 407. For a translation of the entire ghazal, see Davis, 36–37.

27. From ghazal 184. The couplet in this ghazal from which the phrase "measuring cups" comes, rather literally translated, is: "Last night I saw that the angels knocked on the tavern door / They kneaded Adam's clay and molded it into measuring cups." Squires translates it as:

> Last night I dreamed that the angels
> were beating at the tavern's gate
> kneading Adam's clay
> they made measures out of it.
> (Squires, *Hafez*, 356)

Also see Davis, 40.

28. References to ghazal 407. Paraphrase of the following couplet: "I said, Oh fortune, you have been asleep and the sun has risen / She said, Despite all this, do not give up your past hope." See also Davis, 36.

29. From ghazal 320. Squires, *Hafez*, 261.

30. From ghazal 357. Squires, 101.

31. Reference to the famous couplet by Ferdowsi regarding his *Book of Kings*: "I set from verse the foundations of a lofty palace / That will not be harmed by rain and storm."

32. From ghazal 319. My translation. See also Bly and Lewisohn, *The Angels Knocking*, 61.

33. From ghazal 175. The quoted line is from the following couplet: "Renounce the thought of disunion to have union / For when the demon departs, the angel arrives."

34. From ghazal 175. Paraphrase of the following couplet: "Listen to me with intelligent ears and strive for pleasure / I heard this at dawn from the messenger of the invisible."

35. From ghazal 368.

36. From ghazal 254. Both quoted phrases are from the following couplet: "Even though others are pleased and happy with merrymaking and glee / For us, sorrowful longing for the beloved is the source of happiness." Squires translates the couplet paraphrased here as: "if others are blithe and gay in their well-being / yearning for my love is the leaven of my joy." Squires, *Hafez*, 53.

37. From ghazal 249. The phrase I have translated as "mirrorlike" is from a couplet that Squires translates as follows:

> how long is it since I saw that longed-for face
> boy
> bring me the cup that serves as a looking-glass.
> (Squires, 242)

38. Paraphrase of lines from ghazal 46. Squires translates the couplet containing the phrase as:

As long as the treasure of my grief
stays buried in the ruins of my heart
so long shall I sit here in this dereliction.
(Squires, 98)

39. From ghazal 44. The quoted line is from the following couplet: "Last night, the religious jurist of the seminary was drunk and issued a religious decree / That wine is prohibited, but better than religiously endowed property."

40. Paraphrase of the following consecutive couplets from ghazal 170:

The reclusive ascetic who went to the tavern last night
Broke his pledge and picked up a cup
The Sufi who in a gathering was breaking cups and jugs
With one sip of wine again became wise and learned.

41. From ghazal 490. Paraphrase of the following couplet: "I made a pledge to repent at the hands of the wine-selling idol / Not to drink wine again unaccompanied by a face that adorns a festive gathering." Squires translates the same couplet as follows:

I took the hands of the adorable wine-seller
in an oath of repentance
swearing never to drink again
except in the presence of a made-up face.
(Squires, *Hafez*, 297)

42. Reference to the couplets from ghazal 490 (see note 41) and ghazal 388. The couplet from ghazal 388 is: "Spring and the rose became joyful and repentance-breaking / With the happiness of the rose's face, uproot sorrow from your heart."

43. From ghazal 477. Squires translates this same couplet as:

listen   neither an ascetic such as you
nor an old lecher like me
can change the way the world works.
(Squires, 63)

44. Earlier in this chapter, Meskoob uses "mirrorlike imagination."

45. From Hafez's, "The Wild Deer." As Meskoob explains, the fish in Persian mythology means the foundation of the world; hence, *mahi-ye kelk* in this couplet, which I have translated as "the reed pen that is the fish," means "the reed pen that is the foundation of writing."

46. In Islamic traditions, Lowh-e Mahfuz, or the Preserved Tablet, is believed to be God's first creation, on which all events and the destiny of all creation is recorded.

47. From ghazal 380. The phrase rendered as "the master of eternal beginning" is translated as "eternal Master" by Squires in the following couplet from ghazal 380:

I am like a parrot placed behind a mirror
what the eternal Master tells me to say   I say.
(Squires, *Hafez*, 292)

48. The original Persian is *ab-e khezr*, which I have translated as "water of life" to make more sense.

49. From ghazal 37. The couplet from which this phrase comes is: "Why are you jealous of Hafez, oh weak versifier? / The delightfulness and beauty of words is God-given." See also Bly and Lewisohn, *The Angels Knocking*, 30.

50. From ghazal 206. Squires, *Hafez*, 254.

51. From ghazal 199. Davis, *Faces of Love*, 79.

52. From ghazal 225. Modified phrase from the following couplet: "See the voyaging in space and time in the journey of poetry / This child traverses a year-long path overnight." Squires translates the couplet as follows:

See how one poem
traverses space and time

how this child of one night
accomplishes a year's journey.
(Squires, *Hafez*, 372)

53. From ghazal 34. Paraphrase of the following couplet: "The songs in your assembly now make the heavens dance / For the poems of Hafez, whose words are sweet, are the songs you sing."

54. From ghazal 258.

55. From ghazal 160. Reference to the following couplet: "What is the need for expressing eagerness / Since the heart's fire is evident in burning words."

56. From ghazal 161. From the following couplet: "How can a despondent heart compose a novel poem? / I have made one point about this, and that is all."

57. From ghazal 149. The phrase I have translated as "fresh sweet poem" is rendered as "fresh sweet verse" in the following couplet as translated by Squires:

I am astonished that the king of kings
having listened to such fresh sweet verse
does not cover Hafez in gold from head to toe.
(Squires, *Hafez*, 182)

58. From ghazal 240. Squires, 195.

59. From Hafez's, "The Wild Deer."

60. From ghazal 261. Paraphrase of the following couplet: "Come, for the nightingale that Hafez favors / Sings once again from the scent of the rosebush of union with you."

61. From ghazal 364. Paraphrase of the following couplet: "Oh rose, you suffered the branding of the wine last night / But I am the anemone who was born branded by love." Bly and Lewisohn translate the same couplet as follows:

Oh, dark-spotted flower, you endure pain all night,
Waiting for the wine of dawn; I am that poppy
That was born with the burning spot of suffering.
(Bly and Lewisohn, *The Angels Knocking*, 3)

62. From ghazals 354 and 440. The phrase "story of longing" that appears in ghazal 354 is from the following couplet: "The story of longing as recorded in this book / Is the same error-free story that Hafez taught me." The phrase also appears in the following couplet from ghazal 440: "At dawn I was reciting to the wind the story of longing / When a voice said, 'Be aware of God's favor.'" Squires translates this couplet as follows:

I confided in the wind   all my fond hopes
trust in God's grace   the wind replied.
(Squires, *Hafez*, 294)

63. From ghazal 222. The quoted phrase is from the following couplet: "Oh one who caused the lost heart, for God's sake, help / For if a forlorn stranger is not guided, he will be gone."

64. From ghazal 255. The phrase "the Canaan of the lost Joseph" refers to the following couplet: "Lost Joseph will return to Canaan, do not lament / The hovel of sorrow will once again flower, do not lament." See also Davis, *Faces of Love*, 29.

65. From ghazal 94. The quoted line is from the following couplet: "No matter which way I went, my fear only increased / Protect me from this desert, this road without end." Squires translates the couplet that contains this line as follows:

lost in the wilderness
at every turn my apprehension grows
beware the desert and its winding trails.
(Squires, *Hafez*, 270)

66. From ghazal 440. Squires's translation is as follows: "no pen can give tongue to the mystery of love / no person express the nature of that longing." Squires, 294.

M. R. Ghanoonparvar is Professor Emeritus of Persian and Comparative Literature at The University of Texas at Austin. Professor Ghanoonparvar has also taught at the University of Isfahan, the University of Virginia, and the University of Arizona, and was a Rockefeller Fellow at the University of Michigan. He has published widely on Persian literature and culture in both English and Persian and is the author of *Prophets of Doom: Literature as a Socio-Political Phenomenon in Modern Iran* (1984), *In a Persian Mirror: Images of the West and Westerners in Iranian Fiction* (1993), *Translating the Garden* (2001), *Reading Chubak* (2005), and *Persian Cuisine: Traditional, Regional and Modern Foods* (2006). His translations include Jalal Al-e Ahmad's *By the Pen*, Sadeq Chubak's *The Patient Stone*, Simin Daneshvar's *Savushun*, Ahmad Kasravi's *On Islam and Shi'ism*, Sadeq Hedayat's *The Myth of Creation, The Neighbor Says: Letters of Nima Yushij and the Philosophy of Modern Persian Poetry*, Davud Ghaffarzadegan's *Fortune Told in Blood*, Mohammad Reza Bayrami's *The Tales of Sabalan* and *Eagles of Hill 60*, and Bahram Beyza'i's *Memoirs of the Actor in a Supporting Role*. His edited volumes include *Iranian Drama: An Anthology, In Transition: Essays on Culture and Identity in Middle Eastern Societies*, Gholamhoseyn Sa'edi's *Othello in Wonderland and Mirror-Polishing Storytellers*, and Moniru Ravanipur's *Satan's Stones* and *Kanizu*. He was the recipient of the 2008 Lois Roth Prize for Literary Translation. His most recent books include *Iranian Film and Persian Fiction* (2016) and *Dining at the Safavid Court* (2016). His forthcoming book is *Literary Diseases in Persian Literature*, and his forthcoming translations include Hushang Golshiri's *Book of Jinn*.